THE TRANSITION
TO A SUSTAINABLE
AND JUST WORLD

THE TRANSITION
to a Sustainable and Just World

Ted Trainer

Published by Envirobook,
7-9 Close Street, Canterbury NSW 2193
Ph (02) 9787-1955, E: pat@envirobook.com.au

© Ted Trainer 2010

**National Library of Australia
Cataloguing-in-Publication entry:**
Author: Trainer, Ted.
Title: The transition to a sustainable and just world /
Ted Trainer.
ISBN: 9780858812383 (pbk.)
Notes: Includes bibliographical references.
Subjects: Sustainability. Sustainable development.
Climate and civilization.
Dewey Number: 333.72

Typeset in ITC Bookman Std 10/13
by Bungoona Technologies Pty Ltd,
Grays Point NSW 2232
Ph (02) 9526-6199, E: bungoona@ozemail.com.au

Printed in China by Bookbuilders

CONTENTS

Part 1: OVERVIEW   1

1.   A Summary of the Argument. 2

Part 2: THE PROBLEM, THE SOLUTION   17

2.   The Situation: Getting The Diagnosis Right 18
3.   The Economy: A Major Source of the Problems 32
4.   The New Economy. 72
5.   Third World Development 128
6.   Government 151
7.   Social Cohesion and Quality of Life. 161
8.   Global Peace and Conflict 186
9.   Education 193
10. Values And Ideas: The Biggest Problem of All? 205
11. Summing Up. 239

Part 3: HOW DO WE GET THERE?   251

12. A Critical Look at Action Philosophies And Strategies 252
13. A Practical Strategy 302

BIBLIOGRAPHY   325

Part 1

OVERVIEW

There is rapidly increasing realisation that the global problems our society is running into are extremely serious and demand urgent attention and action. However, this book's first claim is that the portrayal of our situation given by almost all analysts is based on the mistaken faith that the problems can be solved within this affluent-consumer society. The argument in this book is that this society creates the big problems and that they cannot be solved in or by such a society.

It cannot be fixed; it has to be largely replaced. This is not only a bold claim; it is also an extremely important claim and so the reasons supporting it should be considered.

Part 2 details the nature of our situation and the way out of it. This leads to the Part 3 discussion of the implications for thinking about social change strategies. It is argued that most previous discussion about what we should be trying to do in order to solve global problems fails to identify the path that must be taken to get us out of our predicament. Chapter 13 discusses previous thought and action on the question of transition and Chapter 14 derives a practical strategy.

Chapter 1

A SUMMARY OF THE ARGUMENT

Following is a brief summary of the main themes argued in the book.

This society is grossly unsustainable.
Although the basic facts are well known, few recognise the magnitude of the overshoot, that is the extent to which this society is unsustainable. Chapter 2 shows that we are far beyond levels of resource use and environmental impact that can be maintained for long, let alone spread to all people. Our levels of commercial production, consumption, and resource and environmental impact probably have to be cut by 90%. This general conclusion is directly given in some of the basic statistics that are familiar to almost anyone concerned about the fate of the planet, but the profound significance of those facts and figures is not recognised.

This society is built on a hugely unjust global economy.
Even if our Rich World way of life was ecologically sustainable, it is not morally acceptable. It would not be possible for us to have it if the global economy was not allocating most of the world's resources and productive capacity to the enrichment of the few who live in rich countries and the elite classes in the Third World. The distributions of wealth and resource consumption are grotesquely unequal, and this is no accident.

Chapter 4 explains that it is due to an economic system which automatically and inevitably lets the rich take most of the resources and wealth. This happens simply because it is a market system. Markets enable the rich to take/buy scarce things and they inevitably devote the productive capacity of the Third World to supplying the supermarkets of the Rich World. A market system cannot function in any other way. If you want scarce resources allocated according to need or justice or rights or ecological principles, then markets cannot do this. Of course the greatest beneficiaries of the system are the super-rich who own the corporations and banks, but ordinary people in rich countries are getting far more than their fair share of world resources and thereby depriving billions of people of a fair share.

The rich countries also ruthlessly use their economic, diplomatic and military power to secure their 'vital interests'. Rich countries force the rest to comply with rules and arrangements which ensure that we get the lion's share of the available resources and business opportunities. For example, the provisions of the World Trade Organisation and the IMF's Structural Adjustment Packages expressly *prevent* Third World countries from devoting their resources primarily to improving the welfare of their people. The rules of these institutions stipulate that the use of resources must be determined by market forces, which means the corporations and Rich World consumers get them.

Our empire-maintaining effort also includes a great deal of very nasty behaviour, such as aiding dictatorial regimes willing to give us access to resources, providing arms, ignoring human rights violations, organising coups, and carrying out military invasions.

The appalling immorality of these processes and systems is almost completely ignored by politicians, officials and the public who benefit from them. Indeed they would be shocked to be told that their high living standards are only possible because they exploit an empire in which billions of people are forced to suffer serious deprivation while their resources flow out to stock our supermarkets.

We cannot expect to see a just, morally acceptable and safe world until the rich are prepared to live on something like their fair share of world resources. If we insist on taking as much as we do now, while everyone in the Third World strives to rise to our levels of affluence, then increasingly fierce conflict and insecurity in the world can be guaranteed, as well as ecological catastrophe.

The fundamental problem is simply over-consumption.

The direct cause of all the big global problems threatening to destroy us is the determination to live affluently, to consume rampantly. This is the supreme value in virtually all societies now; people want to buy, possess, display and use up, a lot of things. They take affluence for granted. They crave more and more of it. No level of income or size of house or amount of travel is enough. Everyone wants more, as much as they can get, the best, the most luxurious, no matter how much they already have. No corporation is ever content to remain as big as it is; they all work hard to grow and become richer. Governments take as their supreme goal increasing wealth, increasing the amount produced and consumed, increasing the GDP... without any limit. In other words, on all sides there is a fierce and unquestionable commitment to constantly raising 'living standards' and to limitless economic growth.

This manic obsession with affluence and growth is obviously the direct cause of all the most disturbing global problems. It generates rapid resource depletion. It means the Third World is forced into an approach to 'development' which siphons resources out to benefit us while condemning most of its people to deprivation and squalor. It destroys the environment by ripping vast and ever-increasing quantities of natural resources from the earth and then dumping ever-increasing quantities of waste into ecosystems. It directly fuels armed conflict by intensifying the struggle for access to resources and markets. Most perversely of all, the quest for affluence and growth is now reducing the quality of life in even the richest societies, partly because it is generating more costs than benefits but most worryingly because the triumph of the neo-liberal ideology of selfish acquisitiveness is destroying the collectivist values without which there can be no society at all.

The defining feature of the coming era – scarcity.
For more than two hundred years the unquestioned world view has taken for granted rising to ever-increasing, limitless material abundance. We are now suddenly plunging into an era of ever-increasing, limitless and irremediable scarcity. We have already seriously depleted stocks of many resources and now billions in the Third World are determined to rise to our Rich World levels of consumption. In the past the rich have easily been able to prevent the poor from controlling much of the world's wealth, but now, try stopping India and China. In the past the general solution to problems of poverty and equity was to produce more. From here on that will not be possible. From here on the good society must be defined in terms of non-affluent lifestyles, frugality and self-sufficiency, and a zero-growth economy. The fact of scarcity radically recasts thinking about the nature of a satisfactory society and how to get to it.

The problems cannot be fixed – in this society.
The problems now threatening to destroy us are caused by some of the fundamental structures and commitments of this society, especially the growth economy, the market system, production for profit, and the cultural foundation of individualistic, competitive acquisitiveness. It is not possible to reform such a society so that it no longer generates the problems while it retains these elements. The problems cannot be fixed in consumer-capitalist society, because that is what is causing them. A society which did not cause them would not be a consumer-capitalist society. This is the fundamental point which most people concerned about our problems fail or refuse to grasp, and as a result most of them support mere reforms-within-the-system, which cannot eliminate the problems. To make this clear is the major goal of Part 2.

It will be explained that the predicament is too big and serious to be solved by technical advance. Already the overshoot is so great that technical advance would have to make miraculous reductions to solve the problems, even without taking into account the effects of economic growth. The quest for limitless growth is bound to overwhelm all likely gains achieved by technical wizardry.

5

There must therefore be huge and radical changes in fundamental systems.

Despite the overwhelming case that this society is by nature unsustainable and unjust, hardly anyone wants to face up to the situation. Almost none of the many analyses of our problems being published recognises that a sustainable and just society cannot be built without change to a radically different economic system, political system, geography of settlements and, most difficult of all, a very different cultural system. Consequently as Chapter 13 will argue, almost all of the rhetoric, expenditure and effort now being devoted to global problems is misguided and cannot solve the problems, because it is focused only on bandaiding the symptoms as distinct from changing the structures and commitments creating them.

The required changes are huge, radical in the extreme, and historically unprecedented. And they have to be made within decades. The chances of us making these changes and avoiding chaotic breakdown are not very good at all, given that at present there is little understanding of the situation despite some 60 years of accumulating literature on the limits to affluence and growth. One could be excused for thinking that humans simply do not have the wit or the will to save themselves.

There is a workable and attractive alternative – The Simpler Way.

If the foregoing account of our situation is more or less valid the basic characteristics of a sustainable and just society are clearly given and are difficult if not impossible to dispute. We must try to move to what is well-described as 'The Simpler (But Richer) Way'.

There are five core principles in The Simpler Way.

1, Material living standards must be much less affluent.

As Chapter 2 argues, in a sustainable society per capita rates of resource use must be a small fraction of those in rich countries today. However, living more simply does not mean deprivation or hardship. It means focusing on what is sufficient for comfort, hygiene, efficiency, etc. Most of our basic needs can be met by quite simple and resource-cheap devices and ways, compared with those taken for granted in consumer society.

Nor should living in ways that minimise resource use be seen as an irksome sacrifice that must be made in order to 'save the planet'. These ways must become important sources of life satisfaction. Ideally people will come to enjoy activities such as growing food, 'husbanding' resources, making rather than buying, composting, repairing, bottling fruit, giving old things to others, making things last, and running a relatively self-sufficient household economy.

2. There must be mostly small scale highly self-sufficient local economies.

We must develop as much self-sufficiency as we reasonably can at the national level (meaning far less international trade), at the household level, and especially at the neighbourhood, suburban, town and local regional level. We need to convert our presently barren suburbs into thriving local economies which produce most of what they need from local resources. They would contain many small enterprises, such as the local bakery, enabling most of us to get to work by bicycle or on foot. Much of our honey, eggs, crockery, vegetables, furniture, fruit, fish and poultry production could come from households, backyard businesses engaged mostly in craft and hobby production. It is much more satisfying to produce most things in craft ways rather than in industrial factories. There would be many little farms and firms throughout and close to settlements, some cooperatives but many could be normal small private firms. They would mostly produce for local use, not export from the region.

Many market gardens could be located throughout the suburbs and cities, e.g. on derelict factory sites and beside railway lines. Having food produced close to where people live would enable nutrients to be recycled back to the soil through compost heaps and garbage gas units.

We should convert one house on each block into a neighbourhood workshop, including a recycling store, meeting place, surplus exchange and library. Because there will be far less need for transport we could dig up many roads, greatly increasing suburban and city land area available for community gardens, workshops, ponds, forests etc. Most of our neighbourhood could become a Permaculture jungle, a complex 'edible landscape' crammed with long-lived, largely self-maintaining productive plants such as fruit and nut trees.

There would also be many varieties of animals living in our neighbourhoods, including an entire fishing industry based on tanks and ponds. In addition many materials can come from the communal woodlots, fruit trees, bamboo clumps, ponds and meadows. These would provide many free goods. Thus we will develop the 'commons', the community land and resources from which all can take food and materials. Many areas could easily supply themselves with the clay to produce all the mud bricks and pottery needed. All the cabinet making wood needed could come from those forests, via one small saw-bench located in the neighbourhood, within what used to be a car port.

It would be a leisure-rich environment. Suburbs at present are leisure deserts; there is not much to do. The alternative neighbourhood would be full of familiar people, small businesses, common projects, animals, gardens, forests and alternative technologies and therefore full of interesting things to observe and do. Consequently people would be less inclined to go away at weekends and holidays, which would reduce the national per capita footprint and energy consumption.

Thus the new economy would be mostly made up of many small scale, local economies, so that most of the basic items we need were produced close to where we live, from local soils, forests and resources, by local skill and labour. Things like fridges and stoves would come from regional factories a little further away. Very few items, including steel, would be moved long distances, and very little (perhaps items such as high-tech medical equipment) would need to be transported from overseas. Given the very austere energy budgets there could be no conceivable alternative to the development of highly self-sufficient localised economies.

3. There must be mostly cooperative and participatory local systems whereby small communities control their own affairs, largely independent of the international and global economies.

We would be on various voluntary rosters, committees and working bees to do most of the child minding, nursing, basic educating and aged and disabled caring in our area. We would also (have to) cooperate in the performance of most of the governing and administrating that state and local governments presently carry out for us, not just maintaining our own institutions, commons parks etc., but actually running our local economies. We would carry out most of our own day-to-day government. In Chapters 5 and 6 it will be explained how we will have to do these things to make sure the economy provides for all. We would therefore need far fewer bureaucrats and professionals, reducing the amount of income we would need to earn to pay for services and taxes. Especially important would be the regular voluntary community working bees to build and maintain the commons, edible landscapes and energy and water systems.

In a context of severe scarcity settlements cannot be viable if all strive as individuals to secure and maximise their own advantage. We will realise that we have to come together to think out what the town needs and then to cooperatively work and organise to achieve these goals. These powerful incentives coming from the situation we will find ourselves in do not operate in the present society. However in The Simpler Way it will be glaringly obvious that the welfare of the individual will depend greatly on how well the town functions. Thus the situation will make us think carefully about the public good, cooperating, giving, and the importance of contributing to social morale and cohesion.

The political situation would be very different compared with today. There would (have to) be genuine participatory democracy. This would be made possible by the smallness of scale, and it would be vitally necessary. *Big centralised governments could not run our small localities.* In an era of scarcity there will not be the resources to enable big government. More importantly our town or suburb could only be run by the people who live there, because they are the only ones who would understand the local conditions, know what will grow best there, how often frosts occur, how people there think and what they want, what the traditions are, what strategies will and won't work there, etc. They have to do the planning, make the decisions, run the systems and do the work.

More importantly people have to 'own' the decisions. The town will not work unless people are conscientious and energetic contributors, aware that they can run the town well, and deriving satisfaction from doing so. They will turn up to working bees knowing they are going to do the things they decided were important. These conditions cannot be created by centralised governments.

Most of our local policies and programs could be worked out by elected unpaid committees and we could all vote on the important decisions concerning our small area at regular town meetings. There would still be some functions for state and national governments, but relatively few. There will be a role for some international agencies and arrangements, but these would not be central in our day to day affairs.

4. A very different overall economic system must be developed, one that is under social control, geared to meeting needs as distinct from maximising profits, not driven by market forces, and without any growth.

There is no chance of making these kinds of changes while we retain the present economic system. The fundamental concern in a satisfactory economy would simply be to apply the available productive capacity to producing what all people need for a good life, with as little bother, resource use, work and waste as possible. Most obviously there would have to be far less production and consumption going on, and there would have to be no growth.

Market forces and the profit motive might have a place in an acceptable alternative economy, but they cannot be allowed to continue as major determinants of economic affairs. The basic economic priorities must be decided according to what is socially desirable, democratically decided, mostly at the local level via participatory local assemblies, not dictated by huge and distant state planning agencies. Centralised, bureaucratic, authoritarian, big-state 'socialism' is not desirable, and could not work in a world of scarcity and localism. However, much of the economy might remain as a (carefully monitored) form of private enterprise carried on by small firms, households and cooperatives, so long as their goals were not profit maximisation and growth. The goals of enterprises would be to provide their owners and workers with satisfying livelihoods, and to provide things the town needs. Market forces might operate within regulated sectors. Local market days could be important, enabling individuals and families to sell small amounts of garden and craft produce. These small private firms would best be thought of as the 'tools' that yield stable and adequate 'wages' to those who own and work in them, as well as satisfying work.

Much of the new local economy would not involve money. Much more economic activity would take place in households than at present. Many goods and services would come 'free' from the commons and cooperatives run by our voluntary committees and working bees, including orchards, ponds, forests, dams, recycling systems, workshops, cooperative firms, stores and aged care. We would receive many things via mutual assistance and as gifts of surpluses.

When we eliminate all that unnecessary production, and shift much of the remainder to backyards, commons, local small business, cooperatives and into the non-cash sector of the economy, most of us will need to go to work for money in an office or a mass production factory only one or two days a week. In other words it will become possible to live well on a very low cash income. We could spend the other five or six days working/playing around the neighbourhood doing many varied, interesting and useful things every day. This would have to be the general form of the overall economy that would enable us to survive and thrive in the coming decades. In the far distant future we will probably move entirely to a rationally planned and socially controlled 'gift' economy (see Chapter 4).

5. None of these changes is possible without radical change in values and world view, especially change away from competition, self-interest and acquisitiveness.

Perhaps the most important goal of this book is to show convincingly that The Simpler Way is not just a path we must take to save ourselves. It would be a *delightful liberation*, enabling humans to get on with what matters. People working for The Simpler Way have no doubt that the quality of life for most of us would be much higher than it is now. We would have fewer material things and would have much lower monetary incomes but there would be many new powerful sources of life satisfaction. These would include a much more relaxed pace, having to spend relatively little time working for money, having varied, enjoyable and worthwhile work to do, experiencing a supportive community, experiencing giving and receiving, growing some of one's own food, keeping old clothes and devices in use, running a resource-cheap and efficient household, practising arts and crafts, participating in community activities, having a rich cultural experience involving local festivals, performances, arts and celebrations, being involved in governing one's area, living in a nice environment, and especially knowing that you are not contributing to global problems through over-consumption.

It should be stressed that The Simpler Way would enable retention of all the high tech and modern ways that made sense, e.g. in medicine, windmill design, public transport and household appliances. We would still have (a few, necessary) big firms such as steel works, and national systems for railways and telecommunications, but on nothing like the present scale. We would have far more resources for science and research, and for education and the arts than we do now because we would have ceased wasting such enormous quantities of resources on the production of unnecessary items.

We will soon move in this general direction whether we like it or not, because the old gigantic energy-intensive centralised systems and the affluence and growth quest cannot continue for much longer. Although the required changes are great, they could be made very quickly, if we wanted to make them. They involve adoption of technically simple ways, they require little capital and they can (only) be built by harnessing the abundant energies of the people presently living in the settlements to be rebuilt.

The Simpler Way vision elaborated in the following pages could turn out to be more frugal and self-sufficient than it will be necessary for us to accept. Nevertheless it is the way I would choose, for its intrinsic benefits. My main concern in elaborating this vision is to show that we could easily achieve enormous reductions in per capita resource use and ecological impact, while enhancing the quality of life.

It hardly needs to be said that the gulf between consumer society and The Simpler Way is so astronomically big that it is not surprising how very difficult it is to get people to consider this alternative. Most instantly dismiss it as not only impossibly unrealistic but also as repugnant since it seems to contradict the prevailing definitions of the good life and indeed progress. But the absolutely fundamental question here is: Do we have any alternative? The foregoing argument (elaborated in Part 2) is that we do not. If our global situation is more or less as has been described then the only possible form that a sustainable and just society can take has to be some kind of Simpler Way.

It should be said again that the argument is not that we will inevitably reach The Simpler Way. At this point in time the prospects must be regarded as very remote. It is discussed here as a vision to be worked hard for, because it is only option that makes sense.

Many and profound implications follow for thinking about social change.

If we must accept that some kind of Simpler Way has to be taken in order to get us out of our predicament, then many extremely important implications follow for thinking about the social change process. Chapter 12 argues that a number of the long-running debates about the process of change can now be settled. The fact of scarcity rules out many of the options that seemed to be open over the last 300 years. For instance we can now see that, contrary to just about all conservative, socialist and utopian thinking, the good society cannot be an affluent or a heavily industrialised society, or a centralised or globalised society, or a marketing society... or one that has economic growth. Similarly it will be argued in Chapter 12 that the Marxist view of violent revolutionary change, and the Green Politics goal of parliamentary solutions, are mistaken and useless now. The coming scarcity renders these theories and much other previous thinking about the good society and how to get to it as inapplicable or valueless now.

As a result almost all of the effort now spent trying to solve the problems and save the planet is being wasted, because it is grounded on mistaken analyses of the nature of our situation. Most is based on the assumption that the problems can be fixed by reforms within and by consumer-capitalist society.

We are confronted by a massive problem of ideology.

In my view the arguments summarised in Chapter 2 supporting the foregoing claims regarding the inevitably unsustainable and unjust nature of consumer society are overwhelmingly convincing and if we had a rational society they would have been accepted and acted on long ago. Yet they are almost totally ignored. Little attention is given to the possibility that the obsession with affluence and growth is the basic cause of our predicament and could very well lead to collapse and massive die-off within decades. A few academic and radical green groups have been saying these things for many years, but they never seem to even enter the minds of politicians, economists, the business world or consumers. Although now there is a great deal of often alarmed talk about the greenhouse and other global problems, virtually all of it takes for granted that there is no need to question affluence and growth or change from the economic, political and cultural systems we have. The dominant ideology is that the problems can be solved by reforms and technical advance which leave the basic systems of this society intact and enable the continued pursuit of higher 'living standards' and greater GDP.

What we are up against here is a massively powerful, wilful delusion, a refusal to even think about the fundamental causes of the predicament, because those causes are the cherished, supreme values of Western culture, i.e. the competitive, individualistic quest for limitless wealth. Thus again the central problem for the people who would read a book like this is, what strategies might best enable us to begin to alter the world view driving consumer-capitalist society? That is the question taken up in Part 3.

Hence the transition problem is defined.

Although the changes required are immense, in most towns and suburbs the essentials could largely be achieved in months, at negligible dollar cost – if enough of us wanted to make them. This is because the alternatives are in general very simple and therefore could easily be built and run –- by people with the will to do so. For instance we could solve the massive and complex transport problem we have now, hundreds of millions of poison-belching cars and trucks, simply by (a) cutting down dramatically on the consumption of non-necessities to be transported and therefore on the need for all that driving to work to produce them, and (b) localising our economies so that little needs to be transported into them and most of us can get to paid work by bicycle, on the two days a week we would need to do so.

But designing and building is not the problem. That's easy. The problem is developing the understandings and values whereby ordinary people will *want* to design and build the new systems, and will delight in doing so. The key to the transition problem is therefore to do with the steps which might best contribute to the development of the required awareness, world view and motivation. If people had the necessary vision they'd get the building done in no time.

What then should we do?

The discussion in Part 2 culminates in the question, what then are the action strategies we should be putting our efforts into? The theoretical answer is developed in Chapter 13 via a critical examination of previous ideas and theories. It can be summarised in terms of plunging into building those elements of the new way that we can in the towns and suburbs where we live, but the reasons why we do this are crucial. We will be beginning to create the required alternatives, the examples people can see and be inspired by, the lifeboats to which people can come across when scarcity impacts, but this is not the most important point. This activity will give us the most effective platforms and arenas for doing the global consciousness raising work, of helping people to see that what we must do is go far beyond creating community gardens and farmers' markets to build radically new local economies under our control.

For some thirty years many people within the Eco-village movement have been pioneering aspects of The Simpler Way. In the last few years many towns, firstly within the UK but now worldwide, have joined the Transition Towns movement. People have realised the coming of Peak Oil means that if they do not develop high levels of local self-sufficiency they will be in great difficulties. However, these initiatives will not inevitably lead to the radical system changes required. They could easily end up as having achieved only reform-within-the-old-system. Our task is to work within these kinds of initiatives to try to ensure that in time they come to be informed by the required radical global consciousness.

This book's quest is to persuade activists, social critics, dissenters, and the many and increasing numbers of discontented people, to adopt the view of our situation detailed throughout the book, and the action strategy outlined in the last chapter. My argument is that these are not options among many that are open to us, because if we think carefully about our situation then we must accept the conclusions argued here.

If you are concerned about the fate of the polar bear, or refugees, or Peak Oil, or economic injustice, or homeless people, please do not put your main energies into protesting, fund raising, getting elected as a green politician, or learning how to handle an AK-47. Please come and join us down at the community gardens where you can get into some really subversive action!

Part 2

THE PROBLEM, THE SOLUTION

The major claim this book makes is that most of the vast literature pouring out on the global situation fails to analyse the situation satisfactorily. The first concern in Part 2 is to make clear the nature of our predicament, and therefore the fact that it cannot be solved within or by a consumer-capitalist society. The second concern is to detail the general characteristics that a sustainable and just society must have, whether we like it or not, elaborating on the sketch given in Chapter 1.

In my view these arguments are overwhelmingly convincing, yet their conclusions are not on the agenda of official or public discussion. This might not be so surprising since they flatly contradict conventional assumptions, values and thinking.

Chapter 2

THE SITUATION: GETTING THE DIAGNOSIS RIGHT

A great deal of literature is now documenting the alarming global situation we are in. However almost all official reports and pronouncements, the government bureaucracies, corporate boardroom statements, media and ordinary people conclude that the problems can be solved without radical system change. That is, they assume the problems can be solved by changes within a system that remains focused on affluent living standards, free markets, competition, private ownership of capital, production determined by what will maximise profits, and the ceaseless quest on the part of individuals and nations for greater wealth, i.e. rising 'living standards' and growth of GDP. This chapter offers an outline of the general argument that this dominant assumption is wrong, that the big global problems cannot be solved without huge and radical conversion to very different systems.

There are two critical lines of argument here. The first is to do with the magnitude of the problems, the extent to which we have already exceeded sustainable levels of production, consumption, resource use and environmental impact, and the rate at which these effects will increase given the commitment to growth. The argument is that this magnitude cannot now be sufficiently reduced given the systems built into consumer-capitalist society. The second argument is to do with global economic justice, i.e. the fact that we could not have anything like the affluence we enjoy in rich countries if we were not taking far more than our fair share of the world's wealth and thereby depriving the majority of the world's people of a fair share. Again it will be argued that it is not possible to fix this situation in a society driven by market forces and the quest for affluence and growth.

FAULT 1: SUSTAINABILITY

The most serious fault in our society is the commitment to an affluent-industrial-consumer lifestyle and to an economy that must have constant and limitless growth in output. Our levels of production and consumption are far too high to be kept up for very long and could never be extended to all people. We are rapidly depleting resources and damaging the environment. Our way of life is grossly unsustainable. The first crucial point on which this book's arguments are built is the magnitude of the overshoot. The key figures here are well known but their significance is not generally acknowledged. Following are some of the main lines of argument supporting these limits to growth conclusions.

Rich countries, with about one-fifth of the world's people, are consuming about three quarters of the world's resource production. Our per capita consumption is probably about 15-20 times that of the poorest half of the world's people. World population will probably stabilise above 9 billion, somewhere after 2060. If all those people were to have the present Australian per capita resource consumption, then world production of all resources would have to be about 8 times as great as it is now. If we tried to raise present world production to that level by 2060 we would by then have completely exhausted all probably recoverable resources of one-third of the basic mineral items we use. All probably recoverable resources of coal, oil, gas, tar sand and shale oil, and uranium (via burner reactors) would have been exhausted by 2045. (Trainer, 1985).

❑ Petroleum appears to be especially limited. A number of geologists have concluded that world oil supply will probably peak by 2010.

❑ If all 9 billion people were to use timber at the Rich World per capita rate we would need 3.5 times the world's present forest area. If all 9 billion were to have US diet, which takes about 0.5 ha of land to produce, we would need 4.5 billion ha of food producing land. But there are only 1.4 billion ha of cropland in use today and this is likely to decrease, and yields are likely to be impacted by the greenhouse problem.

❏ Several minerals are scarce and will probably not be available in three decades, including silver, antinomy, indium, gallium, hafnium, platinum and helium (gas). Not far behind are copper, zinc and phosphorus.

❏ Biological systems and resources are in serious decline, including loss of species, soils, forests, coral reefs, and fish. There are major concerns about the availability of water and food. We seem to be entering an era of massive loss of species, due to the fact that humans are taking so much of nature for our purposes. The World Wildlife Fund estimates that in the last three decades there has been a 30% deterioration in the quality of the ecosystems of the planet. What happens if 9 billion people live as resource-expensively as we in Australia do?

❏ Recent 'Footprint' analysis estimates that it takes 8 ha of productive land to provide water, energy, settlement area and food for one person living in a rich country. So if 9 billion people were to live as we do in Australia we would need about 72 billion ha of productive land. But that is about 9 times all the available productive land on the planet.

❏ One of the most coercive arguments is to do with the greenhouse problem. It is increasingly being accepted that we must totally eliminate all CO_2 emissions to the atmosphere by 2050 (Hansen, 2008, Meinschausen, 2009). There is a strong case that it will not be possible to do this while maintaining consumer-capitalist society, primarily because it will not be possible to run an energy-intensive society on renewable energy, nuclear energy and geosequestration of CO_2. This case is elaborated in Trainer 2007, and put more succinctly in an updated form in Trainer 2008a. An indication of its strength is given in the appendix to this chapter below, (p.28).

These have been some of the main limits to growth arguments which lead to the conclusion that there is no possibility of maintaining present global rates of resource use, let alone of all people rising to the living standards we take for granted today in rich countries. Again the crucial point is the magnitude of the overshoot. These figures indicate that we should be trying to cut present per capita rates by something like 90% or more and therefore we should be trying to move to far simpler and less resource-expensive lifestyles and systems. Again, most people have no idea of the scale of the problem, of how far beyond sustainable levels of consumption we are, and how big the reductions will have to be.

Note that the reference to providing affluent lifestyles to a world of 9 billion is not about the moral desirability of equity. The poorer nations want affluence and are hell-bent on getting it. Consider the manic lunge for growth India and China are making – and shudder. So whether you like it or not you had better think carefully about whether it is possible for all to live as we do and what's going to happen if we don't get off that path.

Now add the absurdly impossible implications of economic growth.

The foregoing argument has only been that the present levels of production and consumption are extremely unsustainable. Yet we are determined to increase present living standards and levels of output and consumption, as much as possible and without any end in sight. In other words, our supreme national goal is economic growth. Few people seem to recognise the absurdly impossible consequences of pursing economic growth.

If we have a 3% p.a. increase in output, by 2070 we will be producing 8 times as much every year. If by then all the expected 9 billion people had risen to the living standards we would have then, the total world economic output would be more than 60 times as great as it is today! Yet the present level is unsustainable.

Population.

These facts and figures confirm that the world is over-populated. However it can be a mistake to focus on the population problem. It is an alarmingly serious problem, but it is not the main problem. The main problem is over-consumption.

World population will probably multiply by 1.5, but if all rise to the present 'living standards' of the rich countries world resource consumption will be multiplied by a factor of about 8, and if they all rise to the 'living standards' 3% growth would provide us with by 2070, the multiple is 60. In other words the factor that will have most impact on the planet's resources and ecosystems is the level of consumption, not population.

'But can't conservation and technical advance solve the problems?'

Most governments, official agencies, and people in general assume that greater conservation and recycling effort and the development of better technology will enable us to go on enjoying affluent lifestyles and pursuing limitless economic growth, e.g. by reducing the energy and resource inputs needed to produce things. However the magnitude of the overshoot makes this impossible.

Obviously there is much scope for reduction of resource use, waste and inefficiency within present procedures. The studies seem to indicate that we might cut one-third off present Rich World figures per unit of GDP. Amory Lovins, perhaps the best known 'technical fix' optimist, claims that we could at least double global output while halving the resource and environmental impacts, i.e. achieve a 'Factor 4' reduction. But it is easily shown that this would be nowhere near enough to solve the problems.

Let us assume that present global resource and ecological impacts must be halved (although we must go much further than that). Remember that if we in rich countries average 3% growth, and 9 billion rose to the living standards we would then have by 2070, total world output would be 60 times as great as it is today. Now do you think technical advance will make it possible to multiply total world economic output by 60 while halving impacts, i.e. to achieve a Factor 120 reduction?

The insoluble energy and greenhouse problems.

It would be difficult to find a more universally accepted yet unquestioned belief than that the greenhouse problem can be solved by replacing the carbon producing fossil fuels with renewable energy sources, etc. An indication that this faith is invalid is given in the appendix below (p.28).

There is an enormous amount of energy in sources like the sun and wind but that does not mean they can meet demand constantly. These sources are highly intermittent; there can be many days in a row in winter when a whole continent is under calm and cloudy conditions. The appended notes are taken from a study which asks how much wind, PV and solar thermal plant would be needed to meet average demand through a mid-winter month, in view of the very low performance of PV and solar thermal systems in winter (Trainer, 2010). The conclusion is that so much plant would be needed that annual investment would have to be over 30 times present total world figure. And there would still be times when little or no energy could be supplied because there has been no sun or wind for long periods.

Conclusion: We have entered the era of savage, irremediable scarcity.

For hundreds of years Western culture has taken it for granted that there will be never-ending, limitless and increasing access to the resources of the earth. We are now fitfully, painfully, realising that this assumption is wrong. There are savage limits to growth and affluence and we are running into them, even though only one-fifth of the world's people live affluently. From here on the defining condition will not be abundance but scarcity. We must come to terms with the fact that there are nowhere near enough resources for all to live as we have become accustomed and that sustainability and the good life now have to be defined in terms of lifestyles, ways and systems which generate far lower rates of resource use and environmental impact. Your choice here is stark. Either you maintain the faith that technical advance will indeed make possible affluence for all, or you must accept that the task is to move to new ways in which we can all live well without consuming much. A major objective of this book is to show that the latter option is possible and attractive.

FAULT 2: THE UNJUST GLOBAL ECONOMY

Markets do some things well and in a satisfactory and sustainable society there could be a considerable role for them, but only if carefully limited and controlled. It is easily shown that the market system is also responsible for most of the deprivation and suffering in the world.

The basic mechanisms are most clearly seen when we

consider what is happening in the Third World. The enormous amount of poverty and suffering in the Third World is not due to lack of resources. There is for instance sufficient food and land to provide for all. The problem is that these resources are not distributed at all satisfactorily. Why not? The answer is that this is the way the market economy inevitably works.

The global economy is a market system and in a market scarce things always go mostly to the rich, e.g. to those who can pay most for them. That's why we in rich countries get most of the oil produced. It is also why more than 600 million tonnes of grain are fed to animals in rich countries every year, over one-third of total world grain production, while more than 850 million people are hungry.

Even more important is the fact that the market system inevitably brings about inappropriate development in the Third World, i.e. development of the wrong industries. It will lead to the development of the most profitable industries, as distinct from those that are most necessary or appropriate. As a result there has been much development of plantations and factories in the Third World that will produce things for local rich people or for export to rich countries. But there is little or no development of the industries that are most needed by the poorest 80% of their people. The Third World's productive capacity, its land and labour, have been drawn by market forces into producing for the benefit of others, especially Rich World corporations and consumers. This is most disturbingly evident where most of the best land is devoted to export crops while millions are malnourished..

The Third World problem will never be solved as long as we allow these economic principles to be the major determinant of development and to deliver most of the world's wealth to the rich. For these reasons, conventional Third World development can be seen as a form of legitimised plunder.

The crucial point here is that these appalling consequences cannot be avoided in the present global economic system. A market system cannot result in just outcomes, or attend to needs, or respect rights, or protect social cohesion or the environment. A market system by definition lets the highest bid take the scarce goods so it will always do what most benefits the rich. If you changed the system so that instead it respected justice and needs, cohesion and the environment, it would no longer be a market system.

In other words our affluence and comfort in rich countries are built on massive and appalling global economic injustice. Few people in rich countries seem to understand that they could not have their high 'living standards' if the global economy was not enabling them to take far more than their fair share of world resources and to deprive Third World people of their fair share. What they are told of course is that development defined in terms of 'growth and trickle down via market forces' will in time lift all to prosperity, when in fact this is the mechanism that deprives them and enriches the rich. (Chapter 6 will deal with the claim that development is indeed lifting the poor out of poverty; all that needs to be said here is that from here on the scarcity of global resources will completely disqualify this solution).

But that is not the end of the unpleasant story. Rich countries work hard to control an empire. They use aid, trade power and especially Structural Adjustment Packages to make Third World countries run their economies in the ways that suit us and not them. We support many dictatorial and brutal regimes willing to rule as we wish, enable and actually engage in terrorism, invade and attack and kill thousands of innocent people, all in order to ensure that regimes and regions keep to the economic and development policies that suit the rich countries. (That might not be the only motive, but it is always the result). Few people in rich countries seem to understand that these things must be done if our supermarkets and petrol stations are to go on being well stocked. How much oil would we get if we did not support the brutal Saudi Arabian dictatorship, or had not got rid of the Iraqi one when Hussein began to behave in ways that did not suit us?

Thus reflecting on the Third World problem makes clear how very unsatisfactory and irredeemable the world economic system is. There is no possibility of satisfactory Third World development until the rich countries stop hogging far more than their fair share of the world's resources, until development and distribution can be determined by need and not by market forces and profit, and therefore until we develop a very different global economic system. Again this must mean huge and radical structural change in our societies, to simpler living standards in rich countries and to an economy that focuses on meeting need rather than maximising profit.

It is not possible to have a good society unless we make sure that considerations of morality, justice, the public good and environmental sustainability are the primary determinants of what happens. But in the present economy all these factors are largely ignored while we allow what is done to be determined by what will maximise profit within the market for those with capital. A satisfactory economy might have a place for private firms and markets, but it must have basic social control and regulation of the economy. (It is made clear in Chapter 4 that this should be via highly participatory local political systems, not centralised states and bureaucracies.

Social cohesion and the quality of life.

In addition to the foregoing global resource, environmental and justice problems, in the richest countries we are experiencing social breakdown and a falling quality of life. This is basically due to the triumph of neo-liberalism. Most people are not given a satisfactory share of the wealth, jobs and resources. Most people are having to work harder, in more insecure circumstances, and many are being dumped into 'exclusion', so it is no surprise that there is much drug abuse, crime, stress, violence, family breakdown, mental illness, alcoholism, depression and suicide. Public institutions are deprived of sufficient funds, especially hospitals, universities, and public transport. Social attitudes are becoming more selfish and mean. Increasing numbers of people believe the future will be worse than the present. Neo-liberal doctrine advocates that all should compete against each other for as much wealth as possible, when the sensible way for humans to relate to each other is in cooperative and collective ways. It is this damage to collectivist values and social cohesion that is the most disturbing consequence of the dominance of neo-liberal ideology. Again these are direct and inevitable consequences of the basic structures and forces at work in consumer-capitalist society and they cannot be remedied in such a society.

Thus the major global problems are explained.

These two basic faults in our society are crucial for understanding the major problems threatening us. For instance we have an alarming environmental problem essentially because there is far too much producing and consuming going on. We have a problem of Third World poverty, deprivation and under-development because the rich countries are taking most of the available resources and forcing poor countries to comply with an economic system which devotes their productive capacity to our benefit. We have problems of armed conflict mainly because some are determined to get hold of far more than their fair share of the world's resource wealth. We have increasing inequality because market forces inevitably enable the rich to take more of the available wealth. We have accelerating social breakdown and deteriorating quality of life because the top priority is maximising production and consumption, business turnover, and GDP, rather than welfare and quality of life.

Conclusions on sustainability and justice.

The evidence referred to in this chapter is widely known and little of it would be subject to major dispute. Yet its significance is not generally grasped. Following are the conclusions which I think are very difficult to dispute, but which for the most part are not drawn.

❏ The magnitude of the overshoot is enormous, much too big for technical advance and conservation effort to solve the problems. Sustainability cannot be achieved without huge reductions in resource use and in commercial production and consumption and therefore GDP, perhaps to 10% of present levels.

❏ Rich world 'living standards' are built on massive global injustice that condemns billions to deprivation and results in misery and death, because we are taking most of the resources that should be devoted to meeting their needs.

❏ Both these lines of argument confirm the essential factor in our situation, which is scarcity. There are nothing like enough resources for all to live as the few in rich countries do now, let alone to live in the fashion economic growth will lead to.

❏ We urgently need to shift to systems that enable us to live well on a far smaller per capita throughput of resources.

❏ The problems cannot be fixed in consumer-capitalist society. They are created by the fundamental and defining systems of that kind of society. They can only be solved by change to different systems.

From here on, thinking about the global predicament and the nature of a satisfactory society must focus on these themes. The remainder of Part 2 will seek to provide detailed support for some of the central elements in this overview of our situation, and to show that there is a viable and attractive alternative way.

Appendix: Can non-fossil energy sources solve the greenhouse problem?

World energy demand is heading for more than the doubling of the present amount, approximately 500 EJ[1] in 2009. Let us assume that by 2050 demand will be 1100 EJ/y. There are only four options for attempting to provide this – conservation/ efficiency in use, coal with sequestration of the CO_2, nuclear energy, and renewables such as the sun and wind.

Let us assume that energy conservation etc. cuts 25% off the supply required to provide services, and that 25% of the reminder is easily provided low temperature heat (which is unrealistic for northern rich countries). The task would then be to provide 620 EJ/y of 'final' energy.

Geo-sequestration of CO_2 can capture only 80-90% of the CO_2 generated when coal is burned and when all sources are included, such as emissions from coal mining, the figure is around 75% (Hazeldyne, 2009). In addition it can only be applied to stationary sources, such as power stations. This means it cannot deal with the approximately 50% of carbon fuels used in other sources, such as transport. These two factors mean that it might take out only 30% of gasses emitted by the use of fossil fuels.

The 2007 IPPC Fourth Assessment Report said we must cut CO_2 emissions to 5–13 GT/y. If we achieved the former figure electricity generated by coal use would have to be about 86 EJ/ y. However it is increasingly likely that before long the general agreement will be that no emissions will be permissible by 2050

---

1. One Exa-joule (EJ) is equivalent to approximately 278 billion kilowatt hours.

(Hansen *et al.*, 2008, and especially Meinschausen, 2009). This is because observed effects of climate change have been much more extreme than the IPCC expected. All warming trends have been running above the upper limits they envisaged. For the moment it will be assumed no electricity can come from coal use plus geosequestration. (We'll come back to this).

Let us assume that 60% of transport energy demand can be electrified. (Ships, aircraft and heavy trucks can't be run on batteries). The task therefore would be to provide 281 EJ/y of electricity to meet direct electricity demand (155 EJ/y) plus the 60% of transport demand (126 EG/y), the remaining 84 EJ/y of transport demand in liquid form, and another 255 EJ/y in non-electrical form.

Let us assume that biomass provides that 84 EJ/y of liquid energy for transport, although this is quite implausible because at 7 t/ha timber yield and 7 GJ/t net of ethanol per tonne of input material (Fulton, 2005) this would require 1.7 billion ha of plantations... when there are only 8 billion ha of productive land on the planet and demands on it for food, etc. are increasing.

What about nuclear energy? There is only enough fuel left to enable the present 8 EJ/y supply for about 80 years. Hydroelectricity is only likely to increase to approximately 19 EJ/y globally.

So the task is to provide 281 EJ/y – 27 EJ/y from hydro and nuclear sources = 254 EJ/y, of electricity, plus 255 EJ/y in non-electrical form. Now where are we going to get that 255 EJ/y, when all the renewable energy sources except biomass provide only electricity? If we get it in the form of hydrogen generated by electricity we will probably need to generate 750 EJ/y. Why? Because converting electricity into hydrogen, distributing it, and using it are extremely energy costly or inefficient. If you run a car using a hydrogen fuel cell you will have to generate four times as much electrical energy as is to go through the wheels of the car (Bossel, 2004).

So the total amount of electricity to be generated might be 254 EJ/y plus 750 EJ/y = 1004 EJ/y. Let's divide the task between wind, PV and solar thermal. We would need almost 640 times as many wind turbines as we had in the early 2000s (Coppin, 2008). Where are you going to locate all that? Not within a very long distance of demand. Europe's total on and offshore potential has been estimated at only 4 EJ/y (Trieb, undated, Lenzen, 2009).

The most difficult task for renewables is meeting winter demand. Wind is at its best in winter but we can't store large quantities of electricity. Our best bet is solar thermal, with its capacity to store heat, located in the Sahara for European supply. The fairly detailed attempt to estimate potential and costs in Trainer (2008b) concludes that after all energy costs are taken into account a solar thermal plant might deliver a continuous flow of only 20 W/m2, or 8 kW per Big Dish (400m^2 in area). The equivalent of a 1000 MW power station would need 125,000 Big Dishes, each costing $146,000 (excluding several components such as transmission lines). This is an estimated future cost (Luzzi, 2000; Lenzen, 2009). One dish would deliver 21 GJ/month in winter.

So if solar thermal was to deliver one-third of the winter load, i.e. 28 EJ/month, we would need (28 EJ)/(21 x GJ) = 1.33 billion dishes, and the total cost would be $195 trillion. Averaged over a 25 year plant lifetime this comes to $7.8 trillion p.a... which is more than 17 times the present total world annual investment in the supply of all energy forms (Birol, 2003). Note that this is just for the solar thermal contribution and the PV contribution would be far more costly. It also only takes into account the cost of the dishes, not that of the associated heat storage plant or the long distance transmission lines.

It must be stressed that these quantities refer only to meeting the average demand through a winter month. There would still be the problem of maintaining a constant supply of energy, for instance through a week of calm and cloudy weather across a whole continent.

The 1100 EJ/y target taken in this exercise is far below what it would have to be to provide 9 billion people with the per capita energy consumption we Australians are heading for. That would be about 4 times as great. You can see how wildly inaccurate the assumptions in this exercise would have to be before it became remotely possible for renewable energy forms to provide all with affluent lifestyles. Even if we assume that geosequestration of CO_2 can enable that 83 EJ/y, or much more, it would not make that much difference.

The widely publicised Stern (2006), IPCC (2007), and Garnaut (2008) reports proceed on the assumption that alternative technologies can sustain a society premised on affluent lifestyles and limitless economic growth, without giving any attention to these issues to do with the limits of renewable energy sources. (For critical arguments see Trainer, 2008c and 2010.)

This is obviously not an argument against transition to renewables. Part 2 explains how we can do that. It is an argument that we can't all live affluently on them.

Chapter 3

THE ECONOMY: A MAJOR SOURCE OF THE PROBLEMS

The alarming range of global problems facing us is due primarily to the economic system we have. This chapter discusses the major faults in the global economy, and the changes needed. The core argument is that these cannot be fixed. The structures built into this economy inevitably generate these problems and if we were to eliminate the causes of the problems we would have a radically different economic system.

The next chapter deals with the kind of alternatives economy we must try to build.

FAULT 1: COMMITMENT TO GROWTH

The most glaring fault built into our economy is the commitment to growth, i.e. to constantly increasing the volume of production and consumption with no limit in view. The taken-for-granted assumption is that economic growth is the key to improving everything, because it means that the 'wealth' produced increases all the time, and this means that 'living standards' are rising.

Not much needs to be said about this issue after Chapter 2 showed we have gone way past the limits to growth. Our present volumes of global production, consumption, resource use and environmental impact are far beyond sustainable levels, and beyond those that could be extended to all the world's people. Remember the footprint situation. It takes 8 ha of productive land to provide one person in Australia with their food, water, settlement area and energy but the amount of such land available in the world per capita is only 1.2 ha, and by the time population stabilises at 9+ billion it will be 0.8 ha. Each person in a rich country is already using about ten times as many biological resources as is possible for all.

This and other lines of argument referred to in Chapter 2 show that we should be reducing resource use and environmental impact to a small fraction of their present levels. This cannot be done in the present economy, because such an economy cannot tolerate protracted reduction in business turnover or sales. In fact unless growth of around 3% p.a. is maintained problems such as unemployment become serious.

So although we are already producing and consuming far too much our economy is obsessed with constant and endless increases! Most people do not understand how much greater the levels of output will become if we continue with economic growth. To repeat, if an economy grows at 3% p.a. then in about 70 years time its total output will be 8 times as great every year as at the start. Economists and politicians want at least 3% p.a. growth. If a) we in rich countries do have 3% p.a. growth to 2070, and b) if the world's population is 9 billion by then as is expected, and c) by then all people have risen to the 'living standard' we would have in Australia, then the total volume of world economic output would be 60 times as great as it is today! Yet the present levels of production and consumption are unsustainable.

Clearly these 'limits to growth' arguments force us to accept some extremely radical conclusions. This economy is grossly unsustainable. It has far overshot sustainable levels of production and consumption. We must not only shift to a zero growth or steady-state economy, we must dramatically reduce production, consumption, 'living standards' and the GDP to a small fraction of their present levels. Yet most people, including most politicians and economic leaders steadfastly refuse to even think about these limits arguments and plunge on, taking the increase in incomes, production, consumption and GDP as their supreme goals. The absurdity of the growth commitment has been the focus of a small number of concerned academics and activists for decades but we have failed to get the issue onto the agenda of public discussion. This wilful ideological blindness indicates how unlikely we are to solve the overall sustainability problem.

The volume of wasteful and unnecessary production is enormous – but essential. This economy involves a huge amount of production that is unnecessary and wasteful. Consider for example, items we do not need much or at all (e.g. cosmetics, sports cars), things that are more elaborate and expensive than is necessary (e.g. cars, houses, clothes), items not made to last, or made to be thrown away, all the packaging that could be avoided, the effort that goes into advertising, the wasteful competition between firms trying to take sales from each other, and the 'defensive expenditure' now required to fix problems caused by over-production or by social breakdown. Advocates of The Simpler Way argue that if we lived more simply in highly self-sufficient local economies we might cut our per capita resource consumption by 90% and we might only need to go to work one or 1 or 2 days a week.

However this economy must maintain or increase the amount of waste. Without waste the economy would collapse. If we decided to stop producing even a few of the things we do not need there would be a jump in unemployment and bankruptcies would skyrocket. The economy would plunge into depression. It is not possible to reform this economy so that it just produces as much as we need.

Advertising and marketing.

Little needs to be said here about the fact that most of the $550 billion now spent each year on 'marketing' is an appalling waste of resources that could be applied to useful purposes or left in the ground. Most advertising is wasteful competition between corporations to take sales from each other in a zero-sum game, most obviously in tourism, car and soft drink sales. In a sane society no effort would be made to persuade anyone to purchase anything. Some few resources could be put into making available good information on products available, via the internet, so that anyone who needs to buy a new item could look up the models that are available. Arrangements might be made within 'news' services to announce new products.

Why do we still have to work so hard?

Over the past three decades the real average GDP per capita in rich countries has more than doubled meaning that we could have 1970s 'living standards' on an average work week of about 17 hours. Yet hours of work are increasing, overtime is increasingly unpaid, work conditions are deteriorating and jobs are more insecure than ever. How can this be? Why is it that despite such an enormous increase in output and average wealth, everyone is having to work harder, try harder to find something to sell, worry more about their future, and to endure less security? Clearly the wealth produced is much greater than it was previously, so why don't we have more of it, or more time to take things easier? How come that no matter how much wealth the economy produces, people still have to struggle harder to produce and sell something?

The answer is, mainly because the super rich are taking the wealth. Yes part of the answer is that people have chosen to spend much more (e.g. on more expensive houses), to take the increased 'wealth' as more possessions rather than as more leisure. But most of the answer is that we have an economy that enables the rich to take most of any increase in wealth while it forces the rest to strive ever harder to earn a sufficient income. Just consider the basic trends in inequality. For instance, over 30 years the average income of the American super rich 1% increased 157%, while the average for at least 40 million fell (see below, p.53).

Conclusions on growth.

It should be glaringly obvious that holding economic growth as a goal is absurd and suicidal, yet few realise this and all governments hold growth as their supreme goal. This is a source of profound despair. The global 'footprint' of a rich person is already about 10 times as great as will be possible for all yet the entire world is fiercely and unquestioningly determined to increase production and consumption, without limit. The core theme of this book should again be obvious. A growth economy cannot be fixed – it must be totally scrapped. It is not possible to solve our most urgent problems while we have an economy that must increase production and consumption all the time and without limit.

The alternative; A zero-growth economy and a tiny GDP per capita

Given that the core global problem is far too much producing and consuming going on we must develop an economy in which not only is there never any increase in GDP but in the short term we must cut it to a small fraction of its present level.

Consider the essential features of a sane economy. It would enable all to contribute to the production of the goods and services that are necessary and just sufficient to give all a good quality of life, with as little work, resource use, waste and environmental impact as possible, and needless to say, without any unemployment. Every element in this statement contradicts the nature of our present economy.

These goals could be achieved with a small fraction of the work, investment, trade, production and consumption and resource use of the present economy, and without any problems of inadequate hospitals or shortage of housing etc., if we simply organised some of our existing productive capacity to the task. If we did so, then there would be a vast amount of work, resource use, jobs and products that we no longer needed, so we could avoid these and devote the time saved to things like arts or sitting in the sun. It is madness that we now work 40+ hours a week when 15 might do, so the point is to develop an economy that makes that possible.

The implications of this first principle for a sane economy are mind-boggling. If we must cut the amount of producing and consuming going on dramatically that means most firms will have to be phased out, most capital will not be needed, and therefore most capital markets will become redundant. If there can be no economic growth then there can be no interest paid on loans. That means almost the whole of the finance industry must be scrapped. It also means that procedures for old age cannot involve superannuation investments and other arrangements will have to be made. You don't like the look of this... don't want to work out such radically different alternatives? Then you had better prove that unlimited growth in production and consumption on a finite planet is possible.

FAULT 2: PRODUCTION IS FOR PROFIT

With modern productive technology we could easily meet all basic needs, yet several billion people suffer severe poverty and deprivation. Even in the richest countries there is huge unmet need. Thousands of people go without basic housing. We need more and better hospitals. Millions of Australians live under or just above the poverty line, going without things most people regard as necessary. Why are these needs not met when they could be met so easily?

The answer is, because it is not an economy in which we ask what needs producing and then organise our productive capacity to meet those needs. It is an economy in which,

❑ most of the productive machinery (capital) is owned by a very few people,

❑ who decide what to produce by asking what will make most money for themselves,

❑ and they can always make most money producing relatively luxurious or more expensive things to sell to people who have higher incomes than they can by producing the cheapest possible necessities for the most needy people, or by producing what is best for society and the environment.

What drives this economy is the determination to accumulate capital, i.e. the intention of those with capital to invest in whatever will make most profit, in order to have even more capital next year to again invest where it will make as much money as possible, in a never-ending spiral. In other words, a fundamental fault in our economy is that it is a system of production for profit and such a system ignores need. If you give people with capital the freedom to produce only what is most profitable to themselves you will inevitably end up neglecting the needs of many poorer people and of the environment. This is simply because the poor can't pay much for products so the factory owners mostly produce for and sell to people with more money. Again such a system cannot attend primarily to need. It cannot be fixed. There is a head-on contradiction between producing what is most profitable and what is most needed.

FAULT 3: THE FREE MARKET IS THE ALLOCATION MECHANISM.

There are only two basic ways to determine what should be produced and how it should be distributed. Either you decide via rational discussion of needs and rights, or you leave it all to the market. Yes, the former option can involve you in difficult problems of planning but the latter option will inevitably result in intolerable problems to do with equity, justice, rights, the environment and future generations.

In the present economy individuals have much freedom to produce, purchase and work as they wish. This seems desirable and there is no doubt that it is an immensely powerful productive mechanism. However the problem is that there is too much freedom for the strongest and richest to buy and do and take and develop what they like.

It is easy to show that most of the waste, human suffering and ecological destruction in the world is due to the working of market forces. In a market system what is produced and who gets it at what price is determined by who is prepared to pay most. The result is that in a market system scarce things always go to those who can pay more. Those who own resources will sell them for the highest price they can get, and richer people can pay higher prices. Poor people have little or no 'effective demand'. Need or justice is totally irrelevant and will not influence the outcome. In a market system it does not matter how desperately something is needed, it will go to whomever can pay most for it.

This is why one-third of the world's grain production, more than 600 million tonnes is fed every year to animals in rich countries, while around 850 million people are hungry. It is why the rich countries take three-quarters of the world's resource output and consume resources at a per capita rate that is fifteen to twenty times that of the poorest half of the world's people. Richer people take most of the valuable resources because they can pay more for them.

Even worse is the fact that market forces ensure that the wrong things are developed. For example in the Third World where there is an urgent need for development of farms and factories to produce for the majority of people who are poor, very little development of this kind occurs while almost all the investment

38

goes into developing farms and factories to export goods to rich countries. Why? Simply because these are the purposes that will yield most return on investment. Investors will never maximise their profits developing industries to produce what is most needed, because the most urgent needs are felt by poor people and it is always much more profitable to produce what relatively rich people want.

This is the main mechanism that has developed the world into the forms and structures that serve the interests of the rich countries and especially their corporate elites. Most of the productive capacity in the Third World now produces things that benefit only the transnational corporations, the few richer people in the Third World, and people who buy coffee in Rich World supermarkets – because producing to satisfy their demand is the most profitable aim for those with capital to invest.

'But the market makes the most efficient allocations.'

Conventional economists claim that the market makes the most 'efficient' allocations of resources and investment. This is absurdly wrong. It is only true if we define 'efficient' in terms of the monetary return on investment. If on the other hand we are concerned with using resources and capital to meet needs most effectively, or to do what is morally right, or to develop what is sensible or best for the environment, then market forces are not only appallingly inefficient, they will almost always result in precisely the wrong outcome! Resource producers never sell vital resources to those in most need. Foreign investors never develop industries to supply what most poor people need. Market forces never result in just outcomes or those most likely to preserve the environment.

Every winter in Britain many old people die of hyperthermia. They cannot afford sufficient home heating. It is not very profitable to produce cheap hot water bottles or insulation. It is however very profitable to built weapons and luxury housing, so this is what is done instead.

Conventional economists, and most people, think the market system is working well, but this is because it has had such desirable consequences... for most people in rich countries. What they overlook is the fact that they are rich. They are among the few in the world who win and take wealth when markets determine production, distribution and development. The market system does work well – for them. They have 'effective demand', i.e. the money to buy things. There are three large groups who have no power to bid in the market and therefore will get nothing from it – the poor majority of people on the planet, all future generations, and all other species. Before you claim that the market works well ask those groups how well it works for them.

'The freedom of enterprise'

Conventional economists claim as a merit of this economy the fact that it gives people a great deal of freedom to buy and sell and invest as they wish. But the foregoing examples show that in our economy there is far too much freedom of enterprise, freedom of purchasers and of investors, and freedom for market forces to determine what happens. Corporations and richer people have far too much freedom to do and to get what they want. Third World plantation owners are free to plant coffee for export rather than food for local people. Transnational corporations are free to invest in luxury production and to avoid investing in what most needs producing. Richer people are free to take most of the scarce resources and goods on sale by being able to pay more for them.

It is of course desirable in principle to ensure that people have considerable freedom to do what they want, but obviously in a good society there must be many restrictions placed on individual freedom. There are many things that it makes sense for us not to allow each other to do if we want an orderly, sensible, just and sustainable society. For example it is not a good idea to allow people the freedom to drive on whatever side of the road they wish. This would reduce the freedom from danger that we all want. When those who own most of the Third World land have the freedom to produce what they like this undermines the freedom of most people to have sufficient food.

The basic question should always be, 'What arrangements will maximise the overall social benefit?' In general these arrangements will restrict some freedoms, especially those of the few who are most rich and powerful and therefore most able to take much more than their fair share and thus to deprive others. Yet conventional economists proceed as if the fewer restrictions on economic activity the better, and we are in an era of globalisation when the giant corporations and banks are trying to reduce the remaining capacity governments have to regulate their activities. When they call for more 'freedom of trade' and investment they mean they want more freedom for corporations to go where they like and do what they like without regulation, and thereby more freedom to take all the resources and markets available.

Thus the dominant neo-liberal assumption that a society functions best when all are free and encouraged to maximise their own individual advantage in competition with all others, is patently ridiculous. This is a recipe for vicious grabbing, winner-take-all, increasing inequality, the deprivation of the poor and the eventual destruction of society and its ecosystems. You cannot have a good society unless you make sure that the strongest few don't take everything and unless you make sure that what is done is what is best for others, for society as a whole and for the environment. This often means individuals and corporations must not be allowed to do whatever will maximise their own benefit.

These have been arguments against the acceptability of a free enterprise or capitalist economy. It does not follow that the alternative has to be a 'communist' or 'socialist' economy in which all productive property is owned by a state which totally controls the economy. The next chapter will show that the economy of The Simpler Way is quite different. In a satisfactory economy there might still be considerable scope for markets, private firms and freedom of enterprise, but there would have to be social control (exercised in mostly small local economies through open and participatory processes) whereby all people share equally in making the decisions. These decisions will include allowing many domains to function without much or any regulation.

'Move over, pal – find something else to sell'.

One of the worst faults in this economy is the fact that everyone strives to take over as much of the productive activity as they can, without any limit. People with little firms try to grow, to get more sales, taking markets from competitors if they can. Gigantic corporations put huge numbers of firms out of business all the time, by selling more cheaply and taking the sales and customers the others used to have. These displaced people then have to search hard for something else to sell. (Most people only have their labour to sell). In recent years much of the foreign investment in the Third World has not set up any new operations, it has just taken over existing firms. As a result there is constant high pressure on all to find something to produce and sell, even though the total amount of work done and stuff produced and sold are far greater than would be necessary to provide well for all.

The conventional economist says this situation motivates everyone to work hard, innovate and produce goods that are cheaper for us to buy. It is true that the most energetic and efficient producer can offer goods more cheaply than the little people he drives out of business, but that should not be the only consideration determining what happens. What about the social consequences? What about the possibility that it is not as important to have cheaper goods as it is to have all people happily in jobs or running little businesses, or to have a more equal society, or to head off the long term loss of social cohesion we are witnessing? What about the possibility of avoiding all that hard work, stress, anxiety and unnecessary competition? And what about the possibility that this system pushes us all to produce far more than is ecologically sustainable?

All that production, wealth and the income which many little people used to enjoy has been taken by the owners of the successful firms of course. Once, many little shopkeepers in the town shared the sales opportunities and the income that could be made there – but then the big supermarket chain came in and took those markets and sales from them. Now the business, income, purposeful activity and satisfaction that was shared between many all go to a very few. This mechanism is one of the main forces at work constantly making incomes more unequal, because the few are most able to win in the struggle to take sales, so they then take over more and more of the business to be done and the money to be earned. The rest are then forced to scramble to find something else to start selling. This is very difficult, so it is no surprise that many turn to illegal ways of getting an income, or that many individuals and corporations do morally questionable things to get more sales. However if we simply shared the producing among all the people who want work and incomes, all could have a satisfactory livelihood without this constant pressure to increase the volume produced, and without fuelling growth of GDP and inequality.

In a sane economy we would make sure that there were strict limits on how much one person could take. (Some tribes do this). We would have rules which stopped the few who are most smart, competent, powerful, rich or energetic from taking much more than they need, and thereby taking scarce things others need and forcing many others to get by on less than their fair share. We would work out ways of somehow sharing the work and goods, to make sure all were provided for. Especially important, we would make sure that all people had a livelihood, a way of earning a reasonable income and getting satisfaction and self-respect from being able to work and contribute.

'But', I hear you say, 'society benefits when all are free to maximise their self interest. Adam Smith said so. If someone develops a much better way of doing something, that will benefit society. Shouldn't he be free to market it and get the reward?' In a good society we would grapple with problems like this, working out how best to provide for all, encourage and reward innovation while not allowing such processes to leave anyone without a livelihood. In a very good society the innovator would be happy to give his new idea to society without expecting to become very rich from it, i.e. in a situation where wealth was not idolised and he knew he and all others could always live well without having to struggle to be one of the few winners.

Humphrey Davey invented a safe light for miners. The lights previously in use caused catastrophic methane explosions which were killing many miners all around the world. Davey didn't patent the light, enabling it to be produced cheaply and quickly used everywhere.

Of course people in a capitalist society would reject the suggestion that there should be such social control over both the economy, and how rich some individuals could become. Both the few who benefit most by the system and people in general would fiercely insist on a system in which a few are free to get very rich taking more than they need, in which they all try to be one of the winners, and they all cheer the winner who becomes a tycoon, with no concern for the many who lose their livelihoods in the process and the many who can't keep up.

Endless, mindless, un-winnable competition.

This economy forces us all into constantly competing against each other for scarce jobs, markets and export sales opportunities. It makes corporations waste huge amounts competing against each other for the same limited sales opportunities, e.g. through soft drink advertising. Even though we already do far more working and producing than would be necessary in a sane economy, everyone has to struggle all the time to be more productive, efficient and competitive, with no point in sight where we can ease up because we have developed a sufficiently productive economy.

Why do people go on working frantically at things that are not important or desirable, such as making weapons, digging up gold, selling cigarettes, advertising junk food, pushing drugs, running gambling casinos? Why would anyone do these things if they could gain a sufficient income doing something worthwhile? But in this economy that can be very difficult and for many impossible. In a sensible economy we would a) think out what needs doing, b) share out the necessary work, and c) share out what we produced. If we got all this done by Wednesday afternoon we would just shut the factories until the following Monday.

Similarly, nations are increasingly dependent on competing against each other to export, mostly into markets that are already glutted. Huge efforts are made to find things to export, and to beat others to markets. A country's entire economic situation can collapse if it does not constantly strive to produce and export more cheaply than everyone else. Meanwhile the rich countries can buy commodities at the low prices set by the fierce competition between poor nations trying to win export markets for their limited range of crops or minerals.

It is absurd to organise the world and the fate of all people in terms of competing to sell. Not all can win in a competition. Only the strongest win and then take more than their fair share while many miss out altogether. In a sane world nations would produce mostly to meet their own needs, at a relaxed pace, and would export only a few things in order to be able to import the few necessities they could not produce.

Privatisation.

As neo-liberal doctrine has become more dominant since the 1970s it has increasingly been taken for granted that governments should not run enterprises because these are more efficiently run by private firms, i.e. left to market forces. Consequently there has been a huge transfer of operations such as railways and power supply from governments to private corporations.

The assumption that private firms run things more 'efficiently' than governments is a myth. The evidence from studies of firms that have been privatised does not clearly show that they then perform better, nor that the total social benefit has increased. It seems clear that some kinds of enterprises are best left to private firms but governments can run many things quite well (see Hodge, 2000).

More importantly, 'efficiency' is not the only factor that matters. Governments should retain control of many industries in order to achieve social goals, such as making sure all have access to satisfactory services like water supply, health care and pharmaceutical goods, keeping prices down by competing with private firms, and locating factories in needy areas. If governments give up their operation of enterprises they reduce their capacity to influence the development of society. In the Third World neo-liberal doctrine, especially imposed through the Structural Adjustment Packages, forces governments to give up much of their power to make development decisions, by insisting that governments should not own firms and that development should be left to private corporations. This means governments can't make sure national resources are devoted to developing what will meet national needs. As a result, when Bolivian water supply was privatised the profit-maximising corporations cut supply to poor areas.

Governments can retain, or set up, firms in areas where jobs are needed or where the services are needed, whereas corporations will dump those areas as soon as they can make more profit somewhere else. One of the big Australian banks recently closed its branch in a country town, because it was only making 17% profit! The fact that the town might need a bank was of course of no concern, whereas if the government had owned that bank it could have been kept open at no cost to society. Note how this reveals the absurdity of conventional economic theory which asserts that allowing profit maximisation to determine everything results in what is best for society.

A similar illustration comes from drug R&D where the problems affecting most people on earth are ignored while drug companies focus on new hair-restorers and cough syrups to market in rich countries. Malaria is one of the most deadly diseases in the Third World, but drug companies hardly devote any research to anti-malarial drugs, because in rich countries hardly anyone suffers from it. Only about 1% of new drugs developed are relevant to the major Third World illnesses.

Unemployment

Unemployment is a central element in a market economy, because labour is treated as just another commodity that can be bought and sold in a market. Unemployment reveals some of the economy's worst irrationalities and injustices.

In this economy it would only be possible to solve the unemployment problem if there was a huge increase in the amount consumed and therefore in the amount produced and in the jobs required for that. But we do not need anywhere near as much produced as there is now, and present levels of production and consumption are beyond sustainable in view of the resource and ecological limits of the planet. If we only produced as much as was sensible, with modern technology the unemployment rate might be well over 80%! In a satisfactory economy we would organise to share the rather small amount of necessary work among all who wanted work.

In this economy labour is treated as just another 'factor of production', like bricks or land, to be used in production according to what will maximise the return on investment. But labour should not be treated as just another commodity. Labour is people. It is alright to leave a brick idle or to scrap it. It is not alright to leave a person unemployed and without a reasonable income. It is not alright to let market forces determine whether a person is dumped into unemployment. The fault here is in excluding from economic decisions all but money costs and benefits when such costs should be given much less attention than considerations of justice, morality and the welfare of people and ecosystems. The misery of unemployment, the damage it causes to morale and self-concept, are serious costs, which economists and people with capital completely ignore. In a satisfactory economy we would keep people in jobs even though this was less efficient or more costly in monetary terms (although we would help them move to other activities if that made more sense).

It is easy to organise an economy without there being any unemployment. There is none in the economy of the Kibbutz settlements, or in tribal societies, communes or monasteries. In those economies people simply arrange to share the work that needs doing among the people who want work. Only backward, brutally callous and uncivilised societies allow unemployment. Right now we could easily have a system whereby the government employed all who could not get jobs in normal firms to work on producing things they need and on important national needs, such as environmental protection. They could be paid partly by the present unemployment benefits but also from increased taxes on the rest of us if necessary. In a good society we would be quite happy to pay more tax if this was necessary to eliminate unemployment.

It is also worth pointing out here that the real unemployment rate is usually about twice the officially stated rate. If you want full time work but were only able to find one hour's work in the week that the survey was taken, they put you down as employed! Studies of the numbers who want work but have given up looking etc. find that by any acceptable definition unemployment is typically twice as high as the government says. Consider how many social needs could be met if the workforce was usually 10 - 15% larger, and if these people could work on socially desirable projects.

Unemployment also shows how it is an economy that suits the owners of capital much more than it suits workers. It is great for the people who own factories to be able to hire workers when that's profitable and dump them into misery and deprivation when they wish. Also note the powerful ideological forces at work here. Unemployment is very bad for people. It has bad effects on health and families. But it is not seen as such a bad thing that we should get rid of it.

During the Great Depression millions of people suffered idleness and poverty for a decade, yet the 'leaders' of society would not take any steps to organise these people into cooperatives where they could put their labour and skills into producing for themselves many of the basic things they need. They could very easily have been helped to develop gardens and small cooperatives to build houses, furniture etc., and provide entertainment and services for each other, at almost no dollar cost to the state. This was not done simply because it would have been contrary to capitalist ideology; it would have been seen as 'socialism'. Conventional economists would have said it was voodoo economics. It would have been very much against the interests of the rich for the working class to have found that it could provide for itself in these ways which contradict the market, 'private enterprise' and the assumed need for capital.

At one point the NSW Premier Lang refused to pay interest on the public debt to British banks, arguing that the money should be used instead to benefit the people in great deprivation. This provoked a serious conflict. Even the Australian Federal government fought against him. During the Irish Potato famine conventional economists argued against assistance to the starving peasants because this would interfere with the normal working of the economy... at a time when Ireland was exporting food. These are powerful illustrations of the toll in human misery caused by the domination of conventional economic doctrine... which, surprise surprise, typically recommends what suits the owners of capital.

It suits the owners of capital if labour is treated as a commodity to be bought and sold in a labour market, like bricks, and just left idle if no one wants to buy any of it. But many important things should not be treated as a commodity that can be bought and sold, including children, friendship, the judgments of courts, loyalty, national defence, good health care, prison sentences, fire protection, clean air, safe water, public parklands... Again the power of capitalist ideology is apparent. Almost everyone, including unemployed workers, accept without question that whether or not people can have a livelihood and an income and thereby escape the misery of unemployment should depend on whether employers can make more money giving people more jobs. The fault here is not greedy, nasty employers. It is an economic system that treats labour as a commodity to be traded in a market, and it is the failure of people in general to see that such a system is unacceptable.

Inequality.

The market mechanism built into the foundations of this economy has a powerful tendency to create and increase inequality. The market heaps goods, income, wealth and opportunities on those who are richer in the first place, and if much effort is not made the poor majority will be deprived and dumped. Fifty years ago reducing inequality was an important goal of governments but in recent decades the surge of neo-liberalism has pushed it off the agenda, and we are seeing rapid polarisation. Consider the following statistics.

❑ One-fifth of the world's people get 86% of world income, while the poorest one-fifth get only 1.3%.

❑ The average dollar income for half the world's people is about $2 a day. For one billion it is $1 a day.

❑ In 1991 there were 274 billionaires; by 1996 there were 447. Their assets equal the annual income of the poorest 3 billion people on earth (Korten, 1999).

❑ Almost all of the world's productive capital, i.e. its corporations and banks, are owned by about 2% of the world's people.

❑ 1% of Americans hold 33% of American wealth (North, 2001, p.83). They have doubled their wealth since the 1970s (Wolff, 1999). However the wealth of the median American household fell 10% between 1989 and 1997. The poorest 80% of Americans have only 14% of wealth (Dyer, 1997).

❑ Between 1971 and 1997 the income of the poorest 20% of American families fell 1%, while that of the richest 5% rose 157%.

❑ About 28 million Americans work but are paid the minimum wage of $5.15/hr, less than the poverty level income. More than 47 million Americans cannot afford health insurance. About 400 Americans, 0.0013%, own as much wealth as the bottom half. In 1955 the income of the richest 400 averaged $125 million p.a., but by 2005 it had risen to $263 million, inflation adjusted. In that period their average tax fell from 51% to 17%, and corporation tax payments fell from 33% of all tax to 7.4%. Over 30 years the top 1% doubled their real income, while that of the bottom 90% fell. Productivity increased 45% but the median wage was below that for 1979 (Monkerod, 2009).

These appalling figures are an inevitable consequence of an economy which allows a few to own resources and productive capacity and to put them into whatever purposes are most likely to increase their own wealth, and to take the wealth others once had (e.g. the firms, forests, fisheries) by beating them in the competition for sales. In the neo-liberal era of the past 35 years governments have greatly increased the freedom for the rich to take more wealth and to drive welfare and labour conditions down.

Wilkinson and Pickett (2009) have shown that inequality does not just affect those excluded, it damages the whole of society and reduces the welfare of even richer people. They found that the more inequality a society has the worse just about all indicators of welfare and quality of life are, such as rates of crime, illness and stress. The struggle-to-get poisons society. It focuses attention on self-interest and detracts from the socially constructive contributions that enrich us all.

Most people think that great inequality in wealth is quite acceptable because there is 'equality of opportunity', i.e. all have the opportunity to get ahead, to do well at school, start a business, and become rich. There is an important distinction between equality of opportunity and equality of outcomes in society. You could have a society in which a very few were very rich and most were very poor, but all had an equal chance of getting into the rich group. We would not be content just to have given every one an equal chance to become rich or impoverished. In a good society we would not want there to be serious inequality of outcomes and we would not want anyone to be deprived of basic necessities. Again this can't be achieved unless steps are taken contrary to market forces to prevent serious inequality from emerging. Reflect on the power of the ideological forces at work here, ensuring that there is little or no discontent with the obscene wealth this economy heaps on a very few and the deprivation it inflicts on very many. Few seem to think the situation is appallingly unjust, wasteful, destructive of human life, and offensive in the extreme.

The solution to the global problem of accelerating inequality is not redistribution of income. Unfortunately most concerned people think it is. This is 'slap on a patch', 'end of pipe' reformist thinking at its worst. 'Accept the system that generates the obscenity, just get the strongest and richest to allow a little more of their wealth to be transferred to the losers.'

A good society provides well for all its members and does not generate serious inequality. It has arrangements and rules which ensure that all have at least a sufficient share of the work and income and amenity available. This contradicts the basic principles of consumer-capitalist society which enshrines the right of the rich and strong to take as much as they can. You can't fix such a society so that it does not have serious problems like unemployment and savage inequality.

Insecurity.

We are many decades past the point in time when we could have produced all that would be needed to give everyone a good life, with the security of knowing that it can't be lost. But in consumer-capitalist society we are all highly insecure and vulnerable. You could lose your job, or have an accident, or go bankrupt. Will you be cared for when you are old? It is a mark of a primitive and barbaric society that such concerns exist. Tribal people do not have these worries. They are far more secure than we are. That's why there is a thriving insurance industry. Tribal people don't need one. If a house blows away everyone comes over tomorrow to rebuild it.

Consider the insecurity of your retirement prospects when they depend on the fate of the global stock market, which can eliminate your superannuation nest egg overnight. Insecurity is an inevitable consequence of the boom and slump character of the economy. During the boom phase there is no restraint as firms rush to make as much money as possible, then over-reach and the house of cards collapses with devastating consequences on millions who lose jobs, houses, businesses, and lives. None of this is possible in the economy of The Simpler Way, because we all hold the power to continue producing the things we need, even though the global economy might self-destruct.

Immediately after a crash, when everyone is wailing about lost jobs, incomes, firms, houses and economic activity the society possesses exactly the same amount of productive capacity, as many fields and factories as it had just before the crash. But no one seems to see the absurdity of a situation which will then keep all that productive capacity idle for years. Why not just organise to put the idle workers to work in the idle factories? The answer is because that's not acceptable, indeed not even thinkable in capitalist society. It could not be done unless society could somehow decide rationally to plan it and deliberately do it, but this contradicts the principle of leaving things to market forces. Productive enterprisers must only be set up if and when someone with capital thinks that will make good profits. Again it is glaringly obvious that (a) such a system cannot be fixed, and (b) the dominant free market ideology is so powerful that the absurdity of the situation is not recognised.

Globalisation '... is inevitable and good.'

Globalisation has been primarily a response to the most fundamental problem a capitalist economy faces, which is where to find profitable investment outlets for all the capital that is constantly accumulating. In the twenty year boom after World War II this was not difficult, because of the pent up demand and the need for reconstruction. But by the early 1970s it was becoming increasingly difficult to invest profitably.

Globalisation is essentially about corporations and banks wanting to get rid of the barriers hindering their access to more investment opportunities. It involves removing the arrangements which protected local firms, forests, labour, resources and markets for use by local people and preventing foreign corporations from taking them. The corporations are therefore increasingly able to enter markets previously out of their reach, to move to where the wages and conditions are lowest, to drive local producers out of business by undercutting their prices and thereby taking their trade, to take over local firms, to divert previously protected local land and resources into producing for export via transnational corporations. The three major strands in globalisation are deregulating (reducing government control of the economy), 'freeing' trade and investment (allowing more to be determined by market forces), and privatising (selling government run businesses to private corporations).

The problem of where to invest the ever-accumulating surplus has also fuelled the orgy of speculation, that is, gambling that has created futures markets, derivatives and hedge funds, and has resulted in the series of recent crashes – the 1987 share market bust, the Savings and Loans crash, the Asian melt down, the dot-com bust and the 2008 sub-prime initiated global financial crisis. It is a mistake to see these speculative frenzies as due to the greed of the financial managers, brokers, screen jockeys and CEOs. That's there abundantly, but it is not the basic cause. The problem derives from an economic system in which that surplus capital constantly accumulates generating a problem of where on earth to invest it all profitably, and therefore generating a need to speculate in ever more risky ventures.

In the extremely narrow and warped terms that conventional economic theory uses globalisation achieves miracles. That is, it results in leaps in investment, trade, business turnover, profit, technical change and GDP as capital can get into more fields. But as is usually the case with conventional economics, this is highly misleading, and it distracts attention from the effects that matter most. These include the savagely destructive impacts on economies, societies and ecosystems, on the welfare of most of the world's people, and especially the lethal effects on the world's poorest and most needy billion.

A satisfactory government must be able to protect and assist its own people, even though this might mean interfering with the wishes of investors and restricting what they can do. But under the new rules governments have given away their power to block or control what corporations want to do. Typically governments are legally prevented (e.g. by the trade agreements they have had to sign to be able to export to rich countries) from protecting their people against many of the things the corporations want to do. Some governments have actually been fined hundreds of millions of dollars for trying to restrict what corporations are doing, e.g. trying to ban a corporation's ecologically undesirable products from sale. Any such attempt will be judged by the World Trade Organisation as 'interfering with the freedom of trade'. It will even be difficult to stop a corporation from coming in and processing your forests or minerals or water resources to sell overseas, if you want to preserve these... because that would be to 'interfere with the freedom of trade'.

Thus what happens in a country increasingly depends on what it suits the transnational corporations to do there. Small and economically weak countries must compete against all others to earn export income. If the corporations can buy commodities more cheaply somewhere else then the country can't export and therefore can't pay for imports of necessities. If it does not suit corporations to do anything in your country then you can have no development. If your government then decides to develop needed industries itself, Moodys will immediately drop your credit rating and the World Bank will tell you your loans will be terminated. The only kind of development permitted is that which allows market forces to determine what happens, i.e. that which is a delight for the corporations and the shoppers in Rich World supermarkets who purchase their exports. The corporations therefore have an open world in which to do business with little or no restraint or obligation, along with the power to go into any country and produce or develop or buy what they want, and to buy from many economically weak countries desperately competing against each other to sell on any terms.

Another important consequence of this more open and unregulated global economy is that governments have little control over financial flows. Vast amounts of investment capital can now suddenly rush into a country, or out, chasing speculative opportunities, causing very destructive booms and crashes. About 97% of the transfers of money around the world are not to pay for products, trade or investment. They are just to speculate or gamble, on currency rate changes. Thus in the 1997-98 Asian meltdown millions of people who had jobs and could feed themselves one day were plunged into poverty the next day because financial markets suddenly decided to sell a country's currency or withdraw investments. In some cases food prices suddenly multiplied by four. Had appropriate development been taking place these disruptions could not have occurred. People would have previously developed the capacity to provide for themselves in their villages and regions irrespective of what happened within the predatory global market system. Neo-liberal doctrine upholds this freedom for banks and corporations to destroy whole economies in the pursuit of maximum profit.

The world is increasingly governed by a few supra-national agencies such as the World Bank, the World Trade Organisation and the International Monetary Fund. For example the rules of the WTO enable three unidentified bureaucrats meeting in secret to judge on trade disputes and punish governments that 'interfere with the freedom of trade'. They can stop a national government from imposing a ban on imports produced in environmentally damaging ways or containing toxic chemicals. In the famous tuna case, one country was not able to ban the importation of tuna caught in drift nets which kill dolphins, on the grounds that this would be to interfere with the freedom of trade. The new rules of world trade have been extremely favourable to the corporations while contradicting the interests of most of the world's people. Their goal now is to extend the kinds of freedoms they have achieved in the trade area to cover foreign investment, the provision of services by governments, and the purchasing of governments, i.e. to drive back or eliminate government control in these areas and open up more lucrative business opportunities for corporations and banks.

The extreme class division; rule by and for the corporate super rich.

At the top of this society are a tiny number of super-rich who own and run the big corporations and banks, and who in effect run the world in their own interests. They have the resources to wage campaigns, fund the think tanks, bankroll the politicians before elections, pay for court cases and 'educational' campaigns. They own the media. They organise the forums such as at Davos where they decide how the world will proceed, and how to maintain acceptance of neo-liberal doctrine. (For an understanding of how they go about their work, and the vast sums they spend on it, see Carey, 1995, Herman and Chomsky, 1988, and Beder, 1997.)

In the last 30 years they have pushed the neo-liberal

globalisation process through, achieving the most massive and stunning grab for wealth the world has ever seen. Under the guise of 'freeing markets', they have remade the rules of the global economic game to secure their access to far more markets and resources than they previously had. Their triumph has been astounding. Governments have eagerly jumped to do what the corporate and banking elites wanted. Governments have voluntarily given up many of their functions and therefore are less able to control the development of their nations. Development increasingly becomes development of only whatever will maximise the profits of corporations.

Meanwhile even in the richest countries the welfare of most people has probably declined, judged by measures of stress, insecurity, public institutions and quality of life. Even measures of income clearly shown in the US that the situation of maybe 80% of people has not improved in decades.

Naomi Klein's *The Shock Doctrine* (2007) documents in detail the way this ruthless drive to get hold of more lucrative resources and investment opportunities now feeds on natural and social disasters. Immediately after the Asian tsunami, when large regions were devastated, governments rushed through new planning edicts and by the time the bamboozled survivors tried to work out where their huts used to be they found that whole areas had been rezoned for tourist resorts and plantations. When a state fails and there is chaos, by the time the dust clears the IMF and World Bank have been in and helped 'to get the economy going again' with loans and advice – on condition that it be restructured in ways which transfer factories, land, forests and fisheries to corporations and local entrepreneurs.

Hence among the many cases is the tragedy of Mandela's South Africa, eventually liberated from apartheid but immediately trapped by the IMF and the World Bank. The ANC had fought a long and bitter civil war with policies of nationalising the corporations, redistributing land to the poor, taxing the rich, basing economic development on redistribution of wealth to the poor. Within days of coming to power the ANC was politely told by the international corporations and banks that they could not do any of that. If they tried the corporations would close their factories and re-invest in other countries, and no one would invest in South Africa, so the country could produce no exports or pay off its debt. Thus they were locked into conditions which prevented significant action on urgent social problems and which kept the economy geared to the interests of the corporate rich. Now those problems are about as bad as they ever were. Unemployment in many areas has remained over 40% for decades while the resources continue to flow out (Leahy, 2009). The abundant anti-globalisation literature documents the way the same steel trap condemns the Third World to inappropriate development.

Thus the last 30 years, the neo-liberal globalisation era, should be seen as a war for wealth and power – which the corporate super rich won. Again if you doubt it take a glance at the trends in global income and wealth inequality. Never have the rich few increased their wealth so greatly or so quickly. In 2008 there were 700 billionaires in the world. In 2009 there were 1100 (A.B.C., 2010). Of course many in the upper middle classes have been among the big winners too, benefiting from the crumbs they get for serving the elite, providing the professional and managerial services.

None of this can be reversed. It can't be fixed. You can't re-regulate the system. You can introduce a bit of regulating, but not much. Let's go back to basics. As Marx made clear long ago, capitalism is about the constant drive to accumulate capital, to invest in order to make more money, to invest... in an endless spiral. This is the fundamental 'problem of surplus', detailed in Baran and Sweezy's *Monopoly Capital* (1966). They explain the chronic need to find enough outlets in which to invest the ever-accumulating surplus. The building of the railways, the coming of the automobile, and the expansion of the 'defence' industry solved the problems at different times in recent history. However, by 1970 the pressure had built again and to intolerable proportions – hence globalisation. They had to push down the barriers, the regulation, the boundaries blocking them from getting into all the business being done by state owned enterprises and into all the fields previously blocked to them. If you now try to regulate seriously, preventing the corporations from taking the land and forests and fisheries and allow poor people to have more of them, you will be cutting down significantly on the opportunities for profitable investment the neo-liberal push opened up. The system can't tolerate that. Move significantly in that direction and you will bring on a depression. A satisfactory society would need only a small fraction of the production, consumption, factories and capital investment this economy has, so what would happen to all that unnecessary capital? You can't fix such a system; you have to replace it.

Why have our governments let it happen?

There is now a large literature detailing these criticisms regarding neo-liberalism and globalisation. Unfortunately most people who are dismayed about the situation see it as having failed or as being irrational, because it is not solving our problems. This is a major mistake. It is to assume that the World Bank and the IMF are run by bunglers who can't see that their Structural Adjustment Packages and the privatisations, deregulation and enforcement of market solutions do not work. This is quite wrong; these policies do not fail, they work like a dream. But they were not intended to work for the poor, or for you.

The people who work for the World Bank are highly intelligent and highly paid and have access to immense research capacities. Do you think they do not understand that globalisation and the neo-liberal agenda have brought economic and social destruction to many countries over three decades while enriching the corporate rich, and have inflicted increased death rates on the poor nations, when these consequences are heavily documented in a large critical literature, indeed in their own publications?

The situation has to be understood in terms of the limitless greed, ruthless power and brazen thuggery of the rich. They want more of the world's wealth, they want to get into more of the forests and mines and soils of the Third World, they want to be able to invest and buy and sell without interference from government, and they do not want their use of Third World resources to be determined by anything other than market forces, i.e. by any set of rules other than one which allows them to get the resources. The best that can be said for the World Bank and IMF officials and the corporate elites is that they have a blind faith in market forces, believing that despite the problems this is the best, the only, way and that in time the wealth will trickle down.

Why do governments go along, doing everything possible to facilitate globalisation, thereby serving the corporations and banks while betraying their own people? The main reason is because governments have no choice. They must cut corporate taxes (meaning less money to spend on hospitals), entice corporations to come in and invest, have their country judged by the credit rating agencies as a good location for foreign investment, reduce costs of production for exporters... or their country will not be competitive in the global market place. No government now can 'defy the global capital markets'. All must do what the corporations and banks want, or be trashed, i.e. abandoned by investors and unable to compete in trade. One consequence is that the big transnational corporations pay little or no tax because governments compete against each other to lower taxes on corporations to attract investment.

So the massively unjust global economy must be seen not as a result of unfortunate and unintended mistakes, but as the result of a deliberate and stunningly successful drive by the corporate rich to establish new rules which increase their freedom to accumulate wealth at the expense of everyone else. Governments pass the rules, all probably believing the virtues of globalisation and free markets, but even if they didn't global capital market forces give them no choice.

But in fact the economy is highly regulated... in the interests of the corporations.

The central point in the foregoing criticism of the market system is that to the extent to which market forces are allowed to operate then inequality, injustice, social and ecological damage will result, because most scarce things will always go to richer people.

While this explains much about the global situation, in many important areas outcomes are in fact not left to market forces. Decisions to regulate the economy are taken but they are decisions which suit the interests of the corporate sector. This has been especially glaring in the US under G.W. Bush where astounding tax benefits have been given to the very rich, massive contracts awarded without competition to favoured corporations (for example, in Iraq), vindictive labour and welfare laws enacted, and the vast arms sector receive ever increasing contracts. Similarly in Australia the 2006 labour legislation greatly benefited business at the expense of workers, while the screws were tightened on 'welfare', etc.

Nowhere is this regulatory action more glaring and damaging than at the level of the World Trade Organisation, IMF and World Bank. Globalisation can be seen in terms of new rules regulating the way trade, debt, foreign investment, etc. must be handled, but they are rules which suit the corporate sector. For example indebted countries must leave everything to the 'free market'... while rich countries are able to go on massively subsidising their agricultural exports.

So two apparently contradictory forces are at work. The neo-liberal ideology insists on free market policies, and the elimination of government assistance and intervention, regulation, etc. in those areas where the corporate rich benefit from such policies, while at the same time governments often pass laws which settle big economic issues by regulation quite outside the market sphere, again usually in the interests of the Rich World.

Markets are never entirely free. There always have to be rules governing aspects of their operation and governments set these. In the neo-liberal era the rules set have been a delight to the corporations and banks.

What role will be left for market forces?

It is not that market forces must be suddenly and totally scrapped. In the long-term future we will surely have learnt to run societies well without markets. Automated systems will arrange the production of the items needed and sensible collective decisions will adjust the list available. This will be made easier by the absence of growth, the reduced scale of production and consumption, and the fact that humans will have had the sense to focus on better things than consuming and maximising their wealth. In addition most production will occur within the local sphere where there will be well-established routines for depositing surpluses at community centres, swapping, barter, giving and taking free goods from the commons. This will leave relatively little to come from large and more distant factories. (Chapter 4 takes up these issues.)

However, in the next few decades there could still be a significant though dwindling role for market forces. The transition process envisaged here involves the gradual development of non-market economic arrangements beside and underneath those of the normal economy, which might remain in place for a long time. Market forces might also play a role in transforming the economy in accord with set limits, quotas and standards which are left to private firms to achieve.

The morality of the market is unacceptable.

The main reason for moving away from any use of market forces in the long run is to do with their unacceptable social and moral implications. Even if we were able to prevent market forces from generating unjust outcomes, the fundamental motivation within markets is not desirable. Markets require and reinforce attitudes, values and practices which are not merely undesirable but which are socially destructive.

In markets prices are always set as high as possible, which means that the driving principle is profit maximisation, i.e. greed. Price is not set by reference to the cost of production, or the capacity of the seller to make a sufficient income, or by what people can pay. Markets are always about suppliers trying to get as rich as possible, and buyers trying to pay as little as possible. That's selfish. It's not about mutual concern or justice or welfare. The seller does not ask himself what is enough; he asks what is the most he can get. In ancient and medieval economies there was often the idea of a 'just price', but we have no such concept today.

The conventional economist thinks that if supply falls price 'naturally' rises. This is not so. If you are running out of porridge at home the price does not rise. You decide who should have what's left in terms of what's best for everyone. Price only rises in situations where sellers find they are able to make you pay more and therefore choose to raise their prices even when they have no need.

The situation is predatory. You must be careful because the other person is likely to cheat you. If someone is forced to sell you pounce on a 'bargain'. People see no moral problem in taking advantage of someone who is forced to sell cheap, as in a fire sale. That's the opposite of friendly, helpful or caring.

These are not the ways people will behave in the satisfactory society we will have some day. They create an undesirable social climate where the focus is on self interest, competition, suspicion, adversarial relations and beating others. All this is usually mild, but it is not a desirable atmosphere. The attitudes and behaviours required in a market situation contradict the best human attributes, which are to cooperate, help, nurture, be friendly and give. Most lamentable is the way that the acceptance of the market system as normal legitimises unfriendly attitudes and behaviours and absolves us of responsibility for outcomes. It is taken for granted that it is acceptable to ruin a competitor or take more than your fair share by competing in the market. As Bookchin says, '...our economy is grossly immoral... the economists have demoralized us and turned us into moral cretins' (Bookchin, 1987, p.79).

The ideal foundation for an economy is giving and gifting. Most of the economies humans have developed have had this foundation. Anthropologists such as Sahlins, Maus and Hyde describe the enormously subtle and complex systems many tribal societies have whereby things are produced and exchanged by being given to others. The rules and processes are at times unintelligible to us. The first yams might have to be given to one's uncle's wife's mother's cousin. In the Western Pacific the Kula Ring involves the slow movement of ornaments around many thousands of miles of ocean islands. Hyde (1983) explains how the gifts must keep moving and must not be considered as property or saleable, or consumed. If food is received other food items must be passed on. The movement of the gift increases its value. Giving valuable gifts makes you richer. Giving and receiving impose heavy burdens, in keeping track of the many debts and obligations, and in having to meet them.

In the Potlach systems even destruction of wealth increases (social) wealth. Typically debts are not carefully tallied and what is given and what is received over time are not expected to balance precisely. It might be an insult to give back something of equal value; that's just trading. It is not a matter of the reciprocity involved in barter. If I give my friend a gift worth $5 and she gives me a gift worth $5 this is not a zero-sum transaction. A lot more than $5 in value passed between us, and we both become richer in the process. Folklore is full of stories reinforcing these kinds of rules; the daughter who keeps the mother's gift might die or turn into stone. Note the remnants of gift obligation in some of our ceremonies, the wedding, birthday and Christmas gifts. The crucial importance of giving and mutual dependence for social bonding, solidarity and security is evident.

When one encounters these inscrutably complex systems of rules, obligations, and meanings, often inextricably woven into religious belief systems, one is stunned by the insignificance of the merely economic sphere defined in dollar terms. The lives, behaviour and thinking of 'primitive' peoples are typically so crammed with meaning that the business of merely getting sufficient food and shelter seems to be of trivial significance. Yet this getting is almost all that people in consumer society concern ourselves with, and we do it in terms of an impoverished calculus centred merely on self-interested monetary gain.

Giving and receiving gifts binds. The individual experiences strong feelings of appreciation, indebtedness and obligation to respond. Social bonds are formed and strengthened. The process develops familiarity, friendliness, conviviality, mutual appreciation and assistance, interdependence, and a powerful concern for social expectations, rules and structures. At its best giving becomes an end in itself, motivated by desire to see the recipient pleased or flourishing, and there is no expectation of recompense. Selling or trading for money not only has none of these effects, it involves, indeed requires, precisely the opposite kinds of attitudes and behaviours. Obviously our goal ought to be to construct economies embodying as much gifting as possible, and as little selling in markets as possible.

In The Simpler Way we will experience conditions which both require and reinforce nice behaviour, i.e. behaviour intended to help others and to advance the public good. We will realise that our own welfare depends on not how fiercely we compete to win or get as an individual, but on whether we all give for the common good, for instance coming to working bees conscientiously, sharing ideas and taking surpluses to the community centre. We will realise that the richness of our lives derives from public sources, such as the quality of the commons, the concerts and the landscape, not from our personal bank balances. The incentives will be positive and will prompt cooperation. We will enjoy helping and giving, because people around us will benefit and smile and help us in return.

The smallness of scale will greatly increase the extent to which our new economies can embody gift exchange. Home garden surpluses will be given away. We will all give time to working bees and concerts. We will all have several days a week to drop in and help out at the joinery or library. We will interact with and know well many people in our small community, increasing the scope for friendly giving and receiving.

Economics should be thought of as pertaining to all the considerations relevant to production, exchange, distribution, consumption and development. Perhaps the most vicious fault in conventional economic theory is that it excludes from consideration every important factor other than monetary profit and loss. The moral quality of decisions, whether they are just, how they affect welfare or social cohesion or the environment are totally ignored. However in the new economies the main economic decisions will be made by assemblies which will clearly understand that all these considerations need be taken into account. More importantly, we will all recognise the immense importance of the social bonding and conviviality associated with giving so we will try to maximise its role in the economy.

The economic historian Polanyi is well known for his impressive discussion of the socially destructive nature of market forces (Dalton, 1968). He points out that previous to the rise of our present society, no other ever allowed the market to have a very significant role, and that we have made a serious mistake in doing so. Markets involve nothing but self-interest and if unbridled this will drive out and destroy the factors that constitute society. A society is constituted by the forces that transcend self interest. At best these forces and procedures must restrain and limit the scope for self-interest, or the powerful will take everything and consume everything including the environment. Polanyi insists therefore that the market must be 'embedded' in society, and that we have an urgent need to re-embed it.

In the next chapter it will be argued that this is not the ultimate solution. In the context of history, the market has been remarkably effective in driving technical/productive 'progress', and it will be neither necessary nor practically sensible to try to eliminate it in the next few transition decades. The Simpler Way transition strategy is about slowly phasing it down while developing an alternative beside it.

But contrary to Polanyi, the ultimate ideal situation will not be one in which a sphere which is intrinsically and inevitably morally and socially undesirable is embedded within an otherwise good society. The long term goal must be a society which is thoroughly characterised by convivial, inclusive and nurturing relations. It is no good if most of the time we treat each other in friendly ways, but from time to time go into a market situation where we try to maximise our own advantage at the disadvantage of others.

The uncertain issue this leaves is just how fast can we and should we try to move away from market relations in the decades of transition ahead. In the next chapter it is suggested that this will not be such a difficult issue if we constantly think about those needs that can mostly be met through 'gifting' processes. The swapping of surpluses and the contributions to working bees are examples and these will (have to) become major elements in the new economies we will soon start to build. It could be that we can gradually increase the role for these processes.

MONEY CREATION AND BANKING

Another major fault in the present economy is to do with the nature of money. In a normal, growing economy the amount of money in use or circulation, has to increase all the time. If we had in the Australian economy only as much money as we had in 1800 there would not now be enough to enable all the purchasing people want to engage in. So the amount of money in circulation has to increase constantly (in a growth economy). Where does it come from, and how does it get into circulation?

In the present economy it is done when the investment banks lend more money to corporations seeking to set up new ventures. But where do those banks get the money from to lend? If you don't know what the answer is you will not believe it when I tell you. The banks literally create the new money, out of nothing, just by writing numbers in the borrower's account. If they lent money they already had then it would be logically impossible for

65

the stock of money in circulation to increase wouldn't it? What the banks do is in effect just create money and lend it to the borrowers. (Only a small proportion of the money in circulation is in the form of notes and coin; most is in the form of numbers in cheque accounts).

Now there is nothing wrong about the creation of money from nothing. That has to be done. But the process whereby it is done in our economy is outrageous, farcical, and incredible. It defies understanding why the process is tolerated, although the main reason is that few people know what's going on.

The most astounding part is that after the banks have created the money they are allowed to own it and to lend it and get interest on the loans. This is just the same as getting a printing shop to print our bus tickets and then allowing it to own the bus rides the tickets represent, that is, to sell the tickets for bus rides and keep the money received.

Very few people understand that this is the process used almost everywhere, but there are many monetary reform groups around the world working to draw attention to the practice and to get it stopped.

The most ludicrous aspect is that when our governments need to borrow money, which they do all the time, in great quantity, they go to those private banks and borrow money from them, and have to pay it back with interest. As a result many billions of dollars of public wealth is continually drained into the coffers of the private banks and then into the pockets of their shareholders... when the entire process is absurdly wrong and avoidable and could and should be eliminated. In the 1990s Australian tax payers were paying about $18 billion every year to the private banks as interest on the money borrowed by their governments, from the private banks... who got the money to lend just by in effect printing it; i.e. writing the numbers into the relevant accounts. Could there be a more incredible, unnecessary, morally outrageous and ridiculous process? And on such a scale. Governments struggle to find sufficient revenue and many important needs go unfunded, and here we have a process whereby billions of dollars are not just wasted unnecessarily and avoidably all the time, but given to the people who are rich.

One serious consequence of the system is that all new money entering the economy is debt that must be repaid with interest. Now consider the logic of a system in which a certain quantity of money enters circulation this year but more than that has to be paid back to the banks at the end of the year. This is not possible unless even more money is lent during the year. Thus the amount of debt increases all the time. And note that if at a point in time everyone paid off their debts or borrowings from the banks, there would be hardly any money left in circulation, because almost all of it has been borrowed from the banks in the first place.

How should new money be got into circulation?

The way most monetary reformers advocate is for the government to create all new money and 'spend' it into circulation, by for instance paying for the construction of new roads. At first sight this seems to involve some kind of injustice, or con trick. The government gets the roads for nothing, just for adding numbers to the contractors' accounts. But another way of looking at the process is that in the long run, as the new money moves from contractors to the suppliers they buy from, and eventually to the ordinary people in society when those contractors buy things and pay wages, the whole society comes to hold those bits of paper, and thus shares the cost of the roads they now have. All the government has done is get the process to occur by creating the money and putting it into circulation.

There are many impressive examples of this in the monetary reform literature, cases where entire economies were lifted out of depression by a government creating money which enabled economic activity to commence and thrive. A much-discussed case was the town of Wörgl in Germany. Another was the building of public markets in Guernsey which triggered economic recovery. During the American civil war Lincoln desperately needed money to pay for the war effort. The banks were quite happy to lend it to him, but at interest rates that would have bankrupted the government. So Lincoln printed his own money. Possibly the most remarkable case was the way Hitler jumped Germany out of misery and into a thriving and immensely powerful economy in a few years, basically by printing the money that enabled large numbers of unemployed workers to be put to work.

The great merit of governments creating the money and spending it into circulation is that the money does not have to be paid back, and no interest needs to be paid to the government which issued it. The government just facilitates the building of the new roads, etc. built and paid for by society. The most important point about the process is that it enables productive resources that were available but not being used, to be brought into production. Obviously you can't build much with money in the form of bits of paper, they rot in the weather, and even less with electrons in bank accounts. The money should be thought of as just a device used in the process of connecting available productive capacity to needs it could be meeting. If the needs are there but there are no bricks or workers available then it doesn't matter how much money the government prints to pay contractors, nothing will or can be built.

In the present system capital is scarce. There are many socially desirable ventures that can't be undertaken because people can't afford to go to banks for capital at the interest rates the banks are charging. Money is treated as a commodity for hire. If you want to hire $100 so you can use it for a year you can only get it if you are willing and able to pay perhaps $10 for the hire. Consequently many projects that would be very socially valuable but can't make that kind of profit are not undertaken. It is hugely in the interests of the banks that money is kept scarce, because then its price, the interest rate on hiring it, is kept high.

These approaches, spending and giving government-printed money into circulation, have the great merit of avoiding dealing with banks and thus avoid having to repay plus interest. But they have a serious limitation. They stimulate the normal economy to do more of what it normally does, but that does not and cannot solve problems like poverty and unemployment. When the government pays for the new roads with newly created money, that money will mostly go to the people who build roads. Most of it will end up in the bank accounts of the executives and shareholders of the firms winning the contracts, and only a very small proportion of it will go to workers who were unemployed but got jobs building the new roads. The result will be a slightly bigger economy of the same form as before, that is a form in which many are unemployed and many are poor, and an economy in which there is still huge unmet need and many unused resources. This is not satisfactory. We need to think carefully about how the introduction of our own new currency can help us do what most needs doing, things like get rid of unemployment, make the town robust, cut its import dependence and increase its power to control its own fate.

At present there are many desirable ventures that could be set up in towns and suburbs which would do wonders for the quality of life of the people who live there, but they cannot be undertaken because people cannot get the capital, the money to set them up. It is not that the productive capacity is not there. The town often has plenty of land, skills and labour sitting idle. It always has many unemployed, bored, depressed and wasted people with needs which those productive resources could be meeting. But the people can't set up to produce anything because they can't afford to hire the money from the banks, at the interest rates the banks demand. This is the absurd log jam we can break simply by creating our own money. The next chapter outlines a very simple and effective way to do this.

Eventually no money creation at all!

In the longer term future the whole confusing business of money creation will have ceased to exist, simply because it will be a zero growth economy. In a stable economy we will only need a stable amount of money to enable only that stable amount of buying and selling going on.

WE SHOULD BE VERY ANGRY.

We should be extremely angry about conventional economic theory and practice. This economy produces and legitimises many actions and situations that are dreadfully bad. It is largely responsible for most of the chaos, deprivation, illness, waste, misery and environmental damage in the world, especially for the gross injustice generating the poverty of two to three billion people in the Third World. Remember the resources that could eliminate these problems are there but they are not applied to the problems because this economy prevents that. The economy is therefore also responsible for much of the armed conflict in the world, because much of it is caused by the injustice this economy inflicts. The deaths of tens of millions every year are directly due to the fact that this economy lavishes scarce resources on a few while taking resources from the poor majority and gearing their productive capacity to the benefit of the rich. Economic theory leads most people to think this situation is an unfortunate but inevitable side effect of the only kind of economy there can be.

Especially important is the fact that the limits to growth analysis of our global situation discussed above shows that this economic system has all countries on a path that is grossly ecologically unsustainable. Rich world rates of resource consumption are far higher than all could ever rise to, yet in this economic system the supreme goal in all countries is to raise 'living standards' and the GDP all the time.

Even if this economy were not causing injustice and ecological damage it would still be causing social problems and damaging the quality of life. It is dumping increasing numbers into stress, insecurity, poverty and deprivation. It has hooked most people in rich countries on the consumer treadmill (e.g. they have to pay at least ten times too much for a house). It makes you work far too hard, and it condemns you to a much more difficult, insecure, stressful and spiritually impoverished life experience than is necessary. Most if not all of our social, economic and ecological problems are getting worse, at an accelerating pace. Meanwhile the economy delivers obscene volumes of wealth to the super rich and the upper middle classes, and increases their power to ensure that governments rule in their interests.

The basic cause of all these effects is an economy in which abundant productive capacity is not geared to meeting need. The economy has structures and mechanisms built into it which inevitably produce these effects. It is a growth system. It is a system in which market forces determine outcomes. It is a system in which what is most profitable is what is done. It is a system in which the fierce and ceaseless drive to accumulate wealth can only lead to the takeover that is globalisation. Such a system cannot do anything but generate unsustainable resource demand and ecological impact, enrich the rich, increase the political power of the few who run the corporations and media and banks. The genie cannot now be put back in the bottle. Any effort to force the monster to stop clearing more forest, using coal, taking over more Third World land, and vastly exceeding a sustainable footprint, would have to impose dramatic reduction in the amount of production, sales, business activity, investment, trade and GDP. This is not tolerable to the owners of capital or to those who shop at supermarkets, and it is not possible in an economy that is in trouble if growth falls to 2% p.a. Such an economy cannot be fixed, it must be replaced.

People should be extremely angry at the system which has these effects but in fact there is little anger. There certainly is a great deal of discontent with the personal life experience individuals are enduring, with the stress, the overtime, the difficulty in paying the bills or finding work, and the insecurity, but these are not linked to any demand to get rid of the economy that causes them. For instance the immensely destructive Global Financial Crisis of 2008-9 was universally attributed to greedy bankers and hardly any realised that it was an inevitable consequence of a boom-bust economy cursed by an ever increasing problem of surplus. (Magdoff and Yates, 2009, argue this account).

Thus our task is again evident. We will get nowhere until there is rejection of the dominant ideology reinforcing mindless acquiescence with an economic system which even seriously disadvantages most people in the richest countries. The core transition problem is what can we do here and now to make that awakening more likely?

Chapter 4

THE NEW ECONOMY

The previous chapter dealt with the global economic level and the general system changes that have to be made in the nature and functioning of the world economy. This chapter takes up the major implication of that discussion which is the need to develop mostly small and highly self-sufficient local economies, using local resources to meet local needs, and under participatory social control. The main concerns of this chapter are to detail that vision and to show that it is workable, that it could deliver all the goods and services we need for satisfactory lifestyles, achieving very big reductions in resource consumption and ecological impact, and that it would enable enjoyable and spiritually rewarding communities.

It could be that the ways discussed in this Chapter will turn out to be much more frugal, austere and low-tech than we need to adopt. I do not think this will be so, in view of the future anticipated in Chapter 2. My concern is to show that if we do have to go that far, we could do so very easily and without hardship – if we wanted to do it. In other words the goal is to show that we could easily cut per capita resource use and environmental impact right down. If we do not have to go that far, then solving the problems will be that much easier, and material living standards could be that much more elaborate.

Many of the technologies assumed in this Chapter are low, not even intermediate. This means that if the very sophisticated and complex systems of the present globalised economy fail we could still get by well. So the account that follows might be regarded as a fall-back position. It is concerned with the ways we might have to go all the way to, and to show that these would be more than sufficient and satisfactory. Think about the ways we had in the 1950s. They were in general quite sufficient to enable a good life. Add to those the advances current technology make possible, plus sensible, caring social systems.

A satisfactory society cannot be an affluent society.

It is important to begin with a restatement of the fundamental implication deriving from the foregoing analysis of the global situation. A sustainable and just society for all people cannot be an affluent society. It cannot have high material 'living standards'. This contradicts almost all previous thinking about social progress, the future and the good society, including especially that from Left sources. Socialists and communist and Marx himself, let alone the Social Democrats, conservatives and neo-liberals, take it for granted that the ultimate social goal is material affluence. This has been regarded as good in itself, and the necessary means to solving other problems. Even Marx assumed that industrialisation and high material living standards are necessary before problems of inequality, poverty and the environment can be solved. The conventional assumption is that much wealth must be created and accumulated before a society can afford to deal with these problems. But scarcity disqualifies all that. A good society now has to be conceived in terms which contradict affluence and growth. This shreds conventional economic theory and practice

Economies must be mostly small and local.

If the analysis sketched in Chapter 2 is at all valid, then globalisation will soon be over. The two main things necessary for a globalised economy are elaborate IT, and lots of petroleum. The former is useless without the second. It's no good if instant communications can organise global production and trade networks unless the resources, commodities and goods can then be moved in vast quantities all over the world. If and when petroleum becomes scarce this will not be possible. The oil will not be there to fuel much transportation of exports and imports. In a satisfactory world the produce of Third World soils, forests, mines and fisheries will mostly be used by Third World people not by us. We will not be able to travel long distances to jobs or for leisure or holidays. Some things could still be organised globally, especially communications and IT, but there will only be a very small global economy. Whether we like it or not this will bring about the end of globalisation and the start of radical re-localisation. Households neighbourhoods, suburbs and towns will become the economic centres of our society. If we manage sensibly they will be highly self-sufficient, independent and secure, and quite capable of providing almost all the relatively simple things we need for a good life.

There would still be wider economic systems, including national economies and an international economy, because there would still be a need for long distance movement of some goods, such as steel and high tech equipment. The goal is not to make towns and regions completely self-sufficient but to go as far in that direction as is sensible, and the scope for this is extensive. We should think in terms of a process of say 20 years beefing up local sources while phasing down the imports, by transferring functions from big distant factories and plantations to small ones close to where we live. In general this would not involve serious inefficiencies because most of the things we would need can be produced quite efficiently on a small scale, and more importantly, the new ways will increase non-economic benefits such as security, employment and satisfaction from work.

Large numbers of small local economies operating on very low energy budgets cannot be controlled from the centre. There will not be the resources for large central governments and bureaucracies. The many small economies can only be run by local people, because only they know the local conditions and can make the right decisions, can monitor and plan in the necessary detail, can maintain the social conditions necessary for conscientious contributions and good morale, and can do all this without using much energy. (Chapter 6 will discuss the new politics and government).

The co-operative imperative.

The coming scarcity will push us not just towards collective ways, but towards taking cooperative social control over our local economy. We will quickly realise that we must work together to analyse our situation and to deliberately make sure we develop the systems that will meet our needs. The right use of scarce local resources to provide for all will not take place if entrepreneurs and consumers struggle against each other to conquer the available markets, to get as rich as possible and to buy as much as possible.

This can't be over-emphasised. If serious scarcity impacts the present individualistic, competitive attitudes and systems will very quickly lead to chaotic conflict and breakdown. The strongest few will take most wealth and the rest will fall into squalor and mutual destruction. We will soon end up with a kind of feudalism in which war lords control their regions. However, this prospect will be transparently obvious to everyone and people will see the sense of working cooperatively.

There must be considerable social control of the economy.

In other words these changes, far in the direction of frugality, a greatly reduced GDP and no growth, cannot possibly be made in an economy driven by individuals pursuing profit maximisation within free markets. In a difficult world of scarcity a satisfactory economy can only function via deliberate, rational, social decision making and social control of the economy. We would have to collectively phase out many unnecessary industries and radically restructure economies so that what is produced and where and who benefits is decided in terms of what will most effectively meet the needs of all. There is no possibility of a centralised state bureaucracy doing this. It can only be done satisfactorily by participatory democratic processes in the many small towns and regions in which most economic activity will have to be organised.

Therefore we must develop the capacity for local economies to collectively analyse their needs, discuss options, make good decisions about what to develop and how to run things, find as much consensus as possible and implement strategies effectively, while maintaining as much good will and enthusiasm as possible. However far from everything needs to be socially controlled. In the near future our concern would be to organise only those crucial functions that will not be carried out satisfactorily by the market. We would realise how very important it is to maximise the amount of 'private enterprise', i.e. small firms and farms owned by individuals, families and cooperatives, because this is conducive to efficiency and satisfaction. Many people get great enjoyment running their own little firm or farm or hobby industry the way they want to. The task for communities will be to provide as much freedom for this as is compatible with the guidelines, limits and priorities which must be there to make sure the town's needs are met. The social control will be exercised via participatory citizen assemblies well aware of the importance of not being heavy-handed or endangering town cohesion. They are likely to make sure there is only control of those things that must be controlled. Much of the economy will look after itself. For instance there will surely be no need for us to give any thought to controlling tomato supply, because home gardeners will produce all we need, for enjoyment and without any monitoring or quotas from town committees. If there is a shortage one year we will remember to plant a few more next year.

We might need to establish or assist vital enterprises such as bakers and bee keepers with loans and working bees, and help some firms to transfer to more important activities. If our town baker is struggling we will have work out how to help him, because we need bread. If he's not very good maybe it would be best if we organised assistance or training, or helped him move to some other activity but we would not dump him into bankruptcy, because that's a barbaric thing to do, and because we need the contribution he can make somewhere.

There would be many areas where we realised we needed to establish necessary firms, gardens, commons etc. maybe running them as co-ops or leasing them as private family firms. So although we will have to take overall responsibility for developing and running our own local economy this does not mean social ownership or control of everything. It means doing what is necessary to make sure we all get enough good bread, vegetables, water, entertainment... while leaving as many other things as possible free for individuals to do as they wish.

All this represents an astronomical change in the orientation of the people to their town or suburb. They will (have to) come together to take responsibility for controlling their local economy, whereas at present they have no reason or desire to do this. The situation will force us to organise co-operative arrangements, to think rationally about needs and gearing our productive capacities to meeting them, and to focus us on what is good for the town. Individuals will see that they will not do well if they compete against each other to survive, let alone get rich. People will see that their individual welfare depends heavily on that of the town, because the town contains the people who must be in good shape if they are to produce what all need.

The contradiction between this situation and present society could not be more graphic. In consumer society there is little incentive to cooperate or think about the good of the suburb, and there is strong incentive to try to beat others to take as much as possible for oneself. In a world of serious scarcity that is a guarantee of chaos. So it is likely that people will turn up for working bees to maintain the commons, and think carefully about what's best for the town before voting at the town meetings.

One of the many things we would take responsibility for is making sure there was no unemployment and that all had a livelihood. Only brutal and primitive economies dump people into unemployment, poverty and 'exclusion'. Our committees and town meetings would have to work out how to ensure that all of us could make a productive contribution. There is work to be done, there are necessary things to be produced, and there are people who want work. If we saw an unmet need, for instance if the town needed a bee keeper, then we would have the sense to try to organise that as an enterprise for someone. If he needed premises we would use our clay pits and working bees. If he needed capital we'd provide that via the town bank, may be as a grant.

We will at last be able at last to make sure that economic decisions are made with reference to all the relevant and important considerations, as distinct from having them made only in terms of one factor, i.e. what will maximise the incomes of those with money. When we are trying to decide whether to set up a new firm we will be able to discuss what weight to give to environmental factors, to the need for all to have work, the social value of the proposal, and the possible effects on equity, justice, town aesthetics, cohesion and the environment.

No centralised agency could make the right decisions for our neighbourhood or town. These can only be made by we who live there, because we are the only ones who understand the complexities and subtleties of the situation, the history, the people, the whims and oddities, the bioregion and what will and will not work there. We are the only people in the universe who know what landscape we will be happy with when we plant that newly dug up parking lot. Above all the town will not function unless we feel we 'own' the decisions, know we have the power to decide and act, and we feel we are running our own affairs. Without this climate the working bees will not be enthusiastically attended. Therefore the decisions cannot be handed down, even from local councils. (There would be a role for these and for states, although much diminished, for instance in facilitating restructuring and research and in setting health standards).

In the past many attempts to run economies deliberately, as distinct from letting market forces do it, have usually not worked out very well and have in some cases worked out very badly. But the coming scarcity will plunge us into quite novel conditions in which the main factors which doomed previous attempts will not apply. Most of the control will not be exercised by gigantic dictatorial, distant and secretive state bureaucracies, but by the relatively few of us who live around here. We will be under powerful incentives to be sensible and cooperative, and the task will be so much simpler than trying to run all aspects of a national economy in which the goal is to produce and sell as much as is possible and in which there is desperate zero-sum struggle of all against all. It should be clear by now that the social control required does not mean anything like the 'collectivisation' of all property or the elimination of private firms.

Those who are discontented with the present economy often say in despair that the only alternative to a free market economy is one planned and controlled by the state, and that recent history shows how unacceptable big-state, centralised, bureaucratic 'socialism' is. It is tragic that there is an alternative to both, but it is not considered. It is an alternative in which the rational planning and control over those local economic activities that must not be left to the market is carried out not by state bureaucrats but by us.

It will be evident that the new economy is not going to work well unless there is also immense change in world views and values. The arrangements sketched would work very well and very easily, but not unless people in general had the kinds of orientations discussed in Chapter 10.

The new geography, structures and institutions.

The geography of towns and city suburbs would include a great diversity of little firms, farms, factories, pastures, ponds and forests. Most food, goods and services would come from very close by with negligible transport costs. Many present roads within suburbs and towns could be dug up and replaced with commons. There would be much more public property than at present, including community workshops, premises for craft and art groups and all those commons. These would provide much 'free' fruit and materials for craft and small firm production. There will be maximum provision of local water and energy, and recycling of water along with all 'wastes'.

One of the most powerful forces in the new economy will be the voluntary working bees. There will not be the resources to sustain the large councils we have now so towns will have to develop and maintain much of their own water, energy, waste, parkland and other systems and infrastructures, through direct voluntary action. Some of the working bees will be regular and some ad hoc to tackle tasks that pop up, such as windmill breakdowns. The main event could be on Saturday afternoon, following the morning market, where major works are undertaken and maintenance carried out. (After the working bee we might have the weekly banquet followed by the concert).

Another crucial institution would be the neighbourhood community workshop, possibly a converted petrol station. It would have work space, tools and machinery, craft and art areas, an art gallery, meeting places, a large concert area (around the log fire), recycling racks, notice boards, a library and computers, and the coffee and scone making area. This is where the committees will meet. Town assemblies will do the governing in the main town workshop's big concert space. Ideally we would build our own community centres, very cheaply, using logs from our forests and our own mud bricks, then we would 'own' them. Such projects are too important and enjoyable to be left to contractors.

There would be no clear line between the economic and political domains. Our committees and town general assemblies would debate and discuss the 'investment' decisions, taking into account all the relevant factors bearing on town welfare, striving for solutions all agree are the best for the town, and owning the decisions thereby maximising the chances that all will turn up to the subsequent working bees.

These are elements in a totally new economy, one which contradicts the present economy at just about all points. Everyone would participate in running the economy and would be acutely aware that we have to make sure our economy runs well. The less we have to attend to the better so we would try to set up or assist firms to enjoy looking after their venture without us having to bother with the detail. But we would know how important it is to monitor and be ready to come in and assist, or arrange loans or working bees or work out how best to phase out and restructure, making sure no one is dumped into bankruptcy or unemployment. We need everyone to be productive and contented and to feel secure, appreciated and cared for.

Again, ideally most of the economy would be in the form of private firms and cooperatives, because that is likely to maximise the satisfaction people derive from a livelihood. The outlook in these firms would not be centred on making as much money as possible in competition with others. It would be about happily making a valued contribution to meeting the needs of the town, knowing that if we all do this our town will function well for all of us, and about gaining a sense of satisfaction and power from knowing we are running a town economy that provides well for all.

Concentric circles.

The geography should be thought of in terms of concentric circles going out from the household to the neighbourhood, the town or suburb, the region and finally to the national and international domains. The most important of these realms will be the household then neighbourhood and town. These are where most of the things we need will be produced or organised.

Diminished amounts will come from sectors at more distance, so not much will be imported.

Big firms?

It will always make sense to retain some big centralised ventures, such as for the production of railway equipment, steel and vehicles. However most things can be produced quite efficiently in small and distributed factories, even without adding the energy and social cost accounts.

HOW COULD THERE BE PRODUCTIVE SUFFICIENCY?

But how could the required low but sufficient level of material wealth be provided without much heavy industrialisation, transport, resource use, capital investment, trade, IT, high tech or a vast highly trained workforce?

Let us look in some detail at where the things we would need to live well would come from. The claim has been that almost all of them could come from little firms, cooperatives, gardens, farms, workshops and institutions close to where we live, and be produced from the resources around there.

Food.

Most of the good food we need for great meals could be produced within the towns and suburbs where we live, and almost all within a few kilometres. The sources will be intensive home gardens, tiny market gardens within the settlement, 'edible landscapes' and commons densely planted on public land throughout the locality, and the small farms just off the edge of the settlements. The space around your home would be packed with gardens, pens for small animals, fish tanks and ponds, nut groves, greenhouses, orchards, herb patches, bamboo clumps, woodlots and bee hives.

Especially important would be the commons, developed and maintained by the voluntary community working bees. Many of these should be on land that was once roads and parking lots. All food, animal and human wastes would then be easily recycled to the soils via compost heaps, garbage gas units and the animals. When green manure crops were included this would eliminate the need for artificial fertilizer production. Even flour can be produced in small intensive areas growing wheat, corn (or chestnuts, acorns, etc). on small farms close to where we live. Several crops can be produced from the same ground each year.

We would eat far less meat and this would greatly reduce the volume of produce necessary. (About two-thirds of the food produced in the US is not eaten by humans; it is fed to animals). Meat would mostly come from small animals such as rabbits, fish and poultry, living within our settlements and recycling food scraps to the soil. Poultry would live in free-range conditions. One of their jobs would be to clear, cultivate and fertilise garden beds.

'Waste' water, kitchen scraps, crop wastes and animal manures would go to compost heaps, methane digesters and fish ponds. The ponds would sustain a fishing industry, along with water fowl and wetland plant production. Running bamboo would be confined on islands.

Little agricultural machinery would be needed, because home gardening and Permaculture principles largely eliminate the need for ploughing. Horses could do most of the small amount of heavy work needed, although it would make some sense to have a small number of motorised vehicles and some farm machinery running on ethanol produced from biomass. Horses could also help with cartage, leisure and the provision of fertilizer.

Plants would also provide many craft and industrial materials, notably timber and inputs to chemical processing of cellulose, replacing petroleum sources of plastics. Many oils and waxes for industry, paints and cooking could come from the locality, including peanuts, olives, flax, bees wax, and fish oil. Herb cultivation would also provide sources of various medicines. Cheese, olive oil, dyes, tea tree oil disinfectant and soap are among the other items easily made on a small scale from local ingredients. These products would mostly come from small locally-owned firms and cooperatives which gave worthwhile work to people. Where produce was to be sold much of this could be done without sales people; just weigh your beans and leave the money in the tin. Many shops would need to open only one or two days a week. If you will want a new pair of shoes soon you can get them on Tuesdays when the shoe shop opens. That saves a lot of labour. There will be familiarity and trust in these communities.

There would be almost no production of synthetic pesticides, although natural ones can be made from plant inputs such a pyrethrum and tobacco, grown locally. There would be fewer pests in the complex Permaculture landscapes. (Monocultures encourage pest build up). Some bulk items such as grains, flour and milk would come from small farms close to our settlements. Honey would replace most sugar use, eliminating its transport and the ecological impact of sugar plantations.

Relatively little storage, packaging or freezing would be needed because fresh food could come from the gardens and fields just before use. Root crops can be left in the ground until needed. Traditional varieties which crop over an extended period enable picking of a few fruit when they are needed, while the rest ripen and store on the vine. Cellers and cool rooms can store fruit and vegetables, and there would be extensive bottling and drying.

Only small quantities of a few food items might need to be imported over long distances into one's suburb, for example salt. We would only eat fruits and vegetables during their growing or harvesting seasons, so there would not be the year-round supply we can now have from supermarkets. Some items would be problematic, such as bananas and coffee in colder areas and we would reduce dependence on these. However the world contains huge numbers of vegetables, fruits, nuts, herbs that will grow well in your neighbourhood but that most of us have never heard about. We would have community research plots trying them out to see which varieties will thrive in our conditions. We would develop recipes for them, and for the edible 'weeds' that will thrive beside roads and ponds. (New Zealand spinach is almost a pest where I live).

There would be almost no need for energy inputs into the food producing sector of the economy. In conventional agriculture these are enormous. Small farmers and home gardeners are far more energy-efficient than agribusiness. Perhaps all of the 17% of US energy consumption now going into food supply could be saved. There would be little ploughing, harvesting machinery, packaging, freezing, marketing, transport or waste collection and disposal. Households and shops would mostly buy from the local farm gate, thereby eliminating most marketing and advertising costs. The average item of food might travel only about 200 metres, whereas at present in the US the figure is around 2000 km. We would need almost no trucks, tractors, harvesters, silos, crop dusters, ships, supermarkets, advertising, cold stores, plastic bags, home freezers or garbage disposal. Because the food was produced close to where it was eaten all wastes could go back to the soils, serving as animal feed on the way. We could save vast amounts on food preservation, packaging, tins, bottles, labels, and refrigeration. Food could go straight from gardens and animal pens to the kitchen as it was needed, and from kitchens to animal pens and compost heaps without trucks and sewer pipes. Surpluses would be preserved in re-usable locally-made glass and crockery containers (not cans). Damaged fruit and vegetables could be used, whereas at present they are dumped because supermarkets will not buy them.

The much-reduced demand for clothing would greatly reduce the need for fibre production. Small farms could provide much of the wool, cotton, flax and leather needed. Some basic clothing materials such as cotton cloth, leather, threads and canvas might have to be supplied in bulk from more distant farms and factories.

Our food would be superior in quality because it would contain no pesticides or preservatives, it would be fresh, and highly nutritious varieties would be grown (as distinct from those that will store well and look good).. Many people would have satisfying livelihoods as small farmers. The total amount of time and labour needed for food production would probably be much less than at present, given that many now work in the trucking, processing, packaging and marketing areas of food supply which will be unnecessary. The move from heavy use of animals and meat consumption to greater use of tree crops and other perennials would also reduce the need for inputs of time, materials and energy. Water demand would be reduced by use of tree crops, perennials, mulching, drip irrigation and local catchment and recycling. The consequences for national ecological regeneration from these changes to agriculture would be immense. Modern agriculture is unsustainable and a major source of ecological damage.

The productive potential of these small-scale intensive approaches is remarkable, indeed barely credible. According to Blazey (1999, p.18) a family can derive all its vegetable needs from less than 50 square metres, using the best heirloom varieties, intensive organic gardening and multi-cropping. Modern US agribusiness requires 1000 times as much land to produce the same food value in the form of beef...plus lots of energy, pesticides and fertilizer, and then the food is transported to floodlit supermarkets, to be ferried home in the SUV.

Figures on the achievements of urban agriculture in Havana are similarly inspiring. Koont (2009) reports vegetable yields of 21 tonnes per ha per year, without use of oil, machinery or artificial fertilizers or pesticides. Such figures are partly due to intensive research into organic methods. We would always be trying out new varieties and ways, coordinated by formal committees. The task would be to find those varieties which thrived best in our unique local conditions, yielding the most tasty, pest-resistant, nutritious, drought-resistant fruit, with the best shelf life. We would stack our home gardens, commons and forest gardens with these so that we are eventually provided with abundant food, largely automatically.

Thus the topic of food provides a powerful illustration of the potential of The Simpler Way. It would be easy and enjoyable to meet food needs from simple local sources with negligible resource and energy consumption, and without significant ecological impact.

But wouldn't we all have to work long hours in the fields, like peasants, just to produce enough to survive? Emphatically not. At present about 15% of work time goes into food production. Only about 2% of work hours are put in on the farm so most of the time and effort that is taken up in avoidable packaging, transport and marketing could be saved by a localised agriculture. Therefore if we assume we would need the equivalent of say 5% of total present work to go into food production that would be something like only two hours per worker per week. That's much more than would be needed to run a large home vegetable garden, although we should also count time going into the working bees on the local commons and the little farms.

Obviously those who did not enjoy gardening would not

need to engage in it. They would buy what others produced and make their contribution in other spheres, as at present. Home garden surpluses would mostly be swapped, given away or left at the community centre. Committees would keep records and coordinate suburban planting so that all people would more or less know how much of what crops would be needed, what varieties did best last year, etc.

In communities very conscious of the need to make their local economies work well much effort would go into education, R and D, sharing expertise and mutual assistance regarding food production and all other activities. It would not be a matter of isolated householders struggling on their own to grow enough in their backyards to survive. It would be in everyone's interests to make sure that all were helped to run highly productive gardens and that all found the community garden working bees enjoyable.

As with most of the other domains discussed below there are desirable spin off implications for health, community and leisure and education. Gardening keeps you fit and for many it would be a major leisure activity. In addition the field days, shows, talks and research activities would provide sources of learning, entertainment and community bonding.

Furniture.

Furniture would be simple, cheap, robust and durable, made from local materials, mostly wood. It would be repairable, and most would be home-made by ordinary people. Some would come from local craft businesses in which people could enjoy making good solid furniture. These pieces might be relatively expensive, but they would last for generations, and cost would not matter since we could in general cover our monetary needs with two days work a week.

Various other items, notably toys, baskets, garden sheds, wheelbarrows, animal houses, carts, boats and storage sheds would also be mostly made from wood, either via backyard or small firm production. There would be much use of hand tools because craft production is enjoyable, but light machinery would also be used.

Clothing and footwear.

Almost all the clothes we wear could be simple, tough, cheap and durable, and much repaired. Few if any of us would need to work in a suit or tie. One of my hobbies is darning and repairing the old clothes I wear. One of my best jumpers lasted 35 years, until a bushfire got it. We might have a few 'nice' things for special occasions, but these need not be expensive. I have one pair of 'good' shoes, never wear a tie, and haven't worn a suit for about four decades. Those who were more interested in 'nice' clothes than I am could of course make or buy them as they wish but hopefully we would have the sense to scrap any notion of fashion. Some people could specialise in dress making and tailoring as a hobby small business.

Old and worn out clothing items would be recycled, sold via second hand shops or given away. Clothes making and repairing would be much-enjoyed hobbies. A few small local firms might mass produce some basic clothing items, mostly from locally grown fibres, and some basic footwear. Some footwear can be made at home via hobby production, especially slippers and sandals. There would be a great deal of that most miraculous art form – knitting, using wool spun from the local sheep.

Houses

All new housing, offices, premises and community buildings would be made from locally-produced stone and timber, but mostly from earth. Houses would be very small by present standards, with low ceilings. In my view tiny houses are in principle beautiful and big houses are morally ugly. The general building height limit would be four stories, eliminating the need for lifts. Most of the floors of single storied buildings would be made from earth, hardened by linseed oil, turpentine and bees wax. Some roofing would be earth (sod) over timber supports, or domes and vaults from mud bricks, surfaced by a thin layer of cement. Most roofing would eventually be ceramic tiles made from local clay and wood-fuelled kilns. Research would go into the production of durable sealers and paints from plant and animal sources. For instance earth walls can be sealed with a whitewash made from lime and milk.

People would have much more time for home-making, and

therefore for cooking with wood. A more vegetable based diet would reduce the amount of cooking needed. Rugs mostly made from wool would replace most carpets, eliminating the need for vacuum cleaning. (Take the rugs out and shake them, and sweep and mop the floors). Matting, seating and screens, as well as baskets and hats, can be woven from local reeds, rushes and willows.

Remember that we are talking about a stable situation, in which construction only takes the form of maintenance and replacement, not increasing the housing, office or factory stock. In other words most of the present construction industry would not exist and most of the building that was needed could be carried out by hand tools (...because this is more enjoyable). For many people, slowly designing and building their own home, helped by friends and with the advice of local experts, would be one of life's most satisfying adventures. No one would want a house and not be able to have one. At present maybe 100,000 Australians are waiting to get one, and large numbers never will because the only kind the market provides are absurdly big, expensive and ecologically unacceptable.

MY DREAM HOME

For many people, including singles and young couples the following very small cottage would be quite adequate. It is the house I would like to build and live in. However most dwellings would need to be considerably bigger. The purpose is to show how very low dollar and resource costs could be.

The ground floor would be one room perhaps 8m x 3m, plus a 3m x 3m toilet, washing and shower room (no bath), plus some storage. The main room would have a kitchen area at one end, with a wood fuelled stove, and a large table at the other for dining, writing and art purposes. In the middle of the long wall would be an open fire, an easy chair and a reading light.

The solar passive design would provide most heating and cooling, via air ducts and valves built in. A water jacket around the fire would siphon hot water to an insulated tank. Wood boxes would be built into the walls, to be loaded from outside. Ceilings would be low. A tiny stairway would lead to the sleeping area in the triangular attic, which would also provide storage space. There would be a small veranda to catch morning sun in winter, and rain water tanks. (I make tanks from cement plastered over chicken wire against a form, for about 1.5c/l. Plastic tanks cost about 70 times as much).

The walls would be cob, straw bale or rammed earth. Floors would be rammed earth over a plastic membrane, and surfaced. They would have pipes set in for circulating hot water. The roof ideally would be handmade tiles fired in the local pottery (only about 50 square metres needed), but in the near term would probably be corrugated iron over heavy (perhaps woollen) insulation. Roof frames would be from sawn 3x2. Ceiling beams would be unsawn saplings.

I would make all fittings, cupboards, window frames and furniture mostly from wood. Minimal use of metals and plastic. There would be no wall-to-wall carpets but there would be some squares and rugs. No fridge, but a solar evaporation cooling cupboard.

	Indicative dollar and energy costs (Assuming new materials prices, $A 2009)
Attic flooring	1000 - 1200
Roof framing	700
Roof iron	800 - 1000
Roof paint	100
Window glass	150
Wood for cupboards, window frames, furniture	1000
Floor surfacing	200
Water tanks (2 x 14,000 l)	400
Solar space and water heating panel, homemade.	200
Water pump, 12 volt	200
Plus: Small wood stove (could be home-made), sink, toilet, lights, wiring, switches, plumbing, pipes, taps. The table, bed and chairs would be home-made as bush-furniture from saplings at negligible cost.	
Total	**$(A) 5,300 ??**

Use of recycled materials would lower this figure considerably. Labour cost? Zero. The house would be home-made using hand tools as an enjoyable creative activity, partly assisted by local friends and builders, who would be paid by labour contributions. Build at a leisurely pace; move in when the roof is on and fit out slowly. Space for storage, hobbies, crafts, workshop? Simple sheds out the back. Electricity supply would add perhaps $2000 for two panels plus a battery and regulator.

Lifetime repair, maintenance, and insurance costs would be very low, given small scale and simplicity; mostly no tradesmen to be paid for maintenance. If necessary

rooms can be added on later. No significant running energy costs. No anxiety about losing your house because you can't keep up the payments... for thirty years.
Compare a normal house:

    Cost to build, perhaps $150,000

    Total sum repaid to bank, $300,000

    Sum to be earned to have $300,000 after tax, $400,000.

Add lifetime maintenance, heating, water and energy costs.

A normal house would be much bigger than my ideal, but assuming 150 square metres its cost per square metre of floor space would be approximately $2,500. The cost for my home outlined above, might be $170 per square metre.

Much cheaper houses than my ideal can be built from cob. See B. Bee, 1997. Earth built vault or dome dwellings are cheaper still, as curved roofs are also built from mud, surfaced by a thin layer of cement.

About 100,000 Australians want a house but can't afford one. Another 100,000 are homeless and must live in friends' houses, or on the streets. In a market economy profits are maximised building big and luxurious houses, not small, cheap and sufficient houses. The average new house built in Australia is now 220 square metres.

Craft industries.

Most items would be produced in households, neighbourhood workshops and small local firms, and they would be produced in craft ways, not via industrial factories. Crockery provides a good example. It should all be produced by hand in your suburb or town, from local clay, fired by wood grown there, and made by people who love making pottery. How many new plates do you need each year to replace those broken? Again when we recognise that we are talking about a stable population and economy we realise that much of our present production is aimed at increasing stocks and consumption, so in a stable society relatively small volumes of replacement production would suffice. Because people will not need to go out to work for money more than two days a week there will be much time for interesting home and neighbourhood productive activity, including via crafts.

Hand tools are sufficient for most purposes but 240 and 12 volt power tools would be produced. Neighbourhood workshops would have larger machinery including drill presses, blacksmithing forges, lathes and saw benches, for anyone to use.

Factories

Small regional factories would produce bicycles, cutlery, pots and pans, roof tiles, containers (although baskets would be made at the neighbourhood level from rushes, willows and vines), nails, bolts, buckles, hacksaw blades, plate glass, preserving jars, ladders, barrows, needles, tools, brushes, paint (from vegetable and fish oils, milk, lime, earthen colours), beverages (fruit wines, beers and ciders), string and rope from yuccas and sisal, etc. and basic appliances such as stoves, radios and fridges. There would be intensive recycling, and items would be made to last and to be repaired. Only small quantities of items such as electronic devices would need to be imported.

Some materials and tools, notably steel, would still be produced by large centralised plant supplying via railways to many small local outlets. Most steel would be in the form of small scale strip, tube, angle, and roofing iron, rather than heavy gage girders or plate etc, because most production would be of smaller items at the home workshop and small local firm level, not the gigantic level of ships, bulldozers, bridges and skyscrapers.

Attention would go into developing excellent designs for all things, especially models that would last, be easily repaired and save resources. Research would go into studying the effectiveness of designs in use and improvements would be cumulative. (At present much design is shoddy, deliberately flimsy and unrepairable, and new products often fail to benefit from experience with older models).

Water.

Because the new agriculture would rely heavily on permanent crops, especially trees, and relatively little meat would be consumed, the water demand associated with annual crops would be greatly reduced.

Water would be scrupulously harvested locally, from rooftops, catchments and creeks. There would be maximum recycling and reuse. There would therefore be little need for big dams, mains, large pumping stations, and the bureaucracies to run them. Windmills and 12 volt electric pumps would do all the pumping of fresh and waste water.

All 'sewage' would be dealt with at the neighbourhood level, thoroughly recycling nutrients back to local soils, eliminating the need for large systems of mains and pumping stations. Waste water would not contain industrial chemicals. This would be recycled on site. Composting toilets would cut water use and garbage gas units would produce methane for use while both returned nutrients to gardens. Settlements would be landscaped to retain rainfall via earthern bunds, swales and ponds, eliminating the need for concrete sewer and stormwater drains and pipes. Storm runoff would be channelled above ground to soak-in areas, where trees were planted. Few if any underground pipes, mains or concrete works would be needed. Above ground systems are easily monitored and repaired, unlike underground systems. Where possible redesign of settlements would catch water on the higher ground, feed it by gravity to houses, then take nutrient-rich waste water further down to orchards, pasture, ponds and farms, reducing the need for pumping energy.

Materials

Most buildings would be made from earth, straw bales, stone, bamboo and wood. There would be little use of energy-intensive metals and plastics. The reduced quantities glass, steel, cement and especially of aluminium might be produced regionally by solar and wind generated electricity in those periods when there is surplus supply. There would be intensive research into plant sources for chemicals, adhesives, medicines, paints, lubricants and fabrics. Most of the dangerous synthetic chemicals in use today would not be necessary. Design would focus on minimising problematic materials. For instance furniture can be made without metal fasteners, by use of dowelled and pegged joints.

Various materials would be produced in bulk in big regional or national factories, such as fabrics, metals and chemicals, and distributed to many small factories and workshops.

Demand for paper would be greatly reduced and might be met from local forests and recycling. Eventually roofing iron would have been slowly replaced by ceramic tiles from local clay and wood-fired kilns.

Cement would be a problem, given that it is such a valuable material enabling permanent structures, especially water tanks, yet it is energy-intensive. However the quantities needed would be small in view of the stable infrastructure stock that only needed maintaining, not expanding. When a stable settlement's infrastructure of tanks and methane digesters had been established there would be little further need to use cement. No cement would be used in the construction of high-rise buildings, big dams or freeways and bridges. Water can be stored in many small earthern dams along water courses, also enabling pumped storage for electricity generation.

Leather might also set difficulties, in view of the quantity of this valuable material that might be required in relation to the much-reduced use of large animals for meat consumption.

Transport and travel.

There would be little need for transport to get people to work, because most work places would be localised and accessible by bicycle or on foot. The few large factories would be close to towns and railway stations.

Neighbourhoods would be very leisure-rich, containing many little farms, forests, ponds, factories, windmills, craft producers, drama clubs, libraries, neighbourhood workshops and centres, and leisure facilities. Therefore we would want to travel for leisure, holidays and vacations much less than we do now. At present most people live in suburbs that are leisure-deserts.

A few cars, trucks and bulldozers would be needed. The vehicles in most use would be bicycles, with some but relatively little use of buses and trains. Horses can be used for some transport, especially carting goods. They consume no oil, reproduce themselves and do not need spare parts or expensive roads. Most roads and freeways would be dug up, the space used for gardens. The concrete can be recycled as building stone and bitumen lumps can stack as animal pen fences. Railway and bus production would be one of the few activities to take place in large centralised heavier industrial centres.

Very few ships, large trucks or aircraft would be produced because there would be little need for the transport of goods or people over long distances. There would be little international travel, partly because the fuel for that would be extremely scarce, and secondly because there would be relatively little need for it. We might ration international travel primarily for educational and cultural exchange purposes, so that you might get one overseas trip in a lifetime. However we could bring back wind ships, so you might study for your degree while on a leisurely trip around the world.

An intolerable deprivation? At present many would think so, given the taken for granted amount of that supremely luxurious self-indulgence that five billion people can't engage in – tourism. If and when petroleum becomes very scarce we will be jolted into understanding the unsustainability of the present levels of travel, transport, trade and tourism.

The consolation is that in your new enriched neighbourhoods and regions there will be many interesting things to do or observe, so there will at least be much less desire to travel. Electronic sources of information and documentaries could be more elaborate than they are now, enabling exotic leisure experience, cultural learning and exchange without travel. We will research and work intensively to enrich the leisure resources of our town or suburb, developing festivals, concerts, celebrations, picnics, adventures, dances and field days. One of the most important town committees would deal with culture and leisure.

Energy.
Far less energy would be required compared with the present. This would firstly be because we would be consuming far less, living in solar passive mud brick houses, recycling, getting to work on a bike, with close access to local sport, cultural and leisure facilities and therefore not travelling much for leisure, and we would be buying little that was imported. The total volume of production and consumption would be a small fraction of the present amount. Most of our economy would be localised, eliminating most travel to work and most transportation of goods. The reasons why the agricultural sector would use almost no non-renewable energy have been explained above.

Almost all energy would be produced locally, from windmills, watermills, garbage gas digesters, solar panels, and biomass sources of fuel and ethanol for vehicles. These sources would be augmented by larger scale regional wind farms, PV and solar thermal fields, etc., and much reduced grids. Horses, mainly

LOCAL MATERIALS FEEDING INTO LOCAL INDUSTRIES.

MATERIALS

FORESTS: Timber, (sawn, poles, fuel, biomass, mulch, honey, fruit and nuts

EARTH, STONE: Earth and clay for building, clay for pottery, sand, gravel, chemicals.

PASTURES: Wool, milk, leather, fat/tallow.

PLANTS: Food, biomass energy, fibres, flax, yucca, cotton, bamboo, reeds, rushes, willow, vines, cosmetics, air fresheners and deodorants, chemicals and medicines.

ANIMALS: Skins, leather, feathers, manure, milk, bone, wool, fertilizers.

WATER:

INDUSTRIES

FOOD: Baking, butchering, fish (from tanks), bottling, preserving, drying, cool rooms, cellars, poultry, pigs, dairy, beef, herbs, honey, milk, composting, worms, methane digesters.

HOUSE BUILDING: Mud bricks, timber, stone, sheds, shingles, fencing, carpentry, wood turning, handles, hurdles.

FURNITURE, CABINET MAKING:

FOUNDARIES, BLACKSMITHING: Casting, buckles, buttons, cutlery, metal tools (using imported ores and metals but local clays, wood etc. for moulds and fuel).

GLASS WORKS: Sheet glass, containers, equipment.

CERAMICS: Crockery, pipes, tiles.

CLOTHING: Dress making, hats, footwear, sheets and blankets.

CHEMICALS: Oils (from plants, nuts, flax, olives, sunflower, fish), dyes, pigments, medicines, paints, soap, pesticides (pyrethrum, tobacco, nicotine), wormwood, antiseptics (tea-tree oil, eucalyptus, wormwood, Aloe Vera), glues. Wax, creosote, alcohol, perfumes.

BASKETS: Containers, mats, screens, seating.

ENERGY: Wind, solar, biomass, micro-hydro, methane, water mills, solar thermal.

NURSERY, GRAFTING, SEED SAVING. R and D for local agriculture.

CRAFT INDUSTRIES: Candles, jewellry, ornaments, toys (wooden, soft), paper, knitting, sewing, tin smithing, lead light, ceramic pots, pavers, paper mache.

LEATHERWORK: Harness, footwear, belts, hand bags.

HEATING/INSULATION: Using wool, plant fibres, mud.

COACH, WAGON, SMALL BOAT, CART BUILDING

used for the small amount of ploughing and hauling, would also provide some recreational and routine transport functions, in a society where the pace was much more relaxed. Cooking would mostly use wood and biogas fuel from methane digesters taking wastes on their way to the gardens.

Solar passive earth-made buildings would eliminate most of the energy presently needed for heating, cooling and therefore air-conditioning. Stirling heat engines driven by solar reflectors or wood fuel would be power sources for some machinery (e.g. saw mills) and electricity generation. Most of the wood cutting, pumping and freezer boosting would be carried out when the sun or wind was high. The many small local dams might enable most of the (much reduced) electricity storage required.

Extensive forests would permeate and surround our settlements, providing some energy including wood-fired electricity and small quantities of ethanol or methanol for transport. Candles and lanterns using bees wax and vegetable oils would meet some lighting needs. (Candles are remarkably good light sources when backed by parabolic reflectors made from pieces of broken mirror).

'Work'

Most 'work' would be local, varied, interesting, worthwhile, and clearly directly beneficial to one's community. Because the present vast amount of production of useless, wasteful, trivial, non-durable, luxurious etc. items would not be taking place, far less work and production would be needed. Much of the remaining production could be transferred to households and craft industries, making work much more interesting and worthwhile. The household and the commons would provide many necessities without the need to work for money to buy them. Some of our 'work' time would go into voluntary working bees developing and maintaining local public institutions, including the productive commons. Many people who chose to live very self-sufficiently and communally would hardly need to earn any money, being able to pay their 'taxes' in produce or additional working bee contributions.

In The Simpler Way the work/leisure distinction collapses. When we dramatically reduce factory production and have most of the necessary remaining work done in gardens, small family businesses and co-operatives and in craft ways, at a relaxed pace and in an economy that does not dump anyone into unemployment or bankruptcy, then work would be better classified as leisure activity. This in turn would greatly reduce the resource, energy and dollar costs presently associated with 'leisure' industries. Some leisure activities can be highly productive, such as knitting, sandal making, honey production, candle making, cooking, dress making, carpentry, arts and gardening. People who engage in these hobbies are not working, or buying leisure services.

Because of the greatly reduced need to purchase, and because much would come 'free' from the commons and neighbours, we would probably need to work for money only one or two days a week. Those who wished to specialise in full-time paid work could do so of course.

We would still need many highly trained people but one could be a valuable contributor to one's community without much formal 'education' and there would be many useful contributions that could be made by people who do not do well at school, and by 'disabled' and elderly people. Many complex skills would obviously be important and educational institutions would continue to develop these. However one's life prospects would depend, not on one's educational credentials but mainly on how well one could contribute. Thus the present mindless and extremely wasteful scramble for educational credentials would be eliminated (see Chapter 9).

Although the typical 'worker' might focus most of his time on a particular activity, he would be a handy-man or 'jack of all trades'. These are the people you will want most in your highly self-sufficient neighbourhood, able to come over and fix and make and trouble-shoot. Remember that most things will be technically fairly simple and gardeners and handymen accumulate a great deal of technical wisdom over time, especially in a situation where sharing ideas and researching and keeping things in good shape is understood to be important for everyone's welfare.

Work represents one of the most unsatisfactory aspects of consumer society. Many, probably most people get little from work other than money. Many hate it, many endure a life time of boring, unhealthy, intermittent and poorly paid work. Even in good times at least 10% of people are probably more or less unemployed (you can always double the official figure for unemployment). Few people now experience any security in their work situation. The pace of work and the hours are being ramped up all the time, the conditions are deteriorating (more casual positions, more unpaid over-time) and the incidence of stress and social costs such as family breakdown are high. Even those who would now say they enjoy their work could be getting far more benefit from their productive effort if they had access to the conditions of work and spiritual rewards The Simpler Way makes possible.

The Simpler Way would also liberate us from the deeply entrenched and costly delusion that hard work is a virtue. We admire the hard worker, regardless of what he does, whether it be advertising cigarettes or producing Napalm. Of course to be able to knuckle down and grind through when this is necessary is a virtue, but in a satisfactory society no one would have to endure work that is felt to be unpleasant or not worthwhile, and the readiness to do so would be recognised as a personality fault. Yet in consumer society most people have been heavily disciplined to accept a lifetime of hard and often unpleasant, boring and indeed socially undesirable work, without seeing that this ideological flaw enables their domination and exploitation. It is great for the owners of the factories when workers not only work about three times as hard as would be necessary in a sensible society, but also believe that they should!

Pets.

At present large volumes of resources and energy are devoured by pets, most of which are not only rather useless but are ecologically damaging, (e.g. cats kill wildlife). Pets consume large quantities of food that humans could have eaten and take up many of the resources going into veterinary science and services. In our new neighbourhoods there will be many useful animals that can be pets, but there will be few cats and dogs.

Health and medicine.

The entire focus in health care would change from the cure of illness to the promotion of health. To begin with, most people would be much healthier than they are now due to the more labour-intensive lifestyles and the high quality food. Even more important would be the psychological factors, the elimination of insecurity, unemployment, loneliness and stress, the experience of a supportive and cooperative community, of being busy, having a sense of purpose and being valued for making a worthwhile contribution. How high would be the incidence of drug and alcohol abuse, crime, depression, domestic violence, car accidents, eating disorders and random violence?

Health and medical services would be mostly localised, but with a few centralised specialised teaching hospitals. Drugs and medical equipment might be among the items still mostly produced far away and transported into regions. Much of the increased R and D effort (below) would go into medical research.

Satisfactory health provision must be organised primarily as a public service, paid for generously by taxation. We would probably put the town doctor on a salary and make all drug companies into public utilities. (The Australian Commonwealth Serum Laboratories provided an admirable example, before it was sold off in the mania of neo-liberal privatisation). Health should not be seen as a profit making domain (although many elements within the overall health system might be left to carefully regulated private enterprise).

Media and communications.

These too should be largely localised, i.e. providing important local information and facilitating discussion of local issues, while also relaying national and international news and information from more centralised sources.

As will become clearer below, a local community cannot run well unless there is a great deal of discussion, sharing of ideas, sorting out of the best options and awareness of how arrangements are working out. All this contributes to the gradual movement towards consensus on what's best for the town. Much of this communication, clarification and learning will take place informally but good local media, especially locally made radio programs, will be important in facilitating the awareness that is crucial for collective decision making and in reinforcing social cohesion.

The significance of TV would decline markedly. People would find much more worthwhile and interesting things to do with the precious time they now spend watching TV. Yet it could have important informing, communicating and educating functions. Elaborate programs on other countries and cultures would help to satisfy some of the present desire for travel. Use of papers and magazines could be cut dramatically, replaced by electronic sources. Many people could work providing entertainment, arts, documentaries, reports, etc., whereas at present global corporations send a relatively few programs worldwide, employing relatively few creative people. Global media send the same material out to everyone, so can't deal with the issues that are only of interest to your neighbourhood.

Media would seek to focus attention, thought and discussion on the locality and its processes, events, problems, merits and delights. This should be our cognitive centre of gravity, not the distant national or international arena, let alone the trivia provided by the global corporate media networks.

What about the IT realm? Doesn't a sophisticated modern society have to be heavily dependent on computers, complex communications systems, highly trained scientists and wizard technologists? The Simpler Way would make whatever use of this realm was appropriate, and it would be of importance for many functions, but it would not have anything like the centrality it has today. It would have an important role in research, medicine, data storage, education, etc. but the need for it in business, accounting, media, leisure and everyday life and the management of complex systems would be greatly reduced. Most little firms and farms probably would not even need a computer. Relatively little leisure time would be spent in front of one. If the worst came to the worst and the satellites could not be kept up there or the computer factories could not be maintained, we could get by well without computers. Just reflect on how good life could have been with 1960s technologies, assuming a rational and caring economy. Most of the above listed productive activities such as food and furniture production could take place quite well without any IT. We were able to make beautiful dinners, houses, furniture and concerts in the 1960s without it.

Computers and similar complicated devices would still be made in high tech factories, located in a few places in the world.

These products would be among the relatively few things that would need to be traded internationally.

Capital, investment, interest, banking.

Nowhere are the implications of a zero growth and de-developed economy more profound than for the finance industry – because there would hardly be one. Firstly, if there is to be no growth then there can be no interest payments. Sorry, there can be no argument about this. If you have a system in which $1 is lent or invested and as a result $1.10 has to be paid back a year later, this is not possible unless the total volume of production and sales one year later is greater than it was at the start. If however the volumes of production are to remain constant then the volume of money in circulation to enable production and consumption must remain constant. If some were allowed to lend money and get back more than they lent then in time a few would have accumulated most of the fixed volume of money that existed.

In a stable or zero-growth economy the only reason for investment would be to maintain a stable productive capacity as old premises and equipment needed replacing. This could include developing new and better bakeries to replace old ones, and it could involve increasing the number of bakeries while reducing the number of dairies, but the aggregate volume of capital invested would not change over time. Obviously this could not possibly be done well by a free market; it can only be the result of rational community decision making.

So, there goes almost the whole of the finance industry. You were warned; this is about huge and radical system change!

This is not a moral argument, but let's consider the moral situation briefly. It is not morally acceptable that rich people can receive big incomes just because they get interest on their bank or share accounts, while many people cannot do this because they are too poor to have savings or investments. Meanwhile rich people consume goods that are mostly produced by people who have to work for their incomes. This situation is never questioned in consumer society, let alone recognised as morally repugnant. In this society all people would be rich if they could, and live in luxury on their investments without doing any work if they could. But whether or not you agree with this moral point is not the overriding issue here. For sustainability reasons we must develop a zero-growth economy and in such an economy there can be no interest payments.

The role of banks would therefore be limited to providing a safe deposit site for savings, and making available small amounts of capital for development limited to renewing or revising infrastructures. The bank should be a core public institution within the town, owned by the town and run by elected boards with open public meetings on all important issues, including particular loan proposals. These would decide what socially desirable purposes capital would be lent for. (Would you prefer instead that money be lent only to those purposes which distant private banks thought would maximise their profits?)

So if many firms remained privately owned, which I would wish to see, they could go to public banks for loans from time to time. The bank might decide that the proposal is especially valuable and decide to give a grant rather than a loan, and arrange for community working bees to build the premises at no charge. This is the kind of power the Mondragon cooperative bank has. Again recognise that there would be relatively little need for big developments and infrastructure projects, let alone mega-buck take-overs, nor therefore for the large banking and finance industry that dominates in turbo-capitalism.

Note that the new community's 'wealth' in the sense of stuff that can be unvested does not exist in the form of dollars. It exists in the form of local resources (do we have the timber in our forests to build the bridge), the skills (do we have the people who can design it), the labour and organisation and the enthusiasm (the well-oiled working bees) that will get the job done quickly and well. Some money capital from the town bank might be needed to pay for imports of bolts, but that's relatively unimportant.

Retirement, old age.

Older, experienced people would be highly valued contributors to production and more importantly to social functioning, given their wisdom, their knowledge of local people, conditions and history. There would be no compulsory retirement age. People could slowly phase down their level of activity as they wished. Most would want to remain active contributors, rather than cease 'working'.

Much of the care of older and invalid people would be carried out by the community via the committees, working bees, rosters and the informal involvement of people who pop in from time to time. With five days a week to spare many people would drop in frequently to chat and help out. People would be able to remain in their homes much longer, there would be little need for retirement 'homes' and specialised staff. There would be small local hospitals and nursing facilities close to where people had lived, set within the busiest parts of settlements.

The experience of old, infirm and mentally and physically disadvantaged people would be infinitely better than it is now. They would be cared for right in the middle of their communities, able to observe and be involved in the everyday activities going on around them. People would be dropping in all the time. Compare the way present society isolates these people in expensive institutions with nothing to do or to be involved in or contribute to. 'Inmates' are often intensely bored, lonely and convinced they are worthless burdens. Then we have to pay for expensive professional staff to deal with the consequences.

All these people would have watertight guarantees of life time security, unlike today where one's fate depends on the skill (and honesty) of one's retirement fund manager in a predatory financial world that can collapse and eliminate your retirement funds overnight. Communities would have most of the responsibility of looking after all their members, including young, ill, handicapped, mentally unwell, old and infirm. State resources for such functions will be very limited. More importantly, as has been explained, provision for old age cannot come from interest on superannuation investments.

Law.

There would be very little need for legal work compared with present society which is riddled with struggles and disputes generated by competition for markets, property, rights, wealth. The climate would be cooperative, not adversarial. Wealth and property would not be so important to people. The stability of the economy would mean that many legal problems that presently derive from competition for development opportunities would not arise.

Most important is the fact that because all would be provided for, i.e. all would have a livelihood and a productive role, and because there would be no unemployment, exclusion, poverty or disadvantage, then most of the forces generating crime in the present callous winner-take-all society would have been eliminated. For large numbers of people today it is extremely difficult or impossible to get a job or to start a business. It is therefore no surprise that some of them end up stealing cars or mugging people, or selling shonky products, or that many give up hope and take to alcohol or drugs. The savings The Simpler Way would produce here would be astronomical. How many police, courts, prisons, judges, barristers or parole officers would we need if people had a role, a worthwhile contribution to make? How much collateral damage and self destruction would be avoided?

Each town would establish systems of mediation and 'village elders', so that if conflicts began to emerge experienced people could informally help to sort them out. This is the practice in many Eco-villages and tribal societies.

The quality of a society can be judged by the size of its legal industry, its welfare spending, and the amount of charity. It there are a lot of these, we are dealing with a society in bad shape. These are consequences of ways, which pit people in zero-sum conflicts and deprive and dump people. A satisfactory society does not do those things.

High tech and large-scale centralised production.

It will always be necessary to import some items from distant locations. The goal is far from complete local self sufficiency. High-tech medical and communications equipment might have to be imported from overseas. Steel would come from the national steel works. Stoves and fridges and various mass-produced items would be made in regional factories and then transported into neighbourhoods.

The Simpler Way is not opposed to sophisticated technology. We would always be exploring more effective ways of producing better goods, but it is a serious mistake to assume that technical advance is important in solving our problems or enabling a better society. We do not need better technology for this; we need to change to sensible values, systems and lifestyles. We could easily build an ideal society with the technologies we had decades ago.

If we phased out the vast amount of unnecessary production taking place we would actually have more resources to devote to sensible R and D than we devote to it now. This is because some of the resources and effort now going into the huge amount of presently inexcusable production could be transferred into researching important topics, while most of it was terminated.

Leisure.

This has been partly dealt with above, in terms of having leisure-rich communities and a lot of time to pursue leisure interests. At present leisure time is mostly spent in the passive consumption of experience produced by corporations or professionals, especially via TV and IT. The quality of most of this material is 'spiritually' negligible if not negative, evident in the mindless TV soap operas, game shows and crime dramas, and especially the violence. However any town or suburb includes many talented musicians, singers, storytellers, actors, comedians and playwrights, presently unable to do their thing because the globalised entertainment industry only needs a very few super-stars. These people will thrive, having several days a week to practise their art and being appreciated for their (largely unpaid) contributions to the many local gatherings, concerts and festivals.

Much more leisure time will be spent in creative and social activities, as distinct from the increasingly private involvement in computerised leisure pursuits today. In addition much leisure time will be spent in productive activities, such as gardening, making things, arts and crafts.

The minor role for the cash economy.

Although a large sector of the new local economy could be the much-reduced present economy in which money is still used, it is possible that most of the economic activity would take place without the exchange of money. Firstly, a lot of economic activity would take place within households. (Even at present more work time is spent in households than in the rest of the economy, although conventional economic theory ignores it because it does not involve monetary payments). This sector would become even more significant as home gardening, repairing, making things and leisure activities were enhanced. Many goods and services would be 'free' from the commons and we would get many through swapping surpluses, standing barter exchange arrangements and gifts of surpluses.

As has been noted, many people would be able to live almost without earning any money, because they would get most of the few things they wanted from their own gardens and craft production, from swapping surpluses, and especially from the abundant commons. They could pay their taxes by extra contributions to committees and working bees.

Culture, learning, knowledge and 'spiritual' development.

Because The Simpler Way would liberate us from spending most of our time in unnecessary production and consumption there would be a leap in the attention given to personal development, learning for its own sake, cultural pursuits, writing, reading, conversing, performing, researching and community development. This is firstly because we would have the time. Consumer-capitalist society forces most of us to work, grind, struggle and cope most of the time, in conditions of insecurity, generating anxiety and depression. If this burden was lifted we could experience 'spiritual' miracles, being able to devote most of our time to activities which broadened our horizons and contributed to personal growth. Minds conditioned to a narrowness of achieving, producing and coping would have the freedom to relax, reflect, appreciate, create, grow and just be.

Secondly, life in the new communities would be intellectually stimulating. Consumer society is intellectually stultifying, preoccupied with the post-modern culture of TV, pop music, celebrities, spectacles, electronic games, sport, soap operas, quiz shows and trivia. The Simpler Way constantly involves one in experiences that stimulate and inspire thought, planning, design, discussion, criticism, creativity and the pursuit of important purposes.

REDUCING THE ECONOMY

THE PRESENT ECONOMY	THE NEW ECONOMY
NECESSITIES Often too luxurious, wasteful • Houses • Cars • Clothes Often production could be reorganized, e.g., • Food from local sources, • Localised production cuts need for ships, trucks. • Recycling food scraps cuts need for fertilizers. **Largely or totally UNNECESSARY PRODUCTION** e.g. gold, marketing, fashion, arms, law, magazines, aircraft, ships, cars, TV, movies, take-away food, finance industry, shops, factories, bureaucracy, prisons, drug rehabilitation, steel, entertainment,precious stone jewelry, throw-away products, pets, shoddy products, travel and tourism... **NECESSARY Research and Development.** **UNNECESSARY Research and Development.** e.g. arms, marketing, sports cars.	**NECESSITIES** Sufficient production to enable a high quality of life for all. **NECESSARY Research and Development** ...more than at present.

One would predict a surge in cultural creativity of many different kinds. Happy, comfortable, secure people, with time to do what they want, are likely to plunge into art, making, growing and learning. Most exciting here is not the painting and play writing that individuals will undertake, but the collective, cooperative ventures. An era like that in which the great Gothic cathedrals were build would emerge. We could work together to slowly construct beautiful, inspiring community works. Consider the new town hall we could create with our working bees, timber and mud. Consider the townscapes we might enjoy strolling through, appreciating the beautiful diverse, idiosyncratic range of architectural styles and ornamentation, the fountains, pools, towers, follies, statues and ornaments. Pilgrims would come from surrounding towns to marvel at what we had done, and we'd be invited on guided tours of their creations. Imagine the magic landscapes and rambling trails, the adventure tours, the caves and pools and wildlife sanctuaries and sacred shrines we could create. Consider the theatrical performances, the concerts, the festivals, the celebrations, the poetry readings, the comedians, the rituals, scripted and choreographed and performed by all those musicians, playwrights and dancers with five days a week to devote to their obsessions.

There would be a synergism between beautiful surroundings and good behaviour. Art inspires and ennobles the spirit. Living in a beautiful landscape and experiencing institutions and systems one can be proud of would surely reinforce goodness and responsible citizenship. See, The Simpler Way is about liberation to thrive, nurture and flourish!

LAND AREAS AND FOOTPRINT

The following very approximate estimates indicate that the new settlements could have an extremely low per capita footprint. (They are summarised from Chapter 13 in Trainer, 2007).

Assume for illustrative purposes a very small settlement with 1000 people, 250 households, 700 m across, i.e. 50 ha area, but located in a square 4 km in area, i.e. 400 ha. The town centre would be 2 km from that of the next town. The small amount of road space needed might take 2 ha and the railway running through about 1 ha. About 6.5 ha of the space that would normally be given to roads would be converted to commons. Total commons in the town would be 10.5 ha, with much more outside it including forests and pastures. Almost all food could come from within the 50 ha settlement, and most of the rest from the farms, forests, pastures and dairy just outside it.

Grains for flour might require 37 ha outside the settled area, assuming 200 kg/person/year use and 6 t/ha/y yield. However some flour would come from trees such as acorns and chestnuts, on land providing other goods and services.

Wool might take 25-30 ha assuming consumption of 2 kg/

person/y, 25 sheep/ha and 3.2 kg clean wool/sheep/y. Other fibres including flax, sisal and cotton might add a little to this area, and some of this would be imported. (Demand for new clothing would be very low).

Timber needs would be low in a stable economy, called on only to maintain stocks of housing and furniture. Some combined heating and cooking would be by wood fires, in well insulated solar-passive houses. The need might be for 100 kg/person/ha/y, and therefore for 14 ha.

Several areas would overlap in functions; for instance woodlands provide timber, fuel, mulch, fruits, nuts, windbreaks, water, grazing area and honey. The grazing area would also function as parkland and playing fields. The creeks, ponds and dams would be sources of fish, ducks, bamboo, rice and other water plants. This makes footprint calculation complex, and significantly reduces the total area needed because the same area can provide many resources and services.

The town's share of regional industry and service space might be 3 ha.

The above areas add to about 135 ha, not taking into account the overlaps which would reduce the figure. The per capita footprint would be 0.135 ha.

Energy.

This is more difficult to estimate, and sets the biggest supply problems. The following estimates come mostly from my household records. (The location at 34 degrees south sets less challenge than most of the Rich World would face).

■ **Water and space heating.** No significant energy cost. Solar passive house design, heat pumps, wood fires with water heating jackets, solar hot water panels and storage tanks.

■ **Electricity.** One PV panel per person, producing c 0.15 kWh/person/day (.54MJ), which is much more than my house needs to run lights, computer, simple 12 V workshop machinery and water pumps. No other electrical appliances. No ironing. Sawing, water pumping and boosting community freezers would be carried out when the sun or wind was high.

■ **Cooking.** Some efficient wood stoves fitted with water jackets, (and contributing to space heating). A small quantity of methane for quick convenient kettle boiling could come from community digesters taking biomass and wastes. Use of wood-fuelled private and communal earth ovens for baking, including bread. Reduced meat consumption and increased use of fresh fruit, vegetables and salads would reduce cooking energy demand. Assume 2 MJ/person/day electricity, via regional 240V grid (below). Cooking total, 4 MJ/person/day.

■ **Freezing.** Many households would not need a fridge, given evaporative coolers, access to fresh foods reducing storage needs, and neighbourhood freezers. Some small electric fridges, boosted when the sun is out.

■ **Farms and businesses, incl.** pumping and machinery. Relatively low electrical demand given the minimal amount of infrastructures and stocks to be maintained.

■ **Transport.** The very low need for transport might be met by railways (national grid) and ethanol/methanol powered buses between settlements, and mostly bicycles within them and between neighbouring towns. Community cars for hire. Little or no tourism or travel away for holidays. Very few trucks needed, given local sources of food and materials. Some use of horses for cartage, (and ploughing and leisure). If 200 km/day (?) for total town vehicle transport demand, this comes to 0.8 MJ/person/day.

■ **Imported items.** Little movement of goods long distances.

■ **Regional and national electricity grids.** Large scale wind, PV and solar thermal plant contributing to the very low residual demand. Demand management, e.g. running electric furnaces when wind or sun were strong.

■ **Electricity storage.** Very low quantities required would make storage in dams, biomass and possibly hydrogen viable.

The uncertain total of the above items 7.5 MJ person/day, or 2.7 GJ/person/y.

However several national items have not been included here, such as steel production, railways and the inputs needed to maintain stocks, e.g. tools and housing..

So let's treble the total to cover errors. 8 GJ/person/y.

Compare present Australian energy consumption 270 GJ/person/y. The ratio is 35 to 1.*Ratio... 35:1*

As has been noted, if we are lucky we might not have to go

110

as far as this chapter assumes. We might not need to be as frugal and self-sufficient. What I hope has been shown is that it would be possible and easy to cut our resource consumption and ecological impact to very small proportions of present rates if we adopted the ways discussed, and that we could do this while enhancing the quality of life.

WE HAVE BUILT ECONOMY B

This chapter has focused on our need to build a radically new economy within our town, and then for us to run it to meet our needs. This new economy will grow underneath the old one. It will be an economy whose principles flatly contradict those of consumer-capitalist economy. It will be

❏ a local economy, not a national or globalised economy,
❏ designed to meet needs not to maximise profits,
❏ an economy under social control and not determined by corporate boards,
❏ rationally planned and controlled as distinct from leaving everything to the market,
❏ governed by participatory democratic procedures, especially in town assemblies and committees,
❏ organised to enable unused productive capacity to be devoted to unmet needs.

The goal here is to gradually add an Economy B to the old economy, reducing our dependence on it. If the old Economy A then self-destructs, we would still be able to provide basic necessities for ourselves.

Nothing could be more revolutionary. If we don't build such economies we will not survive at all well in the coming age of scarcity, and we will probably not survive at all.

At first we will only be able to build a very small Economy B, capable of providing only a few of the important items we need. But as time goes by and Economy A increasingly fails to provide for us the scale of Economy B will grow.

It is important to see this Chapter as dealing with the steps we could plausibly take in the next few decades to a half way position. The economy described is in my view not the end point of the transition. It is only a form that will enable us to get control and turn off the damage, but it is not the kind of economy that

I think is ultimately desirable and to which we will eventually move.

In the long term future surely we will have had the sense to organise the production of the relatively few things we want in rational and cooperative ways without any reference to markets, wages, wealth or getting. We will make a contribution to production and then simply take what we need from the public stores. There would have to be monitoring, accounting and adjustments, but much of the economy would more or less look after itself. For instance people who like growing tomatoes will keep us all supplied, with no bureaucracy. It will be a gift economy. We will produce and give, to family, neighbours, the community. We will get what we need as 'gifts' from others. The processes advocated in this chapter are the first steps in that direction, and it should not be difficult to build on them over time.

PROBLEMS AND ISSUES

Too austere?

The main point of this Chapter has been to explain that we could easily produce enough using mainly local resources and small, highly self-sufficient economies, given the willing acceptance of frugal but sufficient ways. But at first sight The Simpler Way would surely strike most people in consumer society as utterly unacceptable, indeed intolerably primitive, frugal and deprived, an infringement on personal liberty and the entirely deserved right to purchase and use up whatever one can afford. But the core problem here is 'only' one of outlook. Yes if you have grown accustomed to expensive luxuries you will see The Simpler Way as too austere, however the key questions are, 'What important things would we have to do without?' 'Would there be any important deprivation?' 'Are there insufficient substitutes for expensive possessions and pleasures'. 'Wouldn't we have all we need for a quite sufficient material living standard and a quite rich quality of life?' It's not a matter of expecting people to happily embrace The Simpler Way at first sight, but of gradually helping people to find enjoyment and satisfaction in the alternative ways under discussion. After the new society has been established we will easily raise children to hold the new values, because they will grow up finding them to be normal, and they will understand why they are important.

My personal experience as an impoverished, do-it-yourself, make-do-with-what's-sufficient, scruffy homesteader, and my connections with people in the Eco-village movement, leave me in no doubt that the ways sketched could provide rich, varied and idyllic lifestyles to all, at negligible cost in dollars or non-renewable resources or environmental impact... if we changed conventional visions and aspirations. My personal expenditure is way under the poverty line, my clothes are few and mostly heavily patched, I don't travel, but my quality of life and 'spiritual' wealth are high and could be much higher still in the kind of community described. Many people share this perspective. In Australia magazines such as Earth Garden and Grass Roots dwell on the delights of relatively self-sufficient and simple homesteading. We do not think of this in terms of austerity. I certainly go without nothing I would wish to buy. The full title is The Simpler But Richer Way.

Work motivation, incentive, efficiency, initiative, innovation?

Many would argue that an effective economy can only be driven by cut-throat competition between firms, because that's all that keeps them efficient and innovating, and by fear of no income, because that's what gets people to work. In the present economy these factors are very effective, they do prompt enormous effort, innovation and output, but they are sources of great anxiety, stress, drudgery, bankruptcy, unemployment and waste.

Let's first note again that in The Simpler Way far less work would need to be done, and one's fate would not depend on beating others for jobs or sales, and national prosperity would not depend on beating all other countries in the competition for export markets. We would only have to make sure that people worked effectively enough, that firms were efficient enough, that enough innovation was taking place. Reflect on the fact that in the typical household these are not problems. In household economies people get the work done well enough, usually at a comfortable pace, and they innovate well enough. They do not have to constantly strive to maximise output and efficiency.

113

Secondly people would be in situations where there were strong incentives to produce and be efficient and develop new ways. Why? Because people would be able to work at things they enjoyed doing, such as running their own little bakery or joinery, and therefore they would be able to reorganise and improve from time to time, and they would enjoy being appreciated by their community for their important contribution to its welfare.

Hence we come to The Simpler Way's golden rule of work. You should never work for money. It is alright to receive money for work done, but the reasons why you eagerly go to work should be because a) you love growing or making things or treating patients, etc., and b) because you get satisfaction from providing goods or services which benefit the people around you and are important for the maintenance of your community.

But what if Fred's bakery was becoming a bit sloppy and inefficient? After all he has no competition and he knows his town will not let anyone go bankrupt or become unemployed. What's to stop him becoming lazy? Us, that's what. 'Hey, Fred, lift yer game mate. We're depending on you for good bread. What's the problem? Do you need a holiday? Do you need better equipment, a loan? Would you be happier working in a different line of business. Should we organise a working bee to help you renovate? This town has to have bread so if you don't do it well enough we will have to find someone else to set up another firm or set up our own co-op to do it.' The orientation would be helpful, not punitive, although sometimes firm action would surely have to be taken, such as refusing to buy from a firm that continually refused to shape up or tried to take over all the others in its field. We would know that it is best if we try to help each other to get the town into the best possible state for all. We need everyone's contribution and we need it to be from a happy, valued and respected person.

In addition, among the most important institutions we would have in the new communities would be the research and monitoring committees. Mostly voluntary groups would watch how all sorts of important things were going, including our energy systems, our food supply, meetings, ecological footprint, the experienced welfare of old people and youth, and the many factors feeding into the quality of life. Some would be concerned with whether our firms were functioning satisfactorily. They would advise on new ideas found in their research on the ways being practised in the rest of the world. They might have no power to make changes and their purpose would be not punitive. The role would be to help our firms perform well, and to undertake desirable adjustments.

Also the climate within firms and cooperatives would be quite different to what it is present society. It would not be focused on desperate competition to take sales and beat competitors. Workers and managers would be aware that their firm or institution was providing something important for the community and appreciated by it, and surely this would in general prompt conscientiousness and satisfaction from doing the job well.

Money; We will create our own.

The last chapter dealt with the very unsatisfactory way money is created in the present economy. In this economy we all, including governments, have to go to banks to borrow scarce money to develop ventures, and then we must pay the high interest rates for the hire of the money. Consequently there are many socially desirable projects that are never undertaken because they cannot make the profit needed to pay the interest. So all towns, especially in the Third World, endure unmet needs even though they have the productive capacity that could be meeting many of those needs.

Reference was made to the way some governments have got around this by 'printing' new money and 'spending it into circulation', for example by paying wages to workers for building a new road. Although this strategy can jump an economy out of recession it typically makes little difference to the welfare of the most needy because few of them will have got work building the road.

Unfortunately there is a lot of confusion and obscurity on this issue of local currencies and all too often there is no clear and plausible rationale evident when a scheme is launched. It is not unusual to see that a project is not going to have any desirable effects at all. It is essential that we can see and explain in advance precisely how a new currency is going to have what effects.

Most if not all of the discussion of new or local currencies has only been about stimulating the existing economy. In Chapter 4 it was noted that some of these efforts have been very effective. The economies of consumer-capitalist society regularly fall into recession or depression in which people suffer deprivation even though all the productive capacity they need to meet their needs is still there. If a government creates a lot of money and spends it into circulation building roads etc., this will stimulate the economy, but it will only be stimulating the normal economy to do more of the things it normally does. Those things are always most beneficial to richer people. The road contractors will get most of the new money and only a few who were unemployed will get jobs on the new roads. More importantly, the money-creating process will have made no contribution to any system change. When you understand that the goal has to be change to a very different economic system the question is how might money creation help achieve that goal.

Following is the answer to this question which forms the central element in the transition strategy set out in Chapter 11.

❏ A group, which could be a council, church, charity or just a few friends, organises a productive venture such as a community garden or bakery or workshop, in which previously unemployed or otherwise idle people (and others, such as retired people) can come together to produce some of the things they need, using cheap or costless local resources.

❏ Time contributions are recorded and these entitle people to the associated proportion of the output at a later date. When I work an hour in the garden l receive a piece of paper saying I have put in that much time and have the associated claim to a proportion of the goods produced.

❏ These pieces of paper are a new currency. When we have set up several ventures then the money I 'earn' in one of them, say the garden, will entitle me to an appropriate share of the output from the bakery or the sandal making co-operative, etc.

Obviously the introduction of the currency is not the most important element in this process. Organising the cooperative 'firm' is the key factor. Also obvious is the way the currency works. You can see what its desirable effects are and why they

116

occur. But introducing the currency has been crucial in enabling the arrangement.

What we have done here is create and add on a new economic sector, a mini-Economy B, involving economic activity, producing, buying and selling that previously could not take place, and we have created a simple form of 'money' to enable us to keep track of who contributed what and is entitled to what. Especially important is the fact that all the money we have created benefits those in most need. Benefit for them is not confined to the small proportion that trickles down from the road contractors when a government creates money and spends it into circulation building a road. Also significant is that the money is not debt. The piece of paper I receive for an hour's work in the garden is only a record of the fact that I have provided that input and thus that I am entitled to the associated share of the produce. What's more, this new money can't earn any interest.

This throws light on the way the Third World festers on and on in dreadful poverty. Any poor country has vast but idle productive capacity, in its unemployed people, soils, forests etc., and it also has extreme unmet need. Appropriate Development by definition connects the two. But as Chapter 5 will discuss, the agencies which control the global economy, including the World Bank and IMF, will not tolerate this and they expressly prevent it. The policies they make Third World countries accept before they provide debt relief require reliance on free markets and competing in the global economy, meaning that labour and resources must be available only for use by profit maximizing corporations. Governments are obliged to cut their spending and therefore their assistance to the poor, so any move to set them up to produce for themselves goods they need would not be tolerated.

A commune I know needed a bridge to prevent them from being flooded in when the stream rose. They could have gone to the bank for a loan and hired a contractor to build the bridge. Instead they just built it themselves because they had the trees, their own little sawmill, the skill and the labour. They didn't need to borrow any money. This is often the situation your town or neighbourhood is in, possessing all the productive capacity it needs to develop something important and lacking only the organisation. Often all that is needed is to gear the resources to the need, and this is what is facilitated by creating our new 'money'. The money just enables us to keep track of who contributed what, and to eventually share the costs and benefits.

So we can just create our own bits of paper to get our own co-ops going among those in most need. This is an extremely powerful device, making it possible to lift our town out of the typically absurd stagnation where urgent needs and the resources that could be meeting them sit side by side.

Finally, a note on two mistaken ideas common in the alternative currency literature. What about the argument that local currencies encourage local purchasing because they can't be spent outside the town? This reveals confusion. Anyone who understands the importance of buying local will do so, regardless of what currency they have. Anyone who doesn't will buy what's cheapest, which is typically an imported item. Obviously what matters here is getting people to understand why it's important to buy local; just issuing a local currency will make no significant difference.

Similarly, currencies which depreciate with time miss the point and are unnecessary. Anyone who understands the situation does not need to be penalised for holding money and not spending it. In any case it's wrong-headed to set out to encourage spending; people should buy as little as they can, and any economy in which you feel an obligation to spend to make work for someone else is not a satisfactory economy. In a sensible economy there is only enough work, producing and spending and use of money as is necessary to ensure all have sufficient incomes and goods.

But could we actually run the economy? 'Surely there's no realistic alternative to market forces.'

The conventional, taken for granted belief is that it is not possible to plan and run an economy satisfactorily and therefore leaving it to market forces is the only way. Every day billions of supply, price, purchasing, design, distribution, investment, development, coordination and trade decisions have to be made and it is assumed these can't possibly be made satisfactorily by a state planning bureaucracy. Especially problematic is the coordination task. 'How could deliberate rational planning make sure that enough 50 cm bolts were produced and distributed in time to keep enough on the shelves in all the hardware shops?' Yet the argument in this chapter has indeed been that we must not leave any of the important decisions to market forces. How realistic is this?

Firstly, in a market economy all the decisions are in fact made rationally and deliberately, through shopkeepers responding to demand and feeding orders in to suppliers who contact factories. This is not done automatically by some miraculous and mysterious invisible hand. All this could be done in a largely planned economy via processes that would be little different from those used now. Computerised data collection would enable factories to produce just enough shoes of the required kinds to meet the steady demand. In the 1930s the Spanish Anarchists seemed to have handled the task well, partly by devoting energy to collecting the relevant statistics and communicating them to suppliers (see below). With computers now we could do all that very easily.

Keep in mind how much easier the new local economy will be to manage because it will be small and simple and will involve so much less production, competition and conflict. In a much-reduced economy far fewer decisions would have to be made, and perhaps most of these would not involve monetary transactions. Secondly it will be a zero growth economy, again dramatically simplifying operations and enabling movement towards standard and stable production needs. Third, the decisions will be mostly made on the small local scale, not a national scale, as assemblies and committees assess local needs.

But even in the present highly complex global economy many of the most elaborate problems of coordination are handled very well without resorting to markets. The often-quoted example is the way inter-continental transport systems are integrated through meetings between private firms. The timetables arranging connections between airlines, railways and bus networks in Europe are simply worked out voluntarily by 'delegates' from various interested parties, adjusted where necessary, to maximise mutual benefit. This is the classic Anarchist model, avoiding the need for an authoritarian state or bureaucracy to make all the decisions, or for them to be left to competition within a market place.

When I reflect on my homestead situation and the kind of

economy I'd want nearby, it seems to me that the 'economic problem' would be negligible and very easily dealt with. Just about all the things I want could actually be produced almost without any formal decision making or planning. My tomatoes, furniture, entertainment, water supply etc., would be guaranteed by sensible people recognising the need to plant a few more or a few less tomatoes than last year and the fact that windmill maintenance is due. This is what happens on a commune as sensible members keep their eye on how things are going and what's needed. I can't see why the slightly more complex issues, such as regional pot and pan production, could not be quite satisfactorily handled by committees dealing with figures fed in routinely on demand, breakdowns, suggested design change etc. Would the factory become inefficient without the threat of bankruptcy? Not with the whole community watching and dependent on its performance, and not when its workers realise that everyone's welfare depends on everyone making a reasonable effort... and not when people enjoy their (two days a week of) 'work' for money. The monitoring committees and assemblies would be concerned to identify difficulties and help to solve them, because it is important for us all to remain friendly and to find win-win solutions. Are you sure all this would be better done by private firms operating within markets and motivated by self interest or fear of failure, bankruptcy and unemployment?

'But what about innovation, and venture capital?

The foregoing discussion puts a weighty case that a rational and deliberately run economy could get 'work' out of us and could staff efficient firms. But what about the thing the present economy does so effectively, i.e. stimulate innovation and investment in new and possibly risky ventures? Would there be enough new ideas being tried out? Who would take the big gambles on those products that become winners?

Firstly much and probably most of the commercial innovation taking place is trivial and unnecessary. It comes up with another gimmick or variation that might claw back a little more market share, or allow you to do something else on your mobile phone that no one ever needs to do. But what about those innovations that do turn out to be valuable?

At present those gambles are funded by banks or investors who think very carefully and rationally about the potential before putting up any money. Why would it be any worse if the careful rational thinking was carried out by a public bank or investment board, on which you might sit. At least it would be judging in terms of the social benefit as distinct from the possible profit of an entrepreneur or bank. This is what happens in Mondragon. Since the 1930s that Spanish city has developed many large cooperative firms which succeed in international business. Their own public bank provides the capital and their highly sophisticated 'business incubators' assess, modify and guide the new ventures individuals or groups propose. Why can't we have such public mechanisms making most of the decisions where funding of innovations is required? Most scientific research is funded this way, via committees which grant public resources on their assessments of the likely social or scientific value of the proposals. I would be in favour of setting some funds aside for wildcard ventures, and anyone would be free to put their own savings into a venture our bank chose not to fund.

Profit motivation within private firms, or the prospect of bonanza rewards to speculative capital are not necessary to stimulate innovation. People who work in their own little firms, or in the research departments of big agencies, are usually eager to experiment and innovate and improve their systems. For decades the Australian CSIRO, a government agency, has carried out first class R and D via salaried scientists. Most new ideas come from university researchers, who are paid a salary and are not motivated by profit.

So our basically planned and controlled new economy would have little or nothing in common with 'big-state socialism'. But all this has been theoretical speculation. Let's take a look at real cases which clinch the argument.

Consider the 'mutuals', the co-operatives.

The fact that large, cooperative not-for-profit firms can function very satisfactorily, totally independent of market forces, and contrary to the principles of capitalism, is driven home by a glance at the many mutual and co-operative organizations that were prevalent a generation ago. There were for instance credit unions whose members pooled their savings and hired managers to lend these at low interest to members for home building. Over time funds would accumulate enabling very valuable assistance to be extended to increasing numbers of new participants. The Australian National Roads and Motorists Association was an organization providing emergency roadside service to motorists this way. An excellent example today is the Australian radio station 2MBSFM. Its members work voluntarily to broadcast classical music. Consider the characteristics of this organization:

❏ It is set up and run by people who want the service.
❏ It is not run for profit; profit motivation is therefore not necessary to make this kind of organisation work well.
❏ It is very 'efficient'. It achieves its goals very effectively, especially in saving its subscribers the cost of paying out 10%+ of income to shareholders!
❏ It draws heavily on willing volunteers, thereby reinforcing a sense of mutual assistance and giving.
❏ It does not pay ridiculous salaries to CEO's.
❏ It does not have CEOs in a position to rig operations to their own benefit, e.g. by setting up bonus payment arrangements for themselves.
❏ It is not open to gutting by CEOs who can see that profits can be raised by dumping socially valuable operations that don't maximise dividends to shareholders.
❏ It is highly democratic, not ruled by a dictatorial board as normal firms are, and open to all 'workers' to have a say in operations.
❏ It is not driven by income-maximisation; other goals can be taken into account and can take precedence over mere money making. For instance it can help unknown composers to be heard, or subsidise struggling orchestras, or support socially valuable ventures that would not make much if any money... i.e. it can 'cross-subsidise'.
❏ Its output is available to non-subscribers. It generously gives to help enrich society.
❏ It provides and excellent/perfect product!

Clearly the existence of this organization ridicules the assumption that the best/only way to do things is according to profit motivation and market forces. Indeed it is obvious that if it was privatised its admirable characteristics would be more or less eliminated. (It could of course be made to generate far more income, so the conventional economist would say it is very 'inefficient'). These 'mutuals' are so efficient, praiseworthy and publicly valuable precisely because they are not private firms, driven by profit for the few who own them.

Here's another difficult case for the believer in the sanctity of markets. In 2009 the Australian government's large review of Superannuation funds reported that not one of the top 40 performers operated for profit!

This could be the general model for most if not all our middle to large enterprises, i.e. as mutuals run by and serving the needs of their members, or as public firms serving all (e.g. railways, steel works)... providing their control was not centralised and bureaucratised but under open, participatory arrangements. Yet the neo-liberal push has convinced everyone that it is best to leave everything to private firms competing for profits in the market.

If the mutuals are so good, how come they have died out? The point is that it is precisely because they were so good that they were captured - butchered and plundered! Organisations like the NRMA had slowly built up large assets, in resources, skill, experience, fleets, premises, reputation, users, and funds. These assets were contributed by users over decades and belonged to the organization, and had been given in order to build an organization that could go on providing mutual assistance at no profit. At any point in time the current members or 'shareholders' were not owners but trustees of the accumulated resources and organization. Their role and responsibility was to manage these assets while benefiting from them but then passing them on so they could go on benefiting future members. They didn't create the assets or lend them to the organization.

Then along came the neo-liberal globalisers with their sharp eye for unexploited profit-maximising opportunities, and saw that there was an opportunity for a killing here. All they had to do was convince the current members to privatise the organization; i.e. sell it off to a private firm to run for profit pocketing the sale price. There are many fewer mutuals left now.

Look at what the Spanish Workers Collectives did!

In a period of about three years after 1936, during a civil war, the Anarchists were able to establish 1800 workers' collectives throughout large areas of Spain, containing 8 million people. Often they were able to take over factories and estates abandoned when their owners fled the war. With remarkable speed collectives made up of workers in these firms formed and organized to continue production. Many very large ventures were quickly put back into operation. For instance three days after a battle in Barcelona the trams were running again under cooperative control.

Attention was first focused on the most important needs, such as the setting up of communal dining halls. The collectives plunged into the reorganization and improvement of industries, combining many previously struggling small firms, coordinating and integrating. In some regions they ran the entire fishing industry, from the boats to the canning factories and the distribution networks. They actually organized and ran whole regional economies, including public services such as policing, road construction, flood control, water supply, transport and maintenance of parks. They set up banks, flour mills, theatres, an aluminium industry, organized international importing, printed their own money, abolished interest payments, and ran railways and telecommunications systems. Entire health systems were established, including medical centres, hospitals and sanitaria. In Barcelona six hospitals and eight sanitaria were built. Dental and optical services and surgery was free, provided by doctors receiving set wages. Ordinary people gained access to medical services they previously could not afford when doctors only served the rich. Schools were made free and it is claimed that illiteracy was almost eliminated in a few years. They even established engineering and optical training institutes, and a university. The city of Barcelona with a population of 1.2 million was run in these ways.

Towns exchanged surpluses. Regional federations looked after the weaker towns in their areas, transferring resources to those on poorer soils. Some towns and collectives abolished money, arranging all production and distribution in terms of needs and vouchers. Abundant items such as fruit in season were free, but scarce things were rationed. Remarkably they also put some resources into developing theatres, fashionable clothes and hairdressing salons.

The basic format for 'governing' all this was the weekly assembly of all workers in the factory, reviewing all operations, planning, electing managers and making decisions. Factories would send delegates to meetings handling issues involving several factories, and similar delegations to larger and more centralized assemblies would deal with wider regional issues. These latter gatherings had little or no power because recommendations would be taken back down to the factory assemblies where everyone had a vote. That's the essential Anarchist principle; all power is held by citizens. Centralized issues can be thought out by delegates but the recommendations are taken back to the citizen assemblies for approval. They refused to resort to bureaucrats, let alone paid or professional officials, managers or politicians. Managers were just more experienced workers elected by the assemblies, recallable at any time. Committees mostly met after work hours or on the weekend. In other words the government of factories, farms, industries and entire regions was actually carried out by ordinary people deliberating in citizen assemblies. Of course in all these domains more experienced people had key roles but they were not bosses or privileged.

From accounts such as those in Dolgoff (1990), the production of goods, the efficiency of operations, the effectiveness of distribution and allocation, and the social welfare and justice consequences were huge improvements on what had prevailed before when control was in the hands of privileged elites and most people lived in poverty and oppression. They reorganized and innovated extensively and quickly. Men and women became much more equal. A voluntary retirement age of 60 was set. Unemployed people were paid a full wage. Free housing was made available. Difficult and unpleasant work was rotated among workers. By bringing previously idle and inefficiently used productive capacities into operation surges in output, efficiency and welfare were quickly achieved.

Where wages were retained they were made more or less equal. However in many industries wages were abolished, for ideological reasons. Wages were seen to be elements in the system where capital hires labour, controls production, and takes the product, and workers have no involvement in production other than selling their labour and they can be dumped at any time at the whim of the employer. Instead in some cases they simply organised to provide all workers with listed necessities, sometimes via voucher or coupon systems. These entitlements varied with need, for instance being greater if there were children in a family. Thus they implemented the basic 'communist' principle of allocating according to need not work done, skill or status.

Some farms and businesses chose not to join the collectives. These people received surprising levels of assistance from the collectives, often enjoying the benefits they would have enjoyed had they joined. They were not allowed to own more land than they could work. In other industries shopkeepers for instance met and worked out how to consolidate, what shops to close and how to reorganize themselves to share more secure work. Sometimes those who used to be bosses agreed to join the collectives.

The extremely important point for us in all this is that their achievements demolish the claim that you have to leave the mass of decisions either to the workings of the market or to centralized state bureaucracies. They seem to have shown decisively that rational planning carried out by citizens can run factories, industries and whole regional economies, at least well enough.

Although they did these things without huge professional planning bureaucracies. they did plan and make rational decisions, based on the detailed statistics they continually collected. But apparently they could quickly see what needed doing and then make the necessary decisions and carry them out via grass-roots assemblies and elected managers. Compare that with our vast bureaucracies where if you are lucky you get a letter back in two months.

So there, we can do it! Ordinary people can run economies via deliberate and rational participatory democracy, without states, capitalists, bureaucracies or authoritarian rule.

But it's a bit more complicated that I have made it appear to be. I misled you by saying that in Spain 'ordinary people' achieved all those things. The key to the Anarchist success is to be found in the long history and powerful ideological traditions of the regions. For hundreds of years rural villages had functioned in highly collectivist ways. In addition Bakouknin's Anarchist theory had been brought to Spain in the 1880s and had been widely influential. The movement had grown significantly in the decades before 1930, so when the opportunity came with the civil war large and sophisticated pre-existing forces sprang into action. Ideas, values and practices that had been discussed and rehearsed for a long time could be quickly put into practice by large numbers of people.

The point is that the remarkable achievements of the Spanish Anarchists were made possible by extra-ordinary people. We will not be able to do these things unless the right ideas and values have become widely established. People in consumer-capitalist society are far from having the necessary ideas and values, and that sets the core transition problem Part 3 takes up.

Conclusion: How plausible?

Of course it is possible that the entire discussion in this book is based on far too optimistic assumptions regarding how much sense, cooperation and good will humans are capable of. It should be stressed here that the book is not predicting that the kind of economy envisaged in this chapter will be achieved. It is presenting a vision which could be achieved, which would solve our main problems, and could work out well. Part 3 presents the associated strategic path we should try to take to realise that vision. The book's task has been to put forward a persuasive case that this is our best bet. If you are concerned about the fate of the planet the best thing you can do is to work hard to realise this vision.

But keep in mind the grounds for optimism. The incentives that will come from the condition of scarcity we will soon experience will tend to bring out the best in us, if we have enough sense not to plunge into chaotic competition for the last resource scraps. Those conditions will push us towards localising, cooperating and taking control over our situation, because it will be glaringly obvious that these ways make sense. Secondly, with a little luck we will have the wit to realise that the new economy not only provides a quite adequate material lifestyle but it also enables liberation.

Chapter 5

THIRD WORLD DEVELOPMENT

There can be hardly any field where the perspective argued in this book has more profoundly radical implications than that of Third World 'development'. Almost the entire vast literature on this topic from neo-liberal to far left sources is more or less rendered irrelevant when confronted by the fact of scarcity. The dismissal can be accomplished in one sentence. There is no possibility whatsoever that the Third World can 'develop' as this is conventionally conceived, because there are nowhere near the quantities of resources available for such a goal to be achieved.

Again consider the basic multiples. If all the world's people today were to have our Rich World per capita 'living standards' world annual production rates for all resources would have to be at least 5 times as great as they are, and supplies of many are declining fast. But that does not define the problem. The problem is how to get the quantities of resources needed to give 9 billion the 'living standards' we in rich countries would have by 2080 if we average 3% p.a. economic growth until then, i.e. to enable a global economy with 60 times as much producing and consuming going on every year as there is now, and twice as much every 23 years thereafter, forever. This is the goal implicitly at the core of all conventional development thought and action. It is glaringly obvious that this is farcically impossible and that the whole notion of development has to be fundamentally re-thought.

The goal of development for all people, including those in the presently 'over-developed' countries and those in the 'never-to-be-conventionally-developed' countries, has to be The Simpler

Way. Chapters 1, 2 and 3 explained the simple technologies and systems communities can use to provide themselves with most of the goods and services that enable a materially, socially and culturally abundant way of life, from the resources they have around them and without much if any dependence on capital, corporations or global systems. It is distressing that kilometres of library shelves and hoards of economists and NGOs and academics completely fail to grasp that scarcity renders their core theory and practice irrelevant and futile, and that from here on 'development' only makes sense in terms of goals and means that contradict affluence and growth.

Following is firstly a critical commentary on conventional development thinking intended to clarify the fundamental conceptual mistakes, and secondly the fact that when freed from these traps the alternative way becomes visible and viable. The core taken-for-granted elements in the dominant conception of development are indented in bold type. These are` followed by critical comment and the alternative view.

Development, progress and improving human welfare are essentially about increasing the amount of goods and service people can buy. The more that can be produced and sold the more wealth and benefit there is. Development is therefore basically about increasing the volume of business turnover, i.e. the volume of production for sale, and thus the GDP. In other words economic growth is more or less equivalent to development, or at least this is its overwhelmingly important element.

Firstly consider the extreme narrowness here in not only identifying development as a predominantly economic matter but of assuming that of all the important elements of an economy the overriding factor is whether sales are increasing. Development should be about improving all aspects of a society, including the quality of food and water and health services, the opportunities for leisure and cultural activity, the level of debate and discussion, the processes for government and administration, the moral standards, the geographic and aesthetic conditions in which people live, citizenship and social responsibility, openness and accountability, social cohesion, equity, concern for those less fortunate, the quality of life, security, the conditions of the poorest, and especially ecological sustainability. The implicit assumption in conventional development theory is that if you just crank up more production for sale, all these other factors will improve. But, as will be detailed below, the general rule is in fact that when increasing the GDP is the sole or supreme goal there is a strong tendency for all these factors to be damaged.

When within the above long list of desirable social goals we come to think about the economy, the goal should again be to improve its effectiveness in meeting needs, not just to indiscriminately enlarge it all the time.

Consider further the indiscriminate element. 'Don't worry about what to develop – just free markets and free those people with capital to decide this.' But a sensible discussion of development must begin with crucial questions such as, 'What do we want produced first?' 'Where should development resources be focused to do most good?' 'What should we make sure is not developed?' 'What kind of economy do we want to build?' and 'When will we know we have a well developed economy?' Even if increasing the amount people can buy is a relevant consideration, it is obviously far from the whole or the central concern.

Appropriate Development is not possible unless deliberate decisions are made about goals and means and unless deliberate action is taken to develop what's socially desirable. Often this will require contradicting and preventing what people with capital and what free markets would do and what would add most to GDP. Yet conventional development is essentially about allowing those with capital to do precisely what will maximise their profits and it is about preventing governments from influencing development in any other direction.

In other words, Appropriate Development focuses on developing what is needed, and that is totally different from development defined as facilitating whatever will maximise GDP or business turnover. Many regions that have high rates of growth of profits or GDP have had very little or no improvement in the conditions of the poor, and there are some remarkable cases where the 'poorest' people have a high quality of life despite extremely low GDP per capita, such as Kerala, Cuba and Ladakh (below).

The relation between growth and Appropriate Development is in general contradictory. If the supreme goal is to maximise GDP this will actually prevent Appropriate Development, because it will ensure that development resources will go into producing what will maximise sales to richer people and not into what will satisfy urgent needs. Hence 60 years of conventional development have greatly enriched the rich while the Fourth World of more than one billion people has stagnated or is going backwards. About forty countries now even have lower GDP per capita than they had 20 years ago.

To define development as increasing the GDP is precisely what suits the rich. It puts top priority on the freedom to invest in developing what will result in most sales and therefore what is most profitable, and on freedom for those with more purchasing power to gear production to their demand, and on structuring Third World economies to supply goods to the rich countries. All of these are exactly what the owners of capital and consumers in rich countries want but they obviously shift Third World productive capacity from meeting the needs of Third World people to meeting the demand of Rich World investors and consumers. This is the condition into which conventional economic theory and practice have developed the Third World.

Some of the most appropriate development initiatives would dramatically reduce the GDP. For example if some of the land growing luxury crops like coffee to export to rich countries was transferred to the production of food by and for local people, the GDP would fall.

Development cannot take place unless capital is invested, to set up factories etc. to produce for sale. Therefore it is necessary to borrow capital or to persuade people with it to invest. What is developed is decided by those who own capital. Governments must create the conditions that will attract owners of capital to invest.

Most capital is owned or controlled by a very few people and they decide what is to be developed by investing their capital in whatever will maximise their incomes. Appropriate Development recognises that there can be an important role for capital, and it is not necessarily opposed to foreign investment or loans. But it emphatically rejects development defined in terms of the investment of capital. There are two crucial points here. Firstly it is farcical to assume that if you allow what is to be developed in your country to be determined by what will most enrich a few already extremely rich people living on the other side of the world who have no interest in anything but increasing their own wealth then you will get development of things that are most likely to meet your most urgent needs!

What you will get of course is development of enterprises that will use your land, resources and labour to produce goods to export to Rich World supermarkets, at the lowest possible return to you. And if you are one of the perhaps forty countries where transnational corporations can't maximise their profits producing anything at all, then you will get no development at all. You will be told to work harder, compete more fiercely, drop your export prices, and tighten your belt further, so as to be more competitive in the global economy.

This is absurd, morally repugnant, literally catastrophic for the majority of the world's people, and totally avoidable. All those forty countries have immense productive capacity and could have developed into very satisfactory societies without any poverty and with thriving economies and rich cultural systems and a good quality of life for all, if development had been conceived in terms of people putting the resources around them directly into producing to meet their own needs.

The point here is that conventional or capitalist development inevitably results in inappropriate development, i.e. it does not and it cannot result in development of what is most needed. Again the basic question is 'What is being developed?' Conventional capitalist development develops things that will almost entirely benefit the rich, the factory and plantation owners, and the overseas consumers. A small amount of benefit usually trickles down to some of the local poor in the form of a few jobs in the factories and plantations (see below), but the net benefit for the poor is often negative in view of the loss of access to land etc. that capitalist development inflicts on them.

But the second point is much more important. Appropriate Development contradicts the assumption that capital is an important or a necessary factor for development. This is the fundamental contradiction between conventional and Appropriate Development. Its fundamental principle is little or no money capital is needed for the development that can meet most basic needs and provide all with a good quality of life. Usually all the resources necessary for this are there abundantly, in the land, labour and knowledge of the people. All that is needed is the organization and application that an Appropriate Development vision brings, so that people can work together to devote the productive resources around them immediately and directly to producing much/most of what they need. Note that this is emphatically not about reaching Rich World living standards and consumer lifestyles. It is about reaching satisfactory but frugal and secure living standards via intermediate and low technologies.

It is remarkable that even Marxists take capitalist development for granted. They have a distressingly narrow understanding of what development is, focused on merely economic development in conventional terms. They celebrate the way the West has swept away the complex web of traditional cultural elements determining economic affairs in 'primitive' and peasant societies, clearing the ground for progress towards industrialisation. They are especially scathing regarding subsistence economies. According to Marx the laws of history decree that eventual emancipation is not possible unless there is a long painful march through maturing capitalism to revolution. Thus Warren (1980) applauds capitalist development in the Third World. Marxists take it for granted that there can't be development without investment of capital, although they do not want the capital to be privately owned.

Hence the painfully tragic situation is constantly visible wherein possibly three billion people suffer malnutrition, poor housing, inadequate water supply, poverty, unemployment, depression, illness etc., while there are all around them abundant food producing resources, house building resources, labour and skills. Chapter 4 listed many of the low and intermediate technologies, and the cooperative systems, whereby even the most impoverished villages could be building their capacity to meet many of their own needs using the soil and water labour and skill they have, with little or no dependence on capital, corporations or the global economy. There would be important things they could not do, and they might need much guidance (e.g. from Permaculture teams) but except in the most severe circumstances if they were not prevented they could completely eliminate problems of nutrition, shelter, unemployment, homelessness, leisure and exclusion, along with most of the violence and squalor that come from severe deprivation.

Another mistake deeply entrenched in most critical as well as conventional development thinking is that the core problem regarding Third World poverty is the loss of capital, in the outflow of corporate profits and in falling terms of trade. Again this is to think solely in terms of conventional economic theory which only deals with dollar values, and it is to think only in terms of capitalist development. The mistake is evident in Dependency and Unequal Exchange theory. In fact the net flow of capital has little to do with Appropriate Development. Yes more capital could facilitate desirable development, but Appropriate Development can thrive in a poor country while massive amounts of dollar wealth are flowing out. What matters is that people can devote enough of their local resources to directly meeting their own needs.

Thus the calls for debt relief and 'fair trade' miss the point. Yes if rich countries dropped their protection and subsidies and Third World countries could export more to them, and if they had no debt repayments to meet, then conditions for the poor majority would probably improve markedly, but nowhere near as much as they would if Appropriate Development was taking place. 'Fair trade' is not the problem – trade is the problem. That is, the problem is an economic system in which poor countries must succeed in competition against each other to win limited export markets, in order to earn money to purchase and to develop.

Consider the appallingly avoidable tragedy that is unemployment. Hundreds of millions of poor people in the Third World suffer unemployment or underemployment because conventional economic theory says 'There is too little capital to invest in creating jobs for them. Productive activity can't begin unless capital comes in to set up factories'. Hence the 70%

unemployment rates that generate the Raskall Gangs of PNG and the East Timorese 'rebels', when Appropriate Development would have eliminated the boredom and the anger, harnessed all that energy and given those people a sense of worthwhile contribution. Conventional development theory says they must remain idle until some corporation wants to employ them.

The process of development is best determined by market forces. Market forces must determine what is produced, who gets it and what is developed. Market forces will ensure the most efficient allocation of productive resources. Non-market exchanges must be eliminated. All productive items, especially land and labour, must be made into commodities for sale in a market. Productive activities which take the form of 'subsistence' outside the market must be moved into it.

The market system might be allowed to play a (minor) role in a satisfactory economy, but as Chapters 2 and 3 have explained the market is directly responsible for most of the poverty, suffering, conflict, ecological destruction and underdevelopment in the world. This is because market forces ignore need and what is just or appropriate or ecologically necessary, and respond only to monetary bids. This is by far the main reason why billions of people get a miniscule proportion of the world's resource output. Even worse, when market forces are allowed to determine what is developed the productive capacity of the Third World is devoted not to producing what Third World people need, but to what consumers in rich countries want.

It is infuriating that advocates of the market claim that it is the most 'efficient' way of allocating things. But this is true only if 'efficient' is defined merely in terms of what will make most profit. If on the other hand your goal is to meet human and ecological need, then obviously the market is about the most appallingly inefficient system that could be devised! It allocates to those in least need and therefore it produces the most inefficient allocations of resources and development.

Appropriate development is essentially a matter of organization and harnessing up, not investment of capital. Miracles can be performed if the existing resources of land, labour, and skill can be deliberately and rationally applied (by the people, not the state) to the production of things that people need. But conventional capitalist development will not tolerate this. The only approach that is acceptable is to let the market do the organising, which in effect means, to leave it to what suits the corporations.

Consider the benefit that 'trickles down' when people in Bangladesh produce shirts for 15 cents an hour, part of which they must then spend buying from supermarkets sometimes owned by Rich World corporations. They would be far better off if most of their work time could be going into the production of necessities in small local farms and firms they owned. But rich countries and their agencies such as the World Bank simply will not allow this – development is only allowed to take the form that suits corporations seeking to maximise profits according to market forces.

Obviously the development of what is appropriate in view of the urgent needs of people, societies and ecosystems is not possible unless a great deal of production and distribution and investment takes place contrary to market forces. The most important things to develop are not very profitable and many things should be developed that can never yield profits. The general principle is that market forces prevent appropriate development, but conventional development doctrine emphatically rules out 'interfering with market forces.'

Plunge into the global economy! Individuals and nations must find something to produce and sell, because they can't expect to be able to acquire anything unless they have been able to get money from selling something, including labour. So, crank up some export industries, and entice in foreign investment. Trade! Find something, anything, to sell. That's crucial if you are to be able to accumulate capital, pay for imports and loans and infrastructure development.

Appropriate development minimises involvement in the national economy, let alone the global economy. It will usually make sense to sell a little into these economies in order to be able to import some necessities but the key to Appropriate Development is the immense capacity for self sufficiency within the locality. Conventional development theory and practice have no interest in the fact that households, communities, localities and nations can easily produce for themselves most of what they need outside the monetary economy and with almost no dependence on capital or markets or corporations or banks or trade. (They might not produce as 'efficiently' as distant corporations, but that is of little consequence).

Thus among the principles of Appropriate Development are, borrow very little if anything, export only a few surpluses in order to be able to import only a few important items, never squeeze production of necessities to increase production of exports, allow foreign investors into your nation only if they will agree to produce necessities on your terms, and maximise local and national self-sufficiency. These principles enable security from the devastation the global economy can instantly inflict if export prices fall or if capital moves out. No matter what happens to coffee prices or on Wall St you can continue to provide most of the things you need for a high quality of life.

Conventional development is Trickle Down development. Admittedly those who are rich in the first place will become much richer but in time wealth will trickle down to lift the living standards of the poor. And conventional development works! It is lifting large numbers out of poverty.

This is probably the most offensive aspect of conventional development. Yes conventional development has seen significant improvements in GDP and in living conditions in much of the Third World over the last 60 years. Averages for infant mortality, literacy rates and life expectancy have improved considerably. Average Third World GDP has grown remarkably. Rosling (2009) for instance summarises the impressive movement of national indices up the slope towards Rich World figures over the last forty years. So should we adhere to it because it is working? A number of factors have to be considered here.

A development strategy should be evaluated firstly by how effective it is in solving the most urgent problems, i.e. improving the living standards of the poorest people. But conventional development is about the richest few investing their capital to develop whatever ventures will most increase their own wealth, with only a miniscule proportion of the benefit flowing to those in desperate need. It typically results in rapidly increasing inequality as the rich get richer.

India has an accelerating number of billionaires, while thousands of poor farmers suicide every year because they are trapped in poverty. This is outrageously unacceptable – any satisfactory approach to development would first focus all available effort on helping those in most urgent and desperate need.

Next, consider the extreme slowness of the Trickle Down process. If we assumed that the poorest billion are increasing their $1 a day incomes at 1% p.a. it would take 350 years for their incomes to rise to $232 a year, and it would take something like another 200 years for them to rise to the present average income in rich countries. But by then Rich World GDP per person would be thousands of times as great as it is now!

This also makes clear that conventional development fails the test that the neo-liberals make most fuss about; efficiency. It is an extremely inefficient way to solve the most urgent problems. It takes generations and wastes almost all the resources that could have been immediately applied to the problem by allocating them to the few who need them least.

Appropriate Development emphatically rejects any notion of trickle down, recognising it as a vicious myth legitimising development in the interests of the rich. Its essential principle is that it is possible for all people to meet most of their basic needs and to achieve a good quality of life in a few years if not months. There is no excuse for anyone being left behind, let alone having to wait generations until satisfactory conditions trickle down from development which had mostly enriched others.

How comforting trickle down theory is for the rich! No need to even think about radical redistribution or re-orientation of productive capacity to meet need directly – they can just go on seeking greater wealth knowing all will become rich in time.

Another major problem trickle down apologists gloss over is that it attends only to the gains and ignores the losses. For instance China is booming primarily because it has taken over much of the manufacturing that others used to do. For every new factory it establishes to export brooms to Rich World hardware shops one closes in the Philippines or Indonesia. Conventional development creates massive unemployment and economic destruction. Globalisation condemns large numbers of poor people to deeper poverty by allowing some more energetic corporation somewhere to take their markets, productive activity and livelihoods. Conventional development is in part merely the relocation of production and its advocates typically enthuse about its gross gains when what matters are its net gains.

The most decisive point against Trickle Down is that it cannot solve the problem, because, again, it is not possible for all countries to move up that slope to Rich World ways and standards. The gradual enrichment that Hoseling's evidence shows is the result of a development process in which there are already grossly unsustainable levels of production, resource use, transport, trade and ecological destruction, and therefore a process which cannot continue for much longer, and which cannot possibly lift 9 billion to Rich World levels.

Modernise! Abandon your traditional ways and adopt Western ways.

Conventional development sees many traditional customs as thwarting development and therefore to be abandoned. For instance collective land ownership, failing to maximise efficiency and monetary returns on investment, and especially subsistence production are seen as interfering with development... because they contradict market principles. Tribal and peasant ways are typically highly collectivist, and their economies are governed by customs and traditions, not profit and gain. So these have to be replaced by individualist ways and markets. In effect the advice is to become competitive, acquisitive individualists who will trade in the market and forget about everything but dollar values, and whose top priority is to accumulate monetary wealth without limit, and with no concern for the community or the public go

Central in Appropriate Development is recognition of the value of many aspects of traditional cultures. Indeed those cultures often have more effective technical and social ways than we have in 'advanced' societies. Among these is recognition of the importance of the commons, and of collectivist ways. In most traditional tribal and peasant societies and modern communes the community owns and manages the fields and other resources. for the good of all.

Rich countries help poor countries to develop. They give aid and foreign investment and they trade with them.

Rich countries are certainly very keen to help Third World countries to achieve conventional-capitalist development, i.e. development of the kind that enriches themselves. But they will not tolerate Appropriate Development, and they can't because it would mean their own demise. They cannot maintain their 'living standards' or their economies unless they go on getting most of the world's wealth, and Appropriate Development would put an end to that. What is not generally recognised is that the rich countries deliberately prohibit and prevent Appropriate Development.

What would happen if a poor country opted for appropriate development? It would be prevented from pursuing it by the following irresistible actions and forces.

❏ The IMF and the World Bank would politely remind the government that they have an impossible debt and need new loans and roll-over arrangements, and that they have accepted the loans on conditions which include allowing corporations to come in and do what they like, boosting exports, eliminating government regulation and subsidies to the poor or to local business and spending on national needs, and generally allowing market forces to determine what is developed. In other words, the conditions included in Structural Adjustment Packages explicitly rule out appropriate development and oblige recipient countries to get rid of it.

❏ The credit rating agencies such as Moodys would instantly drop the country's rating, meaning that it's not a good place to invest and that corporations would have to pay high interest on funds borrowed to invest there. The economy would then decline as corporations ceased to invest in it.

❑ The government would have to tax corporations properly to pay for (some of) the appropriate development, so the corporations would leave and the associated export income would cease, making it more difficult to meet debt payments let alone to fund development.

❑ Natural resource investment would have to cease going into building the power stations and ports the exporting corporations want, and start going into building local workshops, gardens and premises for small firms. Again this would cut export capacity and create unfavourable investment conditions for corporations.

❑ The World Trade Organisation would politely remind them that when they joined (which they had to do in order to be able to export) they agreed not to interfere with the freedom of trade. If the government redirected development away from exports it would contradict this commitment, and to increase local self-sufficiency would be to restrict imports, which is not what Rich World corporations want.

❑ The entire development establishment would point out that they are making a dreadful mistake, flirting with voodoo economics. Everybody knows 'socialism' doesn't work and its best to leave things to the market.

The country is therefore totally trapped, locked into inappropriate development. Several powerful forces and agencies explicitly, deliberately prevent Third World countries from devoting their productive capacity to meeting their own needs. They have no choice but to go on facilitating only that form of development which will see rapid production of resource exports and goods imports, increase in the amount of business done in the global economy, opportunities for transnational corporations to do good business in the Third World, and rapid increase in the amount of the nation's wealth flowing out to the Rich World, while ecosystems deteriorate, most of their people remain very poor and large numbers suffer greater deprivation and impoverishment than ever.

The point was illustrated in Chapter 3 by reference to Mandella's South Africa. Having fought and won a civil war with the intention of nationalising resources, distributing land to the poor and focusing development on their needs, the ANC was quickly told that it could not do any of that or international capital would leave and dump the country into squalor. Decades later the problems are about as bad as ever. In many regions, unemployment has been stagnant at 40% for decades, while the gold and the diamonds flow out.

Of course a big part of the explanation is that in almost all Third World countries it is in the interests of the small privileged and powerful class to pursue conventional development. They can be junior partners in the lucrative business deals, owning some of the plantations and mines and sweatshops, and benefiting from Rich World aid, arms and protection when they rule as the rich countries prefer.

So it is crucial to understand that development is not one thing or condition and that there are many different forms into which an economy could develop. The state of the Third World today is the particular condition into which it has been developed. The rules of the global economic game imposed by the rich have developed the Third World into economic forms which deliver to Third World people little of the wealth produced.

In other words, as many now recognize, conventional development is a form of plunder. It gears Third World productive capacity to producing to enrich the rich. It's genius is that few see it for what it is, because it appears to be legitimate. It appears to be the inevitable consequence of market forces, and everybody knows the best way to run an economy is to have as much freedom for market forces as possible. Appropriate development might eliminate most of the suffering of three to four billion people within months if they were able to devote the resources and the productive capacity they have around them to meeting their own needs. But this possibility is emphatically ruled out by Rich World agencies and policies and by the dominance of the free market ideology.

Empire
This has brought us to the nastiest aspects of the way the world works. It is not just that the global economy is grotesquely unjust. In addition rich countries go to a great deal of effort to secure and run their empire.

From time to time poor Third World people object to the

deal they are getting in the global economy and try to change to different systems and rules. Sometimes they seek to take 'national' control over their own economies so they can devote their resources to their own needs. Often this has not even involved any suggestion that capitalism should be abandoned, as the aim has only been to take more of the control of development into national hands. But that is not acceptable. When a move of this kind occurs force will probably be needed to counter the 'subversion'. Rich countries have a very long and very extensive record of assisting Third World regimes to put down threats to their capacity to rule in our (and their own) interests. The most common response in the past has been to label any threat as communist subversion, which gives a watertight entitlement to crush it ruthlessly. The governments, secret agencies and military forces in rich countries provide financial assistance, military equipment and training, organise assassinations, train torturers and undertake direct military destruction and invasion, in order to get rid of regimes that will not rule in our interests, or install ones that will. Anyone who thinks these are mistaken or exaggerated claims cannot be familiar with the vast literature on international relations and modern imperialism. (For a detailed summary of this issue see http://www.ssis.arts.unsw.edu.au/tsw/10-Our-Empire.html, and for lengthy documentation see http://ssis.arts.unsw.edu.au/tsw/DocsOUREMPIRE.html).

The basic relationship between rich and poor countries for the last 500 years has been one of invasion, brutal thuggery and looting. World history has largely been about the struggle among the strongest nations to get control of and to dominate an empire. Thus beginning with Spain and Portugal a series of Western powers has led the conquest, destruction and plunder of the Third World. The population of some large New World regions was reduced by about 90%. The British fought more than 70 colonial wars to conquer their empire. Early in the last century the struggle to control and expand empires generated two world wars, in which the British were exhausted and the US surged into the dominant position. Since World War 2 the US has intervened in the Third World with military force about 60 times, killing more than 16 million people, in order to put down threats to its control. It now maintains the empire from which rich countries in general derive much of their wealth.

It is exasperating that most people in rich countries do not seem to understand that their affluent living standards could not be provided if these dreadful things were not going on. If you want your supermarkets to continue to be well stocked, and your mobile phones to work on Congalese Tantalum, and to have petrol in your car, then don't complain about the vicious foreign policies and the deceit and the brutal military action that rich countries engage in. Unless these things go on your empire and your resource access and your supermarkets and living standards cannot be maintained. Remember, it is utterly impossible for all to live as you do. If you insist on getting the proportions of the world's resources you take for granted then most people must (be forced to) get by on a tiny fraction of them. That can't be done without a great deal of effort to keep in place the regimes, policies and military bases that secure our sources. The West has made most of the effort, but consider the behaviour of the Chinese now, giving generous aid without questions to Burma, Sudan and North Korea, to secure the right to take out resources. Consider also its thuggery in taking the waters from the Tibetan plateau, on which South East Asia depends.

If all this still sounds a little exaggerated and offensive just ask yourself is the oil, timber, copper, fish of the planet equally distributed among all its people? If not, who is getting most of it? How is it that we get most of it?

Again we are confronted by the problem of ideology, the deliberate, stubborn, immovable refusal to recognise the situation. Rich world officials and publics simply ignore the fact that their levels of wealth, comfort and security would not be possible if they did not have and loot an empire. The process is largely an automatic consequence of the fact that the global economy is only allowed to run on market principles, but it also requires a great deal of brutality to keep in place. Chapter 7 grapples with the grotesque lack of social responsibility which enables people to not see or care about such things.

Consider Kerala, Cuba and Ladakh.

Appropriate Development could achieve miracles very quickly.

It is not being claimed that it can solve all problems, nor that there could be no benefit from dealing with rich countries. It is being claimed that even the poorest regions could be well on their way to providing themselves with basic necessities within a matter of months if Appropriate development was permitted. Now add the effect that genuine aid from the rich countries, appropriate technology and expertise could have. What might be achieved if the rich countries behaved like Cuba, which sends tens of thousands of doctors into poor countries?

Instead what do we see all around us? As I write there is more trouble in East Timor. 'Rebel' groups are killing people again. You can't walk on the streets of Port Moresby at night either, because of the 'Raskall' gangs. In any number of African regions children are soldiers in vicious wars. Millions of Afghans grow opium for a living, because there is no other option. Are you surprised these things happen when the unemployment rate for young men can be around 70%. What else do you expect people to do if you have forced them to be idle, poor, hungry and angry, just because you have decreed that no development can occur unless someone with capital can set up an enterprise that will make more money for him there than anywhere else in the world?

There are some very impressive illustrations of the potential of Appropriate Development. One is the state of Kerala in India. Because the development goal adopted there (by an elected 'communist' government) has been equity, ie., ensuring that what the poorest need is the main consideration, astounding indices of low infant mortality etc. have been achieved.

Cuba provides another partial example, especially of the power of Appropriate Development with respect to food. Cuba had become highly dependent on oil imports from the Soviet Union, bought with heavily subsidised income from the export of sugar to the Soviet Union. When the Soviet Union collapsed Cuba's oil-dependent agriculture ran into huge difficulties. The Cubans were jolted into a rapid switch to organic and self-sufficient ways and to local agriculture, and these have been remarkably successful. (There are more than 30,000 food gardens in Havana city alone, some yielding over twenty tonnes of vegetables p.a. Bruce, 2007, 53-8).

One wonders what conventional development economists

from the left and the right would make of Ladakh, a region near Tibet where people live in extremely difficult conditions at around 14,000 ft, with only hand tools, animals and no modern technology, on an average GDP per capita of almost nothing. Yet this is a complex, culturally rich, and admirable society, with a great deal to teach the affluent societies about civility, humanity, community, social justice and ecological sustainability (Norberg-Hodge, 1991).

The Ladakhis are kind and generous. They have extensive community support systems. They look after and value their old people, they have a rich spiritual life, a relaxed lifestyle, and robust and sustainable food producing systems despite fiercely cold winters and a short growing season. Their production is labour-intensive, yet the pace of work and life in general is relaxed, with much time for ceremonies and religious observance. No one is isolated or lonely, they recycle everything and waste nothing. They have no interest in power, domination or competition. They are very conscious of their dependence on nature, they are multi-skilled and practical, and they live simply. There is no crime and no poverty and no drug problem and no social breakdown. Above all they are notoriously happy people.

A strong case could be made that the people of Ladakh have a far superior culture to that of the rich western countries. It is quite disturbing to ask of the Ladakhis 'What development do they need?' With respect to most of the factors that matter the traditional Ladakh villages are in my view, more or less satisfactorily developed. A few possible technical changes suggest themselves, such as to do with improved infant health care and perhaps the introduction of tree crops and windmills. But they do not need supermarkets, television, freeways, cars, throwaway products, and packaged imports, an advertising industry, more lawyers or higher incomes or a higher GDP. In fact it is precisely the coming of these things, the penetration by Western economic forces, that is now rapidly destroying the ancient culture of Ladakh.

Ladakh's impressive level of development has been achieved without movement down the dimension of increasing monetary value of production, sales, incomes, exports, etc and without accumulation and investment of capital. It is due to the organisation of existing resources, especially the labour, skill and co-operative dispositions of the people into forms which enable easy, pleasant and secure production of the basic goods and services which provide them with a very high quality of life. The existence of Ladakh, and many other 'primitive' and 'peasant' societies confronts us with the grossly erroneous and vicious assumption that development has to involve people suffering for generations while capital is slowly, painfully and inequitably accumulated, and while most of the benefit of development flows to others.

The stubborn refusal.

This book worries throughout about the problem of ideology, the myths and delusions that underlie and perpetuate our plight. The worst thing about these phenomena is not so much a failure to critically evaluate taken for granted ideas and assumptions, but the wilful, deliberate, stubborn refusal to even think about the issues. Questions, practices and ideas that scream out for attention simply don't get on the agenda, while grossly mistaken and never questioned assumptions drive thought and action. Nowhere is this more depressingly apparent than in the 'development' field.

Many people who profess concern for the plight of the poor, or who want peace in the world, or who want ecological sustainability, or want to see an end to violent repression in the Third World, will not recognise that their own Rich World 'living standards' are the basic causes of the problems. Such goals cannot be achieved until the rich countries stop hogging far more than their fair share and far more than all can ever have. This is not the only source of the problems, but it is by far the most significant one.

Appropriate Development is of course a mortal threat to the interests of transnational corporations and banks, Third World elites, and people who shop in the supermarkets of the rich countries. It is incompatible with globalisation, and with some of the fundamental elements in Western culture, such as notions of progress, efficiency, 'living standards', the supremacy of competitive individualism, and especially acquisitiveness and wealth seeking. If appropriate development emerged in the Third

World you would not get anything like the proportion of world resources you get now. It is therefore not surprising that the vast development establishment, from the level of the UN, World Bank and IMF down, including the armies of development academics and Foreign Affairs bureaucrats, show not the slightest interest in Appropriate Development, never have conferences on it, never write books about it, and never even recognise that development can or should be thought of other than in terms of capital investment, sales in the market and becoming consumers. I estimate that in my University library there must be 1500 metres of shelf space taken up by books on 'development'. But they only deal with conventional/capitalist development. I have only found two that make even the most distant reference to any notion of Appropriate development.

Daily one is confronted by distressing images of impoverished, suffering millions of people – who are idle while surrounded by abundant productive capacity. Consider the 'drug mules' of Columbia, desperately poor people who swallow heroin capsules and ferry them into the US, taking huge risks in order to provide for their families. Or people who have to sell some of their children. Or those who sit on the sidewalk all day trying to sell a few shoelaces or boxes of matches. Or those who pick our tea or harvest the beans for our coffee and are paid wages we couldn't survive on. All that is lacking in these situations is the organising and the harnessing of the available productive capacity, and the main factor blocking that organisation is the lack of an Appropriate Development vision. Yet almost the entire development establishment and literature fails to recognise the distinction between conventional and Appropriate development, let alone the way it condemns Rich World affluence.

And what are your chances of solving global ecological and resource problems given the conception of development generating them. Billions of Indians and Chinese are manically striving for the Rich World 'living standards' that are already destroying the ecosystems of the planet. Hence the Chinese build one new coal burning power station every ten days. (By the way this isn't China's development; it's ours. China is where our cheap goods are made. The emissions come from our factories and power stations, located over there).

The Chinese rulers now can do nothing but deliver development defined as getting richer, because that's all they and their people understand, and if the people can't get more bicycles and TVs there will be chaotic unrest. That's why the Chinese and the Indians destroyed the Copenhagen greenhouse conference, by adamantly refusing any agreement that might limit their growth in energy use and thus hinder their 'development'. The entire march to the precipice cannot be avoided unless they grasp that there is another conception of development to the one they are obsessed with.

Leahy (2009) illustrates the distinction in his case for a focus on Permaculture systems in South African villages. He describes the pathetic poverty and struggle millions of people there endure. The only solution that occurs to the government is of course to get conventional development going, that is to try to get the villagers to crank up production of agricultural commodities to sell in the international market. The inevitable and chronic failure of this strategy, supposed to triumph against the high tech machinery and billion dollar a day agricultural subsidies of the rich countries, makes no difference to the well-meaning bureaucrats. Leahy makes it painfully obvious that enormous benefits would come if even meagre resources were put into development of simple Permaculture systems to enable villagers to produce much of what they need. But of course this would look like 'subsistence' and everybody knows that's what has to be eliminated.

Almost none of the agencies claiming to work for the Third World are anxious to expose the myth of conventional development. Most think and act within the conventional understanding of development theory and practice. They are doing things like seeking to increase monetary transfers to the Third World or to help poor countries get ahead within the viciously competitive and predatory market system, or to help poor individuals prosper within existing systems, (e.g. the Grameen bank). Yes campaigns for debt relief and fair trade can improve the lot of many poor people, to some extent and in the short term, but they are only about enabling some to compete more effectively within an inherently unjust system which does not and cannot provide for all. Most aid agencies are only working to help the

Third World succeed within the global economy, and they are therefore working on behalf of the system and those who benefit from it most. Whether or not they realise it they are in effect working to get poor people to take for granted and accept the legitimacy of the competitive world market, the inequality and injustice it inflicts, and the goal of consumer lifestyles for all. Above all they are reinforcing the understanding that there is and can be no conceivable alternative to capitalist development theory and practice.

Billions of people are trapped and enslaved in conditions of appalling poverty, exploitation and oppression not primarily by the guns and prisons of the dominating classes, but by the belief that development equals conventional-capitalist development. The single most powerful action that can be taken towards emancipation for the Third World is to help its people to understand and reject the vicious ideology that is conventional-capitalist development theory, and to realise that there is another way. The supremely important task for anyone claiming to be concerned about the fate of the Third World is not to give more aid, or teach them Permaculture, or enable more trade. It is to help people to understand the Alternative Development vision. The Simpler Way defines Appropriate Development for rich and poor worlds.

As Ghandi said long ago,
'The rich must live more simply so that the poor may simply live.'

Chapter 6

GOVERNMENT

There is almost no understanding of the magnitude of the changes that will take place in the nature of government when the coming scarcity impacts. In the context of history representative democracy has been remarkably effective, but as global problems intensify we will move on to participatory democracy... because we will have to.

Consider some of the main problems in representative democracy. Firstly, it is highly centralized. A very few individuals make the decisions, often determining the fate of hundreds of millions of people. Most Australians were firmly against the invasion of Iraq, but one person, the Prime Minister, decided that Australia would take part in it. In the coming era there will be extreme decentralisation and localization, meaning that neigbourhoods, towns and regions will have to make most of their own decisions about development and functioning. These decisions could not possibly be made for them by centralized governments, which will not have the resources to continue doing more than one quarter of the spending that is done now.

Secondly, centralized government is easily enlisted to serve the rich. The rich and powerful can spend large sums on lobbyists, propaganda campaigns, think tanks, publications and expensive lawyers. They do not have to persuade the people in general; they only have to sway perhaps a single minister. If they don't like a government they have great power to devote to getting rid of it. They can turn their media against a government, or support the alternative they want. They can in effect buy governments via their campaign contributions. How transparently corrupt this is when large sums are given to both sides to be sure of having influence no matter which one is elected.

Government is typically more or less closed to the people, thuggish and arrogant. It forces things through despite discontent. The state has its own interests and its comfort and privileges to protect. It is convinced that it knows best, often it will not tell you what it is doing, it will fob you off with deceptive and evasive rhetoric, and when it makes mistakes it never admits them. It strives to minimize bother to itself. It wheels in teams of spin doctors to distract and deceive. Freedom of information rules are designed to protect governments as much as possible from having to provide information. We wage a constant, losing battle for openness and accountability. Democracy more or less means the people elect a few to be their dictators; the government rules, the people do not.

These features are understandable because it is very difficult to govern gigantic consumer-capitalist societies. Governing involves trying to decide between fiercely competing demands, and trying to get things done that many bitterly oppose. Criticism is abundant, understanding and appreciation is scarce and credit is rarely given where it is due. Therefore governments try to ram things through and to protect themselves through secrecy, deception and spin.

The adversarial nature of politics degrades behaviour to appallingly childish and vicious levels. Governments and oppositions constantly search for ways of making the most derogatory interpretations of each other's actions. Dishonesty rules as they tug at every possible thread to find fault and put the most damning interpretations and smears they can think up. Just listen to question time in parliament and try to work out how it is possible for adults to descend to such dishonest and infantile behaviour. This makes it impossible for the public to grasp the pros and cons of policy options and is a patently absurd way to try to arrive at sound decisions. However it is what you must expect when the supreme concern is to get or hold onto power. It is not surprising that most people despise politicians and ignore politics.

But there is a far more important issue. We should not be

governed! It is wrong for humans to be governed. It is infantile, not good for us, dangerous and reflects lack of responsibility and maturity. Humans will not have reached social maturity until they have learned to govern themselves. The goal must be thoroughly participatory democracy, whereby everyone is equally involved in the direct making of the decisions about how things are to be run. This is the classic Anarchist philosophy and the coming of The Simpler Way will make it possible and necessary.

For perhaps ten thousand years since tribal times humans have allowed themselves to be governed by lords, kings, dictators, 'leaders' or elected representatives. This is infantile. Humans will not have grown up until they become capable of and fiercely determined to take responsibility for governing themselves through the direct participation of all citizens in public assemblies. It's no good if governors, no matter how well meaning, govern passive and uninvolved masses. The problem of good government is not about finding good leaders or good procedures to follow.

We have no difficulty in seeing that as a young people move towards personal maturity it is appropriate that there is increasing autonomy, readiness to think for oneself, make one's own decisions and take moral responsibility for decisions and actions. The concept of personal maturity is not compatible with someone else making the decisions for you. Yet most people do not see the contradiction between this and the political situation where we let a few decide for us and tell us what to do, force us to do what they decide, and punish us if we do not conform. That's the way you treat children. Tolstoy looked forward to when '... humans outgrow the governmental stage in history' (Marshall, 1992, p.372).

It is difficult to practise participatory democracy when systems are large, but in the coming situation of mostly small towns it will be easily done, it will be essential... and it will be enjoyable. Only the town can govern itself satisfactorily. Only the people of the town know the situation, the climate, the soils, the history, the likes and dislikes, what will and won't work here. The right decisions can only emerge from informal processes of discussion among the townspeople, that is, the decisions that are not just technically valid but that the town is happy with because all understand the reasons and helped to arrive at the decisions through a process designed to accommodate all desires as well as possible. Resentful people who don't own the decisions are not going to turn up well to the working bees to implement them.

It will also be clear to all that voting will not be very important, and usually will not occur. The intent must be to discuss until the option that is technically and socially best for the town becomes clear to all. In other words the goal in principle must be to reach consensus. This is not the goal in our present society where the norm is the adversarial, zero-sum struggle for scarce resources or favours. In that context voting makes sense and 51% decisions can be made to stick. But this is not so in a town where the overriding concern is what decisions will keep our town solidarity and morale in good shape.

Three factors will greatly facilitate our capacity to govern ourselves in these ways. Firstly our small local economies will be far less complex and therefore far easier to manage. There will be no economic growth and this will eliminate much of the political struggle that occurs now, especially the ruthless competition to win development approvals and access to things like building sites. There will also be much less zero-sum conflict to get decisions that advantage one party at the expense of another. Mostly the political task will be to work towards agreement as to what is the best decision for the town.

There can be no argument that the ways being outlined are impractical or too problem-ridden. They are the ways many small communities do govern themselves. Hundreds of Eco-villages, monasteries, communes and Kibbutz settlements proceed as it is being argued our new town economies will have to. Anyone who doubts this vision should come to terms with the way the Spanish Anarchist collectives governed themselves. Chapter 4 explained how they ran whole regional economies very effectively through thoroughly grass-roots participatory democratic practices giving everyone a direct vote on issues and policies. Our task will be much easier than theirs was.

There is a strong case that the self government of small communities results in much better government, both with respect to the technical issue of sound decisions, and to the issue of community solidarity. As Morris says, 'There is not one public service, not one, that could not be better supplied at the local level where the problem is understood best and quickest, the solutions are most accessible, the refinements and adjustments are easiest to make and the monitoring is most convenient' (Morris, 1987). 'Smallness is simply essential to preserve the values of community as they have been historically observed – intimacy, trust, honesty, mutuality, cooperation, democracy, congeniality.' (Institute for Self-Reliance,1982, p.189).

Colin Ward makes the point that the more the state does the less society there is. The more functions that are performed by the state then the fewer there are requiring people to get together and carry out, generating thought, concern, mutuality and responsibility. 'If we want to strengthen society we must weaken the state' (Ward, 1973, p.20). The coming scarcity will force this good fortune on us.

There will therefore be no need for professional politicians, let alone parties. There will be some professional bureaucrats and experts to look after the technical aspects of things like water and energy supply, but their role will only be to advise us and do what we tell them. We will get the preliminary reports from the review committees, giving us all the relevant technical information. Because the systems will mostly be small and technically simple we ordinary citizens will be able to assess the reports and proposals. We will all be acutely aware that to engage in the childish nonsense that typifies present political 'debate' would be to jeopardize our chances of finding the right decisions for the town. We will have worked out the systems best designed to facilitate good decision making – the committees, consensus-seeking processes, town meeting and referenda provisions, the conflict resolution systems and public hearings on technical reports.

Easily overlooked here is the educational significance of participation in our own government, its importance for personal growth. Bookchin explains how this was recognized within Ancient Greek society through the concept of 'Paidea'. When the ordinary person is trusted with thinking, discussing, deciding, implementing, monitoring and reviewing, and understands how important it is to get the decisions right, he is under a strong incentive to be conscientious, well informed, considerate, disciplined and tolerant. The experience of governing therefore contributes to personal growth. 'Participating in the political life of the self-governing Greek city state... was the 'school' in which the citizens highest virtues were formed and found expression... Politics in turn was not only concerned with administering the affairs of the polis but also with educating the citizen as a being who developed the competence to act in the public interest.' (Bookchin, 1987, p.59. See also de Hart,1984, p.27).

All this is an assertion of the validity and importance of Anarchist political theory and practice. The above argument has been that if we are to cope in the difficult conditions we will soon have to grapple with we will (have to) move to classically Anarchist principles and practices of government. We will have to run our own small communities and we will not do this very effectively unless we do it via thoroughly participatory democratic practices. This will be quite feasible and it will be enjoyable – and it will be good for us.

It should be emphasized that the appeal here is to the Anarchist approach to government and that there are other strands within the tradition that are not being advocated. It should not need to be said that the association with violent means advocated and practiced by a few Anarchists has no value in the approach being taken here. (This association runs contrary to the strong concern major Anarchists have shown for peaceful means, notably Tolstoy and Gandhi). Nor does the recommendation some have made for the abolition of private productive property seem to be necessary in the economic arrangements suggested in Chapter 4.

The main classical Anarchist thinkers adamantly insisted on freedom for the individual and denied the right of authorities to restrict this. They thought that order would derive from the voluntary mutually beneficial arrangements people would come to as they needed to exchange goods and manage local affairs. They saw antisocial behaviour as primarily generated by the poverty and oppression the state inflicts as it rules in the interests of elites. They believed that in an equitable society there would be little or no crime. Kropotkin especially argued that the natural condition of humans is one of cooperation and mutual benefit. I think these are plausible assumptions, but many would reject them as being unrealistically optimistic. In the long term future it is likely that good social systems and good pro-social behaviour will reinforce each other so well that people will be happy to behave in ways that eliminate any need for power to correct disruption. However advocates of The Simpler Way do not have to settle this debate and we can therefore avoid criticism for being impractically utopian on this issue. If in the near future we find a need for some coercive laws, police, courts and jails, as I expect we will, then so be it but that does not affect the way we must govern ourselves.

Marxists have scathingly rejected Anarchism for its optimistic assumption that the revolution can be about ordinary people taking over social institutions and running them without the state and without leadership. Whereas Anarchists would get rid of the State as soon as possible, Marxists see taking state power as essential if the change is to be driven through despite strenuous resistance, including resistance from those being saved. Issues of this kind are discussed in Part 3 but it is appropriate here to note that the key problem is to do with the consciousness of people in general. In Spain large numbers of people did in fact quickly take over the running of society and did so remarkably effectively. But in this special case a long tradition and much educational work had built the necessary ideas and values in people in general. In more common revolutionary situations it is plausible that revolutionary leaders would have had no choice but to take state power and use it brutally to push change through given that the masses did not have the 'right' vision.

One wonders why both sides in the depressing history of Marxist vs. Anarchist conflict could not acknowledge the validity of the other's perspective on this theme, and focus on the absolutely vital preparatory task of developing the required consciousness. Both parties have the same long term goal, a society that does not need a coercive state (as distinct from a purely administrative apparatus without power) because there are just arrangements and because people have the right world view. A society which runs without a state, power, coercive authority and law because its citizens are happy and cooperative and work out mutually beneficial arrangements, might be the ideal but it obviously has no possibility of working unless a remarkable level of personal awareness and responsibility has been achieved.

When an opportunity to take power arises it is understandable that the Marxists seek to seize it and to drive major structural and cultural changes through, and take up the reforming of ideas and values later after the dictatorship of the proletariat is no longer necessary. Bookchin (1990) points out that Marx thought the personality of the worker and peasant was unimportant and could indeed be left until later. The Spanish Anarchists however saw it as crucial, and their success was largely due to the attention given to the task over a long preparatory period. If presented with an opportunity to take state power the Anarchists would instead urge people to turn away from the state and run things themselves. Whereas the Marxists work to take the state and smash it, Anarchists work to develop in people the consciousness that will lead them to ignore it. (On Tolstoy, Gandhi and Bookchin on this theme, see Marshall, 1992, pp. 372, 417, and, 615 respectively).

Marx can therefore be criticized for taking a too narrowly economic a definition of the problem, i.e. for thinking that the task is just to take control of the economy from the bourgeoisie. In fact the main task is to change the dominant ideas and values to those which will both enable a good society, and lead people to dump the old economy and power structures. The arguments in this book align with the Anarchists in thinking that it is an inexcusable and fatal mistake to assume that the consciousness raising can be left until later. Again this conclusion is given by the new situation scarcity will bring. Viable communities will have to govern themselves and this cannot be done effectively without aware, responsible, willing citizens.

Given that this general problem of consciousness is the absolutely crucial factor for achieving a satisfactory society, both the Anarchist and Marxist Movements can be strongly criticized for giving it nothing like appropriate attention. The history of both reveals concern to trying to stir up or capitalize on social unrest, hoping that this will lead to the revolution (for instance, Kropotkin, Bakounin and Proudhon running around Europe to this and that insurrection), with little or no effort going into the enormous, difficult and lengthy task of building widespread adherence to the ideas and value without which a satisfactory society cannot come into being. Today we are in a far worse condition regarding awareness of and discontent with the system than was the case one hundred years ago, so the educational task is that much more daunting.

Perhaps the main worry raised by this vision of government is to do with 'populism'. What happens if the assemblies in a region agree on procedures that seem to the rest of us clearly unjust or otherwise intolerable? Isn't there some need for an overarching power of law to make sure certain rights and principles are respected everywhere? The approach argued for in this Chapter accepts general laws and sanctions so long as the power to make and enforce them lies with participatory assemblies, and is attended by detailed provision for due process, review, conciliation etc.

The focus in this Chapter has been that of the town, neighbourhood, suburb and region. In addition there would be the need for the government of those state and national affairs that remain after so much has been devolved to the towns and suburbs. In a stable economy geared to meeting needs national affairs would not involve titanic struggles over mega-buck developments and construction contracts but would be largely about administering national systems of law, communications, research, transport etc. The Anarchist assumption is that this level too can be run via mechanisms which take all proposals down to citizen assemblies for direct participatory votes. There would need to be expert professional bureaucracies, completely open and accountable and without any power.

The Anarchists are understandably criticised for being much too optimistic. Many people in dog-eat-dog society would not believe humans are capable of the conscientiousness and mutuality which some Anarchists assume will totally eliminate the need for social coercion, law, prisons and armies. In my view the optimism is warranted. Social conditions which provide well for all, especially spiritually, and in which the supreme concerns are mutual assistance and the public good, are likely to bring out the best in us. The Simpler Way vision sets a far easier problem of government than we have now. The task is only to govern small local communities free from the conflicts produced by the manic quest for affluence and growth, and communities forced by circumstances to focus on consensus and mutual aid.

In addition the quality of life implications will be conducive to the good will and cooperation that must be strongly present if a society is to work well without much if any coercive or top-down power.

Chapter 7

SOCIAL COHESION AND QUALITY OF LIFE

Even if we did not have alarming problems to do with resource scarcity, poverty, war, sustainability and global justice we would still be confronted by profoundly unhealthy societies in which many are unhappy, deprived, insecure, stressed, depressed or dumped into 'exclusion'. The quality of life most of us experience is nowhere near what it should be. Social cohesion and community are in poor shape. This chapter concludes that our sorry state is a direct and inevitable consequence of the mistaken commitments to affluence, growth, competition, the market and individualism. That is, some of the core ideas, values and ways of consumer-capitalist society are inevitably socially destructive. These problems of cohesion and quality of life cannot be fixed within such a society.

The disintegration

The living conditions most Australians enjoy are probably among the best in the world, and there are many aspects of our society we can be proud of, especially to do within political freedoms, the rule of law, security and health. Yet there is a long list of disturbing observations regarding the state of social cohesion, including the breakdown of families with almost half of marriages ending in separation, drug and alcohol abuse, crime and violence, almost the world's worst youth suicide rate, an epidemic of stress, anxiety and depression and mental illness, and of eating disorders and obesity, unemployment, homelessness and poverty suffered by millions, the decay of rural life and decreasing security from violence and in old age. There is political apathy and cynicism. The situation with respect to indigenous people is an embarrassing disgrace. In addition most environmental conditions which impact on the quality of life are deteriorating, such as traffic congestion and pollutants.

In a satisfactory society there would be high levels of cohesion, solidarity, integration cooperation, common values, and community. There would be strong agreement about important ideas, ways and values, and a strong concern with the common good, the public interest and the welfare of all, especially of those least advantaged. There would be care, giving, generosity, and the desire and the good will motivating actions to benefit others. Underlying these behaviours there would be strong inclinations to cooperate, help, give and nurture.

These issues are to do with the dimension from individualism to collectivism. It is not possible to have a society made up of individuals pursuing their own self interest. A society only exists in so far as individuals have concerns for other than their own interests. If there is no concern for social values, no control of individual thought, feeling and action by social considerations, then there is no society. Obviously there can be societies in which the focus on the good of the collective is too strong and unnecessarily interferes with the interests of individuals, or binds the clan into hostility against outsiders. The former is what we rightly reject in the case of totalitarian societies where the common good has been identified with the state or a dictatorial elite. Reference to collectivism these days is usually taken to be a recommendation of greater state control, but that can be avoided. The task is to find a satisfactory balance between the good of all and the freedom of individuals to do what they wish. Unfortunately Western culture with its long capitalist history has come to put far too much emphasis on the freedom of the individual and far too little on the welfare of society.

A society is like an ecosystem with many components, inputs and feedback mechanisms that determine its condition. Unless they are all chugging along well, meshing, providing each other with what they need, in the right quantity and at the right time, then the whole thing won't work well, and could die. That's what we see in a rainforest. An enormous number of organisms and processes generates and maintains the conditions making it possible for each of them to exist. The insects pollinate the trees and the trees give insects their food.

In a satisfactory society conscientiousness, cooperation and helpfulness are required, but they are also rewarded and reinforced. It's all about cooperation and mutual benefit. Your helping is pleasant, appreciated, and makes your own existence go well, so it is encouraged and reinforced. The rainforest requires the bat to eat the fruit and spread the seeds, but bats don't do it grudgingly, they like doing it. The action is reinforced. There is a harmony of purposes and actions, an automatic agreeable meshing and integration. There's no need for artificial force to get things done. No one makes that bat do the pollinating. In a tribe there's no need for police and a bureaucracy to make people do what's necessary. It's largely automatic and voluntary, not thought about.

In a healthy dog functions are well coordinated, they mesh. When a cat appears feet do their stuff, blood is diverted from stomach to limbs and growl apparatus clicks in. Back left leg never decides to go at right angles to front right. All parts work together smoothly for the common purpose, each making its precise contribution. This is how a good crew gets a sailing ship to work well. No need to detail scarce sailors to go below and rouse the rest of the watch out of their bunks when they were supposed to be on deck by now. In a well integrated system problems tend not to arise or are dealt with by the routine functioning of the system so there is little or no need to add on solutions. In the traditional village of Ladakh many formal and informal processes enable conflicts to be identified early and to be quietly resolved by family and community as they go about their everyday activities. There is no need to apply a patch of social workers or counsellors. Most tribes have been highly stable and cohesive for thousands of years without any need for police forces. The controls are internalised and automatic. People have within them the ideas, values, habits and dispositions that ensure integration and cooperation. But in our present society the integrating conditions and forces are weak and damaged, by some of the major structures and processes of our society. As a result there is a lot of breakdown so we need to add on armies of social workers, police, counsellors, courts, judges, prisons, parole officers and lawyers... and still the problems multiply.

The result is increasing system complexity and cost as society becomes more encrusted with inadequate patches on patches which require more and more resources. This contributes to the diminishing returns Tainter (1988) identifies as the essential cause of the collapse of complex societies. It is as if more and more of our crew members have to be set to rounding up those who fail to come on deck and guarding them in the ship's lock up.

In *The Way*, Edward Goldsmith (1983) discussed the conditions which enabled many societies to remain stable over very long periods. He saw that these societies were cooperative, cared for their members, prevented significant inequality, cared for their environment, were not hierarchical, and were not greedy. That's The Way, and we have lost The Way. Indeed our way contradicts all these crucial prerequisites, and it is therefore no surprise that our society is at such conflict with itself, creating problems that then require such effort to deal with, in a losing battle.

The fundamental cause of the malaise is of course the competitive, individualistic acquisitiveness and an economy based on these values, which not just condemns many to struggle and exclusion but damages the whole of society. (See below on Wilkinson and Pickert, 1990). The disintegration is a direct consequence of this society's fundamental structures and processes. It is not a superficial effect that can be righted by the application of patches while those structures remain.

A central concern in this chapter is to show that the conditions of a society following The Simpler Way would strongly require and reinforce integration and cohesion. Those conditions would provide powerful positive incentive to think, feel and act collectively, to want to do what is good for society. This would firstly be because all would be acutely aware that their own welfare and quality of life would be due, not to their own wealth or talent or effort, but to the richness of their society and its landscape, infrastructures, festivals, artists, public works and climate of support and community. Secondly all would know from experience how satisfying it is to participate in and contribute to a thriving caring community. They would know the miracles of synergism from everyday personal experience. They would know that the more they give the more they receive, especially spiritually. The goal should be, not seconding the wishes of the individual to the good of the collective, but aligning the good of both so that clashes are eliminated or minimised. One way of doing this is to get individuals to love Big Brother, but a better way is for us to work together to develop social systems and rules which can be seen to maximise the long term welfare of all of us.

It is commonly assumed that there is an inevitable tension between individual and society. In competitive consumer society doing the socially appropriate thing is often difficult and unpleasant, because you have to go against your immediate self interest. You pay your tax but that means you have to send in money you'd rather keep. You stop at red lights, but that clashes with your desire to get there fast. Individual interests are felt as clashing with the good of society. However in The Simpler Way, with its sensible organisation of resources to meet needs, to do what is good for society is much more likely to be to do what you like doing anyway. Consequently there is not likely to be significant tension between individual and society.

Thus the motivation in a good society is almost entirely positive. There's not much point in trying to force people to be good, creative, helpful or conscientious, by threatening to punish them if they aren't. Things can only go well if people want to give, create, help, take responsibility and come to working bees, because they find these socially-crucial activities satisfying.

Collectivism does not need to imply docile compliance with the herd or the state, or absence of criticism, dissent and deviance. A robust society needs these, to ensure that assumptions are challenged and possible problems identified and arrangements are improved.

The disintegrating forces at work

Consumer-capitalist society is structured in terms of fundamental, irreconcilable, zero-sum conflicting interests, which at best can only result in the exclusion or destruction of many. In other words this society has conditions and forces built into it which have a strong tendency to damage cohesion and cause breakdown. (Of course there are also some forces at work which tend to integrate). It is a society in which individuals strive to maximise their own advantage, to get more wealth, status and power. The welfare of the tribe or the public good are far from the focal concerns guiding thought and action. It is accepted that those who are energetic, fit, lucky, rich and/or who work hard can end up with much more wealth than the rest, and that many who are less so will end up with too little.

It is in other words more or less a winner-take-all society... with miserly provision for some of the winnings to be transferred to the biggest losers. All compete and it is quite alright for the few rich and powerful to win and take things many poor people need, such as materials for their too-big houses, and fish for their pet food. It is not just alright but it is a sign of admirable success to drive business competitors into bankruptcy and take their sales and markets, leaving them without a livelihood. If you insist on having a society structured on such principles then it follows as night the day that you will have many serious problems. For instance, if you exclude a lot of people from a livelihood, a worthwhile role, self respect, decent housing or supportive communities, don't be surprised if they do turn to crime, drugs, alcohol, depression and self-destruction, and cost you billions.

Our society then puts patches on these festering sores. It does not try to eliminate their causes which lie in an economic system that is not designed to provide for all. It just tries to get the failures and deviants to shape up, get back into the system, compete against others and perform properly. When it can't do this satisfactorily it manages the irritants in order to minimise inconvenience. Thus we have vast 'welfare' industries including prisons, remedial schools, drug and alcohol clinics, and mental health institutions. Then there are industries the employed and respectable middle classes turn to for coping advice, from the books on self-help to the consulting and life coaching and depression clinics. None of this questions a culture of far too much work, competition, risk, stress and insecurity in order to consume far too much. The biggest health problems we have now are probably to do with depression, stress and anxiety. The fact that on average we work about three times too hard and have houses at least ten times too expensive is not on the agenda.

Agencies representing disadvantaged groups then plead to the state for assistance. The state a) ignores them as best it can, b) gives some assistance to the squeakiest wheels, c) and bandaids, administers, manages the problem but never solves it. Dissent and discontent are kept low, and in any case are experienced as individual misfortune or defined as due to personal error (drugs or alcohol abuse...) so the system is not threatened no matter how bad the experience of individuals. The fact that most of the bad behaviour is due to the bad conditions the system inflicts is not considered. The existence of social problems is normalised, and anyway rugged individuals don't complain, they just soldier on.

'Welfare' therefore takes the form of compensation, always grudging and inadequate, for those who lose the competitive struggle. The existence of welfare proves that the system is charitable. 'End of pipe' 'tech-fixes' are applied. Bandaids and patches are put on the spots where trouble breaks out, and then patches have to be put on the patches. So, build another freeway, bury the CO_2, build more prisons, send more police to deal with drunken Aborigines... but don't ask about the connections with an economy which automatically creates and impoverishes losers, ignores the need for livelihoods and dumps whole regions into unemployment and boredom. Drug abuse provides a perfect example. Declare 'war on drugs', develop more high-tech equipment to detect the shipments, impose higher penalties for the pushers who are 'killing our children', but don't ask what is so seriously wrong about a society where the most attractive thing many young people can find to do is to take drugs.

The quality of life.

It is well established that increasing economic wealth does not raise the quality of life, so long as wealth is above a very low level. Long ago Easterlin (1972) reviewed more than 30 studies and found that the experienced quality of life does not increase as the GDP increases. Even with a doubling of the US GNP per capita (in deflated terms) over recent decades there has been no increase in the experienced quality of life. We are about three

167

times as rich as our grandparents were but it cannot be said that we enjoy life any more. Richard Douthwaite's The Growth Illusion, (1992) and Short Circuit (1996) argue in detail that not only has economic growth not increased the quality of life, in Britain it has reduced it since 1955 (pp. 3, 9). Hamilton (2000), Hamilton and Dennis, (2005), Eckersley (2004) and Speth (2001) are among those reviewing the extensive and convincing evidence that above a relatively low income, quality of life does not increase with increasing income. The above list of social problems aligns with the indices suggesting that in general the experienced quality of life in the rich countries is now actually deteriorating as GDP increases.

These facts should be a policy bombshell, but their significance is largely ignored. They show that there is a head-on contradiction between prioritising economic turnover, profit maximisation and growth of GDP on the one hand, and on the other seeking to raise the quality of life.

The supreme goal of all governments and of just about all people is still to increase monetary wealth – yet it is clear that this does not increase happiness, or the quality of life, while it is the main cause of damage to social cohesion and the environment. Politicians do not ask 'What policies might best increase the quality of life?' They only ask, 'What will maximise the GDP?'

Politics should be driven by concern to improve the quality of life of all, and effort should constantly be going into researching and monitoring the conditions which do this. By making growth of GDP the supreme goal social policy is instead geared to the interests of those who benefit most from selling things. Many of the actions taken to raise the GDP damage the quality of life, directly by for instance driving workers harder, and indirectly by increasing the climate of insecurity and callous selfishness.

Community.

Community is a most important element in a satisfactory quality of life, yet its significance is rarely given the attention it deserves. Many of the problems our society is encountering can be explained in terms of the lack of community. It is an imprecise concept and is not well understood, but it would seem to involve the following elements.

168

❏ Having many familiar personal relations. Important here is friendliness and feeling connected to many people, 'face to face' communication, meeting, talking to, and sharing with other people (so an internet group or people with the same religious outlook who do not meet would only constitute a weaker kind of community).

❏ Identification with a place or group. 'This is my town. I like this place. I feel at home here. I belong here.' Earth bonding.

❏ Solidarity, support and security. Having comrades. Concern for the welfare of the place and its people. 'There are people around here who would look after me if I were in need.' In an individualistic society your security depends mostly on your own strength or wealth because you can't depend so much on others coming to your assistance. Mutual concern and assistance, Concern for the public good. People care about and do things for each other. Especially important are common values and responsibilities, such as the need to keep the town bushfire equipment in good order. Hence a sense of civic responsibility.

❏ Traditions, rituals and celebrations. A sense of our local history. Events and dates that are significant in the history of this town. Things we celebrate together.

❏ Moral debts and obligations. In a strong community people often do things for each other, giving and receiving 'gifts' and help. There are voluntary contributions and there is reciprocity; you give and you receive. This creates appreciation, strong moral debts and social bonds, feelings of desire and obligation to repay, to give in return.

Note how none of these elements has anything to do with money or conventional economic theory and practice. They are all about the social forces, structures, bonds and rewards that make a society harmonious and robust – and satisfying and noble.

These factors are also sometimes thought of as making up 'social wealth' or 'social capital'. In a strong community people have much social wealth, i.e. relationships, habits, past experience and climates of good will and expectations which will guarantee access to friendship, security, cooperation, civil interactions, assistance and pleasant social experience. These sorts of factors are much more important in enriching life than merely having financial wealth. In pre-industrial societies people devote a great deal of time to maintaining these social relations, which then give them community, support, security and satisfactions.

WE SHOULD NOT USE THE TERM 'SOCIAL CAPITAL'.

Social cohesion is utterly different to mere monetary capital and it is important not to think about social 'wealth' in the way that conventional economists think. They collapse everything into the single dimension of monetary value, and thereby grossly distort understanding. The stuff sometimes referred to as 'social capital' is extremely complex and largely incomprehensible, involving many mysterious factors such as pride, friendship, memories, morale, manners, social connections, history, ideology, tradition, emotional bonds, religion, trust, and feelings of security, reciprocity, obligation, debt, gratitude and generosity. It is impossible to think of all these in terms of one dimension that can be quantified, like monetary value. You can't take a quantity of this stuff from one place and invest it or spend it anywhere else, as you can with money from a bank. You can't bank social wealth. If you hoard money it grows, but if you don't use social wealth it wastes away. For instance you must renew friendships or they will cease to exist. Often when you 'spend' social wealth you then have more than you had before, such as when you give assistance or a kind word or tell a joke. Money transactions are zero-sum; what I get you lose, but when I give you a friendly smile we both gain. Social wealth has no financial value and does not behave according to the 'laws' of the market place.

So don't let the economists with their impoverished conceptual tool box (containing only one thing) take over the discussion of social phenomena and the nature of a good society. Their paltry and misleading theoretical apparatus cannot deal at all satisfactorily with the field.

How do we rate on community?

How much community is there in the typical city suburb? Some of us do enjoy considerable experience of community, e.g. in football clubs and churches, but many do not and this is a major source of social breakdown.

❏ Many people live very privately, as isolated individuals or in nuclear families, having little or nothing to do with the people next door. Many of us live in dormitory suburbs hardly knowing anyone who lives nearby.

❏ Life in our society is a competitive struggle between individuals pursuing self interest, as distinct from being organised in terms of working to provide for the welfare of all, especially

170

those in most need. In a good society effort would be made to provide for all, to make sure no one is dumped, excluded, or without a livelihood. The basic nature of individualistic-competitive society therefore militates against community.

❑ We move a lot and this reduces the tendency to 'put roots down' and to become identified with a place. We also move to work each day, meaning that we are not interacting with our local community most of the time. The significance of mobility is most evident when it comes to the care of old people. This is best carried out by the members of a community, such as the whole tribe as distinct from the members of as single family, many of whom were cared for as children by the people who are now old. They would then know that they will in turn be cared for many years hence when they are old. These understandings cannot develop when people come and go rapidly from a locality. That makes it impossible to build up and pay off moral debts and obligations between young and old.

❑ Because we live in cities we have many impersonal relations, with relatively few familiar people. How well do you know the people you buy your food from? In a city most of the people we meet might as well be robots. Hence the term 'the lonely crowd'. Familiar personal relations are more likely in small settlements.

❑ Many people have little access to emotional support. Large numbers are lonely and depressed. Many people are allowed to become unemployed, homeless or impoverished, therefore it is no surprise that many turn to alcohol and drugs. Many self-destruct or become socially destructive.

❑ This society deliberately and energetically teaches children hostility, violence, predation and contempt for others. Many TV shows (e.g. cartoons) and electronic games, are about little more than aggression, violence, destruction and delight in defeating and trashing others. We also teach people to be fiercely competitive rather than cooperative, especially in sport, school, social life and the economy. By comparison little effort goes into encouraging people to be friendly, cooperative and helpful to each other let alone into making these our top priorities.

❑ Many people have too little time to become involved in local affairs.

❑ There is little identification with one's area or place of living. Suburbs are dormitories. Houses are often just temporary conveniences or commodities.

❑ People have few community tasks and responsibilities. We do not spend much time working together in our neighbourhood to improve it or perform useful public functions. Distant bureaucrats and corporations do all that.

❑ The public sphere is being reduced, especially as state spending is cut and state institutions and services are 'privatised', i.e. taken over by corporations and run for profit. Shopping malls are private spaces. Museums, railways, schools, prisons, hospitals, aged care facilities, universities and leisure spaces are increasingly being funded and run by private corporations. Therefore we are less able to think of these as 'our' public institutions, services and spaces, functioning to serve us (as distinct from existing to make profits).

❑ There are few meaningful festivals, rituals and traditions. Those we do have tend to be spectacles provided by states and privately consumed. Compare the impoverished spiritual and cultural life of white Australia to any peasant or tribal society.

The lack of community most seriously affects people with problems, notably the single parent, the disabled, poor people and the aged. The young and the affluent can to some extent find or buy alternative satisfactions, but without community many old people are condemned to a life of isolation and boredom. Elderly men have a high suicide rate.

The community is a crucial and irreplaceable agent of socialisation. As people interact with others in a satisfactory community, social values are reinforced. People experience the benefits of helping and cooperation. Children hear their parents discussing important local issues, expressing concern for the welfare of each other and of the area, and for standards and traditions. We experience parents and friends helping each other, cooperating to do important things for our community, expressing concern for others. We get satisfaction from participating in the festivals and civic duties that we can then see contributing to the welfare of all. We come into frequent contact with many others and share their perspectives on the locality. These experiential learnings about the way the world is and about what is important cannot be learned from books or from the pronouncements of parents and teachers. Contrast this with the socialisation experience of children who live in high-rise units without contact with neighbours and whose parents shop as isolated individuals in supermarkets.

Especially perverse is the way we neglect adolescents. They have no important role in society, no valued status and no contribution to make, precisely at the time when they need to form a healthy identity. It is a time when they should be learning to be useful and appreciated contributors to society, committed to it and eager to serve. But instead adolescents in present society are alienated and excluded. No effort is made to include them in socially useful activity. The work to be done is allocated to paid workers, and there are always too many of them anyway. This society's only interest in them is as consumers. So young people turn to spending their time with each other doing things that are at best time-consuming entertainment, and often physically and socially destructive. They also spend hours every day on average playing computer games, unconnected with the real world. In tribal societies young people are not ignored and cut off like this. They are part of society, working and playing with all the others, doing useful things, under the eye of older people, learning by experience what it is to be a solid member of society.

This again reflects the lack of integration. We isolate the toddlers in day care, the aged in nursing homes, the workers in factories, the housewives in kitchens, the teachers in classrooms. In The Simpler Way they would all be rubbing shoulders most of the day, engaged in important, purposeful and mutually beneficial contributions, fuelling the synergism.

At the bottom of the heap are the angry alienated many. More than 200,000 teenage Australians are not in work or in school. This is no way to form a good citizen. It is not surprising that many turn to drugs, alcohol, hooliganism, car stealing, body piercing, graffiti, over eating or under eating, fast cars, to achieve identity and status and to defeat boredom.

As Illich (1973) pointed out so well, much of this trouble is due to the way the economy has taken functions from us. Long ago everyone in the village had to think about the management of the well and the commons. Now just about everything is done for us by councils, professionals and corporations. The economy constantly needs to enable them to do more business, which means there is constant pressure on us towards more passive consuming. Hence another blessing that will come with scarcity; we will again have to get together, from toddlers to the aged, to do many of the things now done for us.

Much of the disintegration can simply be put down to lack of purpose. Nothing matters more than having things to do, interests, projects, goals which one is keen to work on. This is another reason why arts, crafts, gardening and hobbies are so important. The tragic situation of many native people, homeless, drug addicts, unemployed and depressed people is in large part due to circumstances which have left them without purpose. In winner-take-all society there's little interest in making sure no one is left without interesting and worthwhile things to do.

We pay a high price for our poor level of community, not just in terms of the isolation many people experience, but in terms of the costly social problems it generates. If people experienced more community fewer people would become depressed or turn to drugs or crime. Friends and neighbours would foresee many problems emerging before they became serious such as domestic violence, mental illness, suicide and child abuse.

Market relations drive out and destroy desirable social relations.

If the top priority in a society is merely increasing the amount of production for sale then many things that undermine community will occur. Many industries and regions will be 'restructured' as factories close down or open in new areas, changing familiar townscapes, depriving people of livelihoods and requiring many families to move and break emotional ties to people and places. Freeways will be put through stable neighbourhoods. Peasants will be displaced as foreign corporations come in and take their land and their markets.

Especially important is the increasing pressure to commercialise as many functions as possible, i.e. for corporations and professionals to take over the provision of many goods and services we once produced for ourselves outside the cash economy. The more they do this the more the GNP rises, but individuals and communities lose functions, connections, control, autonomy, livelihoods, self respect and the incentive to interact and to take responsibility. For example we are now preparing less of our own food while buying more take-away food and we purchase entertainment, furniture, child minding, counselling, insurance, security, education, aged care...

The social relations which used to govern all this economic activity, for instance determining how things are shared, how help is given, how less able people are provided for, are eliminated and replaced by market forces and the activity of governments and professionals.

It is of course very much in the interests of the corporations for us to exist as isolated individuals who do less and less for ourselves and have to buy everything from them. So they spend vast sums on advertising to persuade us to buy products but no one makes any effort to persuade us to get together to do things for our neighbourhood or town. Most of our society's capital and development resources flow only into ventures that will increase production for sale and therefore lead to more passive, private consuming. Few resources go into projects that might stimulate more community self-sufficiency, mutual aid, cooperation and sharing. For example almost no resources go into developing neighbourhood workshops, drama clubs, commons and leisure-rich environments. Such developments would not only contribute nothing to 'getting the economy going', they would actually reduce GNP by enabling people to live better while purchasing less.

However by far the most destructive force eliminating social values is the market system. When buying and selling within a market situation is allowed to become the main mechanism whereby people acquire the things they need, then desirable social attitudes, bonds and relations are damaged or driven out.

When you enter a market situation to buy or sell you have to be selfish. You go into the market to get things for yourself, and you must focus on how to maximise your own advantage and to minimise that of the other person. Markets allocate things to those who can pay most for them. The situation does not encourage thought about what would be good for other people or for society as a whole. But it is impossible to have any society, let alone a good one, unless there is much more than self interest, i.e. unless there is concern with what would be good for others and for the society as a whole. Self-interest is only one of the many motives and values people have, and the quality of their society depends on their social and moral values, not on their self interest, competition and acquisitiveness.

To repeat, a society is not possible unless people have concern for more than their own self interest. There must be concern for social values such as being honest, doing the right thing, seeing justice done, standards, the public good, what is good for others, traditions and customs, cultural values and practices, equity, and the situation of the least fortunate, morality and decency, pride in society, respect for law, appreciation for good institutions, concern for the environment and to see social progress. These are the things that constitute society; if they are absent you do not have a society. Yet the relations you have in a market situation contradict and prohibit these relations. The more emphasis we put on mere market relations, i.e. trading to maximise individual monetary wealth, then the less attention and value will be given to the other-regarding values that make society possible, let alone satisfactory or admirable.

What would happen if mum made the toast and sold it to the highest bidder?

Dad would get the toast, because he can pay more for it. The kids, and grandma, would starve.

The things that make a family satisfactory are precisely the many non-market values and relations, the giving, mutual aid, and concern for the welfare of others, and the satisfaction that comes from doing what will help others thrive. When you let market relations determine what happens you drive out good human relations and replace them with self-interest, suspicion and predatory behaviour.

Thus we can see the serious mistake in allowing the market to have much influence in society, let alone in identifying a society with its economy which economists are strongly inclined to do. Markets, wealth-seeking, trading, investing and making money

176

are dangerous to society, because they are about individuals pursuing self-interest. It might be acceptable to have a large market sector within a society, so long as it is a minor part of the society and moral, pro-social values and rules are much more important considerations.

The neo-liberal scourge.

Over the last 500 years there has been a titanic struggle for freedom for the individual, i.e. freedom from rule by tyrants, kings and popes, and freedom to do one's own thing and to believe what one wishes. This has been of immense significance for human emancipation. The trouble is that it has also freed acquisitiveness from moral/social control. Once for instance lending money to receive any interest was regarded as a mortal sin, banned by the Catholic church. In the Medieval period feudal lords were bound by moral laws to provide for and protect their serfs. But in the capitalist era there are only weak moral considerations restraining some from taking more and more. Over a period of a hundred years or so the labour and 'socialist' movements managed to institute stricter controls over the freedom of the entrepreneur, by giving the state power to regulate. But by the1970s capital's ceaseless and fierce drive to find more investment outlets was increasingly being thwarted by state regulation in the interests of the less powerful – so capital determined to get rid of it. Hence globalisation.

The worst thing about globalisation is not society's loss of capacity to regulate the economy in order to meet needs (not that it this was ever done very well), or the resulting economic catastrophe afflicting millions and killing thousands of Third World people every day. It is the ideological shift that has come with neo-Liberalism and globalisation, the increased affirmation of the desirability and legitimacy of individuals having freedom from social regulation to maximise their own self interest.

Neo-liberalism makes us all into individual entrepreneurs who must focus on our own self-interest and survival in a difficult and hostile market place, working against all others, knowing that not all can get jobs or prosper or be secure. It causes rapidly increasing inequality. It makes altruism and cooperation and concern about social issues irrelevant at best, or liabilities holding us back. It generates a more selfish, mean, unequal, predatory, brutal and callous society, destroying the fundamental social bonds, solidarity and cohesion. The result has been the accelerating destruction of society itself, of the attitudes, habits, ideas and institutions which assume and reinforce the importance of other than self interest.

It should be clear that these problems of cohesion cannot be solved in or by consumer-capitalist society. The problems are caused by the fundamental elements in such a society, by the competitive pursuit of affluence and economic growth and especially by the excessive and increasing freedom given to market forces. Again markets cannot attend to justice, equity or the needs of society or the environment or future generations. Solving the problems the market creates is not possible unless there is a vast and radical change to another, very different kind of society in which markets are very minor determinants of what happens, if they exist at all.

THE SOLUTION?

Following is an indication of how some of the main factors that are important for social cohesion and quality of life are central in The Simpler Way. It must be stressed that this is not a wish list of desirable things. These are conditions which come with the definition of The Simpler way. They are integral to it. The community-reinforcing effects, the benefits to quality of life and cohesion and the automatic avoidance of problems are characteristics and consequences of the normal functioning of a satisfactory society.

Small, highly self-sufficient, cooperative communities running themselves.

The Simpler Way is about small communities which take control of their own affairs and organise local resources to meet local needs and such economies cannot function satisfactorily unless there is a high level of community, social responsibility, mutual aid, concern for each other and the common good. The day to day functioning of these communities will have a strong tendency to reinforce these good values and ways.

Because of the severe resource limits, we will have to come

together to cooperatively organise our own local economic affairs, and this will help to create interaction, familiarity, mutual concern, sharing, responsibility and therefore community. We would have transferred much economic activity into a large non-cash sector where giving, cooperatives, mutual aid and the working bees would automatically build community, social bonds and cohesion. We would have taken control over much of our own government, i.e. of determining how things will be organised and run. Because all would have a valued, rewarding contribution to make, a livelihood, no one would suffer unemployment, or lack of purpose or self respect. We would organise such a cooperative economy, under social control, because we would have to, because local productive capacity must be geared sensibly to meeting local needs. The new economy would have many free goods, commons, working bees, committees and town meetings, and it would (have to) be driven by citizens focussed on what is best for all. These radically new economic structures and processes would have a powerful tendency to generate mutual cooperation, concern and solidarity.

Especially significant here is the smallness of scale. Settlements would be walkable. We would therefore be constantly engaged in face to face contacts with familiar neighbours as we walked or cycled to work, shops, leisure and events. There would be a vibrant street life, including things like the evening 'promenade' as a significant leisure event. To leave one's front door would be to run the certain risk of convivial conversation, which would inevitably get onto important community issues, reinforcing awareness and concern and spreading ideas. When you have to get into a car to go anywhere these things don't happen.

Giving.

Many of the exchanges of goods and services taking place would not involve cash sales but would take the form of giving (and therefore receiving). For example the surplus from your fruit trees or any left-over materials from a repair job would be given to others or left at the neighbourhood recycling centre for others to use. We would also give our time to voluntary neighbourhood working bees. The artists, gardeners, comedians would give and enrich the landscape and concerts.

The distinction between giving and getting is important here, and easily overlooked. In consumer–capitalist society the dominant outlook and motivation is to get. People work to get money, they go shopping to get things, the compete to get, they live as individuals who have to get what they want in competition against others. Outside the home their lives do not involve much giving. However in The Simpler Way this situation is reversed. All will give much time to working bees (voluntarily), will give surpluses away, and will give attention to social issues and needs and will give help to each other. If they don't do these things their society will not work, but more importantly the giving will be enjoyable. This situation will build solidarity. The society requires giving, but it also rewards and reinforces it. Giving brings out the best in us, and makes us feel good. If people are doing a lot of giving, they are also doing a lot of receiving. More importantly, giving creates the right climate and outlook. It creates the generosity that releases and multiplies goodness. In The Simpler Way giving is the basic economic mechanism – most of the things you need will be given to you, from others or from the commons and social institutions, rather than bought.

Security.

The fear of insecurity that consumer-capitalist society increasingly imposes on everyone generates great pressure to accumulate monetary wealth as an individual. Unless you can pay for insurance, educational credentials, superannuation, health cover, aged care, etc., you are vulnerable and will probably suffer serious deprivation, because your fate depends on your individual capacity to buy the things you need. But in a tribe anyone who suffers a loss will be helped by all the others. Most tribes people are far more secure than we are in western society.

The Simpler Way involves a mutually supportive community, in which everyone knows that everyone is needed and that it is vital that everyone is in good shape. They know everyone has an interest in looking after each other. We need a baker so if he has a problem we have a problem. In addition we will know him personally and would want him to be content even if we didn't need him.

Dependence.

In The Simpler Way there would be intense mutual interdependence between people in their small settlements. We would all clearly understand that our individual welfare would only be secure if we could get many goods and services from each other, especially via bonds of familiarity. In consumer society we are highly dependent on others, but in a quite different way. We could not last more than a few days if the vast, complex and fragile global supply networks bringing everything to us broke down. This is dependence on people you don't know and have no bonds with, and who have no concern for your welfare. It is dependence on oil tankers and satellites. It makes you extremely vulnerable. By contrast the tribesperson is least vulnerable and most secure because of dependence on familiar people close by who care for him and who are in full control of the systems for providing everything they need. Knowing that your quality of life depends entirely on whether your local ecosystems and social systems were functioning well would feedback to reinforce your eagerness to contribute.

'Welfare'.

The dominant assumption in consumer society is that what matters most is economic or monetary wealth. If this is high and increasing then everything else will either be OK, or much better than it otherwise would be. From the perspective of The Simpler Way wealth and welfare are seen in a totally different light. In the present 'social-democratic' systems of the rich countries people compete to get and take as much as possible, a few succeed most and become obscenely rich while most struggle, then those with incomes pay taxes to enable some of the wealth to be redistributed to those at the bottom. In this process the most successful few take livelihoods from many others; e.g. many little shops are wiped out as supermarket chains take their business. Therefore there is a strong tendency for the numbers of people needing welfare to increase. Even in the richest societies large numbers are dumped and 'excluded', without employment, in lousy jobs, homeless etc. The avoidable economic cost (e.g. in bureaucrats and social workers), let alone the social cost, is enormous.

The Simpler Way scraps this entire concept of 'welfare' as

compensation. Income, inequality of income and redistribution of income are not important. Instead, The Simpler Way ensures that all have access to the things that enable a high quality of life regardless of monetary wealth. This is not about having big enough incomes to purchase all you want or need from the normal economy. It is about not having many material demands in the first place, and more importantly it is about establishing a new cooperative and socially controlled economy which provides well for all in the locality, including basic goods, a livelihood, purpose and abundant leisure and cultural activities. The most important things it provides are public, the commons, landscapes, and workshops and activities. Thus it is possible for people with extremely low monetary incomes to be very 'rich', i.e. to have access to the things that make their lives very satisfying.

This approach has been partly evident in the history of 'Distributivism' (Matthews, 2009), which seeks to spread productive capacity widely among people, as distinct from redistributing the wealth created by unevenly owned productive capacity. Perhaps its most spectacular instance has been Mondragon where workers own their firms. The Simpler Way goes much further, distributing to all the opportunity and responsibility for providing most social services and infrastructures, and in distributing to all access to the many intangible benefits of community.

Synergism.

In a good society there are mutually reinforcing effects, positive feedbacks, i.e. synergism. Consumer society is very competitive so if you beat someone to a job or a deal he's resentful and the relation between the two of you is damaged, and then he won't be inclined to help you or be nice to you, or to others because he'll be in a bad mood. Often therefore the outcome is less than zero-sum. But in The Simpler Way all the incentives and the rewards are the other way around. If I help you get what you want, or do things that make our institutions function well and enable you to thrive, then you're more happy and therefore more inclined to be nice and helpful to me and to others, and if you're nice to someone else then that person is more likely to be nice to me. So goodness multiplies. If I show you how to grow good strawberries then there will be more people in town who can provide us all with good strawberries. But in consumer society, if I show you how to grow good strawberries you might then put me out of business. The goal in a good society must be to foster those conditions and arrangements that require and reward cooperation, conscientiousness, helping and giving, so that positive knock-on effects multiply.

Synergism can't thrive in a competitive situation. Synergism flourishes only in an economy of giving. It dies in an economy of getting. Consumer society has an economy where individuals struggle against each other to get income, goods, wealth, prestige, property and power. Goodness can't multiply there. But when I give you something then the value received is more than I gave. Miserable, stingy, warped, narrow conventional economic theory can't deal with any of this. It's only good for accounting zero-sum transactions in monetary wealth.

Self-government.

Chapter 6 stressed that in a sustainable and just world most government will be of and by small communities, through intensely participatory democratic processes. This is not an option; our new communities will have to be highly self-sufficient local economies and the right decisions can only be made by the people of the town. The right decisions are those which suit the town's conditions, especially its social conditions, and only we who live here can work those decisions out. This situation will make us develop the necessary skills and attitudes, and these will inevitably focus us on the public good. You will realise that you can't have a good quality of life unless the town thrives. Our 'political' situation will push us towards cohesion and integration.

Can we restore cohesion and community?

No we can't, in consumer-capitalist society. The fundamental structures and processes of this society have a powerful tendency to destroy cohesion and community. The obsession with the individualistic pursuit of wealth, in a competitive market situation, inevitably generates ever-increasing polarisation. Too little is then grudgingly redistributed to those who lost, and then we wonder why there is a plague of drug abuse, depression, crime, family breakdown and violence. The economy does only that which will maximise profits for those with capital and it ignores what is most urgently needed, especially what is needed to protect social cohesion. The economy forces us to cope as individual entrepreneurs competing against each other and not only will not prioritise community-reinforcing developments, but expressly facilitates development that destroys community.

In an economy with these fundamental structures and dynamics it is not possible to have healthy levels of cohesion and community. The best you can do is stick on pathetic patches that redress a little of the damage. Give more funds to Meals on Wheels, hire some more community workers, set up a Youth off the Streets charity... while the fierce individualistic quest for wealth goes on generating the ocean of alienated and angry youth, drug abusers, single parents, lonely old men, depressed people, alcoholics and over-eaters. Community and cohesion are not things that can be added on or fixed up later, as if it were a coat of paint or a spray on deodorant. They are integral characteristics of the whole system, produced by the myriad conditions and interactions within the system. They are like the thriving evident in a healthy rainforest. You can't take an unhealthy forest and add on some thriving. Only if the many conditions and interactions and relations are in good shape will you see thriving. Consumer-capitalist society is built on foundations that thwart and damage and drive out social thriving (while they promote a thriving economy).

Strong community derives primarily from the productive situation. One of the great but easily overlooked virtues of The Simpler Way is the 'poverty' it imposes. When you are affluent you can be independent of others and you do not need to get together to think about and organise collective supply and security. But the great scarcity is coming and soon we will have to take these collective actions to provide ourselves with the goods and services we need, and this will generate community. The interactions will not be optional or matters of charity; we will have to get together and cooperate and share and organise. It will not be a matter of feeling that you might give a little time to Meals on Wheels, when you don't have to, you are busy, and most other people won't do it. If the getting together is only a matter of charitable good will not much of it is going to occur in a society which preoccupies us with looking after our own interests in competition with everyone else. But in The Simpler Way the required getting together will be enjoyable.

Chapter 8

GLOBAL PEACE AND CONFLICT

Throughout history conflict and war have mostly been caused by the intention to take the resources of others, or to take more than a fair share of the available resources. Armed conflicts in the world today are mostly explicable in these terms. To a large extent the problem of peace and war derives directly from the quest for affluence and growth.

To go back to the basics, our high 'living standards' in rich countries would not be possible if we were not getting far more than our fair share of the world's resources. The global economy automatically allocates most of the world's wealth to the rich few and condemns many to deprivation and squalor. Most if not all of the important resources are rapidly becoming more scarce and costly, yet only 1.5 billion people are rich and if all 9 billion expected were to have our present per capita use demand for resources would be 7 – 10 times as great as it is now. Add the fact that everyone, including even people in the richest countries, is obsessed with increasing living standards, economic output, production and consumption as fast as possible and without end! It follows as night the day that if we insist on living more and more affluently we will have to remain heavily armed and ready to use force to preserve our access to more than our fair share of the world's wealth.

In other words, global peace is not possible unless we develop a society in which we can all live well on far lower per capita resource use rates than at present.

Injustice means violence.

The massively unjust nature of the global economy directly generates a number of different forms of conflict and violence. Firstly consider the effort that many Third World elites make to preserve their privileges by keeping their people down. In some cases this has resulted in millions of deaths. These brutal and greedy regimes are usually eager to sell their national forests etc. to the corporations from rich countries. Often rich countries are propping up these governments, i.e. supporting them in a war against their own people.

Rich countries go to a great deal of effort to keep in place in the Third World the governments and policies that benefit the rich countries, including the supply of military equipment and actual invasion. Brutal Third World regimes are often supported or installed by the rich countries because they are willing to give the rich countries the access they want to Third World resources and markets. Rebels, war lords and rival factions fight ruthlessly to get control of the supply of diamonds, timber, oil etc. Often they are funded and armed by Rich World governments and corporations in an effort to come out aligned with the winning side, or just to have their mines protected.

The Structural Adjustment Packages inflicted on indebted poor countries by the World Bank have contributed to many serious conflicts by, destroying the Third World government's meagre capacity to provide assistance to its poorest and thereby provoking discontent and conflict. This was an important cause of the Rwanda genocide and of the break up of Yugoslavia. (See Chussodovsky, 1997). Those SAPs force countries to give corporations greater freedom to access the country's resources, markets, again fuelling discontent and desperation.

Rich world military force is deployed in the world's 'trouble spots' to be used against or to deter 'rebel/communist/subversive/insurgent/terrorist' groups who might disrupt 'order', and to deal with those '... threatening our vital interests.' For example how long do you think we could go on getting most of the world's oil if we did not have huge military forces patrolling the seas, in bases in the Middle East, supporting ruling elites who are hated by many of their people, e.g. the Saudi royal family? It is in our 'vital interests' that most of the world's oil continues to flow to us and not to benefit the ordinary people of Nigeria, Iraq, etc. Anyone calling for radical redistribution of these wealth flows so that poor people get more/some of it, is of course an insurgent, communist, terrorist... etc.

Then there are the outright massive invasions rich countries carry out, usually justified in noble-sounding terms such as 'humanitarian aid', 'preventing genocide', 'resisting communist advance', 'getting rid of a dictator', and 'opposing terrorism.' Sometimes there is some validity in these claims but always the action achieves important economic or political goals for the rich countries. There are many cases where the rich countries have totally ignored the need for humanitarian intervention (notably Rwanda and East Timor), and where they have not only ignored but supported dictators or taken no action against genocide, or supported regimes that murder their own people... because these actions were in their interests. Where they do launch military action you can be sure they will end up with resources, markets, military bases and control they didn't have before. For instance Yugoslavia and Iraq were socialist states, with no private ownership of major industries and resources and no participation by foreign corporations, but now these economies and firms are in the hands of western corporations operating in a market economy. Before the invasion Iraq oil was controlled by the state, but early in 2007 the industry was 'restructured' and most of the oil revenue will now go through western corporations.

In other words, arms and violence are needed to maintain our empire, to enable our access to more than our fair share of the world's resources. If we insist on having a way of life that is far more extravagant than all can share and that is only possible for the few of us, then we will need a lot of military force and the readiness to use it. We also have to supply arms to the Third World regimes that will keep their societies to the economic policies that suit us.

> Speaking to American soldiers at Camp Stanley, Korea, President Johnson said, 'Don't forget, there are two hundred million of us in a world of three billion. They want what we've got – and we are not going to give it to them!'
> If that is our attitude, and it seems to be, then we had better remain heavily armed!

To put it another way, we cannot have global peace without global justice and we cannot have global justice unless the rich countries cease grabbing so much of the world's wealth.

Think about security

We all want to be secure from armed conflict. The conventional solution has always been to try to build up the armed might to defend against attack... while doing nothing to change the factors that ultimately cause armed conflict. There can be no security in a world where no one questions the drive to get richer when it is totally impossible for all to be rich, or where the push for greater wealth must lead to conflict over resources and markets.

The best way to be secure is not by increasing military force but by enabling all to live well without taking more than their fair share. Thus a peaceful and secure world order cannot be achieved unless we shift to The Simpler Way.

In general the Peace Movement does not attend to the focal theme being stressed here. It has been largely made up of middle class people in rich countries who are pleading for an end to armed conflict while they go on living affluently... which they do not recognise as the main cause of conflict in the world.

Most people fail to grasp any of this. They wonder why there are conflicts and poverty and poor nations. Every now and then their leaders tell them their children must go to war and to slaughter the children of other people just like themselves. They don't like this much but it never occurs to them that they have brought it on their own heads by being enthusiastic supporters of and beneficiaries of the grabbing that has led to the conflict. They have been enthusiastic about the empire building, the quest for more markets, the pursuit of national prestige, and they want to be members of 'a great and powerful nation'. Why can't they be content to be members of a noble and admirable nation, or a humble nation or a caring nation? Above all they want the high 'living standards' they can't have without taking more than their fair share. But they would angrily reject the claim that they are greedy; they only want normal, 'nice' things. They don't realise that lifestyles regarded as normal in rich countries are far more resource-expensive than all people could ever have. We can't solve the problem until people who go to supermarkets realise what they are doing; i.e. understand that they are participating in and reinforcing the injustice and the plunder that requires and generates armed conflict in the world.

The failure to question – The refusal to ask why.

One of the most puzzling and surprising things about our society is the almost total absence of interest in the question, 'Why do we get into wars?' A tiny number of historians delve into the question but governments, military establishments, soldiers who fight in wars, the civilians who get minced, and publics in general show not the slightest interest in the question! Consider the massive amount of time and energy and rhetoric and emotion that goes into the 'celebration' of wars, the remembrance services, the recognition of bravery and endurance and sacrifice. Consider the number of books describing heroic campaigns. Consider also the massive investment of brains, resources and dollars in military policy and preparation, such as the time that goes into building another destroyer. Governments spend more than $1000 billion every year on preparing to fight wars. They do spend on 'peace keeping' but this is only about preventing some conflicts that have arisen from becoming more violent. They spend almost nothing on trying to prevent conflicts from arising in the first place.

War is an astronomically costly business, in dollars, effort, options foregone and destroyed lives. It killed about 160 million people last century. It has plagued human society for about 12,000 years. (It appears that there was little of it before humans established settlements). Wouldn't you think that the overwhelmingly focal concerns for human beings would then be, 'Why does war occur?', and 'How can we make sure it does not occur again?' Yet almost no one shows the slightest interest in these questions! The books and movies describing and eulogising and lamenting pour out continually. Where are the books trying to explain why war occurs and how to avoid it?

The ideological forces at work here are extraordinarily powerful, mysterious and perverse. Huge numbers of people go off to kill each other when they are told to, evidently without any interest in whether or not there is a good reason do so, whether someone has made a mistake, whether there might be another option, whether their leaders are dolts or thieves and whether their own mindless greed has led to the situation. They seem to feel no need to check. They certainly show almost no interest in asking whether their own lifestyles or their nation's foreign policies might be the source of the trouble.

If I told you to go and kill someone would you do it? Or would you ask 'Why?', and expect a very good reason before you did it? The military mind is trained never to ask such questions, but people in general seem to need no training.

In World War 1 many Australians walked hundreds of miles from country regions to cities to enlist, to fight against young Germans and Turks on the other side of the world enlisting with surely the same appallingly unsatisfactory reasons. Many of them actually said they enlisted for adventure. Many enlisted '... to defend the Fatherland.' Many on our side enlisted '... to defend the glorious British Empire'. Did they not understand what an empire is, and that you are not supposed to invade and plunder, and that stolen property should be returned?

How many of them would have had the faintest idea why the war had broken out or whether there was a good reason to enlist, or whether the politicians who presided over the creation of the war were the ones who should have been shot. How many would have enlisted if we could have sat down with them for half an hour to explain a little about international relations, imperialism, the military industrial complex, the class interests that generate war and the history of war? The British fought 72 colonial wars to conquer their glorious empire, slaughtering how many dark-skinned millions who got in the way. World Wars I and II were about the Germans challenging the British for dominance of the global system, i.e. for looting rights. A major factor leading to the outbreak of the war with Japan was that country's effort to get access the resources of the region, and the determination of the British and the Americans not to let them into the spheres they had previously taken control over.

The politicians always say we are taking this action '... in defence of our interests', but this mostly means 'in defence of the access we have taken to distant resources and which we don't want to extend to anyone else, except on our terms'. It is now in the 'vital interests' of Americans that they should be able to go on getting and squandering 25% of the world's scarce and dwindling oil, while about 4 billion people get almost none of it. They have said they are prepared to go to war against anyone who threatens this access, (The 'Carter Doctrine').

Thus we can explain most foreign policy, international relations, diplomatic activity, 'defence' planning and activity, invasions, and the vast 'security' industries including spying and CIA skulduggery and assassinations, and most if not all of what was called the 'Cold War', and most if not all that goes under the headings of countering 'insurgency', 'liberation movements', communist subversion', and now 'terrorism'. All of it is more or less about the ceaseless drive to get and hold more access to resources and markets and business opportunities than others, to outsmart and out manoeuvre and bully, politely if possible but via thuggery if necessary... and about the resistance of the many who object to all this and are trampled into the dust.

If soldiers were inclined to demand very good reasons as to why they are being told to slaughter others just like themselves, and what international relations had led their leaders to tell them to do it, and knew a little about the history and causes of war, then there probably wouldn't be much war.

Clearly there cannot be a peaceful world before we have adopted some kind of Simpler Way, enabling all to live very resource-frugally, within highly self-sufficient local economies, thereby eliminating the main cause of armed conflict. Essential to The Simpler Way is the understanding that affluence is not possible for all and is the basic cause of global problems.

Chapter 9

EDUCATION

In consumer-capitalist society 'education' has little to do with Education. Following is a brief summary of the general critical perspective radical education theorists have been elaborating. (For a more detailed account see, for the radical view, http://ssis2.arts.unsw.edu.au/tsw/D30EducationRadView.html and for a view of Education, http://ssis2.arts.unsw.edu.au/tsw/D31 EducationHoweShdWCncvIt.html.)

Schools and universities
❏ Train workers, very well. They develop the skills and more importantly the dispositions required to staff the industrial machine with obedient, diligent and skilled workers who will accept hierarchy and authority, turn up on time, work hard, do what they are told, consume, and not expect to have control over their situation.
❏ Legitimise social position and inequality. Those who fail at school learn that they do not have 'brains' and therefore do not deserve good jobs and life chances. This helps to make inequality in society seem inevitable and legitimate.
❏ Turn out competitors; people who believe in and love competition, and therefore accept winner-take-all society, see themselves as deserving their hard-earned privileges, see losers as deserving their fate, focus on advancing their own welfare without much interest in the public good or collectivism and who see as legitimate a system which allows the super rich to thrive.

❏ Help to produce enthusiastic consumers, people who are keen to get ahead, succeed and get rich, identify modernity and progress with affluence, who see Western ways as the goal for the Third World, and who accept the market system and think technical wizardry will solve all problems. Just as they have passively consumed the activities, work and decisions presented by their teachers, so they passively consume the products, services and decisions presented to them by government, corporations and professionals.

❏ Produce masses of politically passive, compliant, docile, uncritical 'citizens', largely by devoting almost none of the standard 15+ years of 'education' to serious examination of their society's fundamental faults. After that much schooling in intensively authoritarian conditions it is no surprise that they leave the functioning of their society to leaders and experts, show no inclination to take control over their collective fate, and do not question let alone protest the social injustices that their rich-world comfort inflicts on the rest of the world. They are well disposed to staff hierarchical organisations and do what their superiors tell them, to think in power terms, to strive to rise and then boss inferiors around.

These are not the only outcomes of schooling and they are not intended effects but they are outcomes of the 'hidden curriculum' that radical education theorists have pointed to. Years of experience within 'educational' institutions automatically, unwittingly, condition inmates to these dispositions. For years students slave through mountains of work in the quest for credentials, knowing that these are the keys to good jobs and when the exams are over they burn their notes. Try testing them one year later to see if they remember any of the stuff 'learned'. But no one cares about this because the grade is all that matters. 'Poor students' are forced to 'learn' even when they hate it. Teachers punish them with righteous indignation at the lack of gratitude. Billions of children are forced to learn heaps of things they don't want to learn. This constitutes the world's greatest human rights abuse (not the most savage but the most widespread), but resistance is regarded as a stupid failure to appreciate the importance of 'education'.

Some good things happen at school, indeed even a little Education occurs. Highly skilled technocrats emerge, but a thoughtful, critical, responsible, caring and Educated citizenry does not. On the dimensions that matter graduates from our educational systems are appallingly ignorant, insensitive and uncaring. Would a well Educated Australian society have tolerated what the Howard government did to refugees, would it be so grossly unaware and unconcerned about the Rich World's exploitation of its empire, would it be so suicidally unaware of the limits to growth predicament, would it have gone along with the Neo-liberal globalisation hijack and the murderous policies of the IMF and world Bank, would it have allowed Menzies to get Australia into the Vietnam War or Howard to get us into the Iraq war? Would it have felt not the slightest need to make amends for the millions we thereby helped to kill. Our 'educational' institutions are remarkably good at turning out acquiescent hard working competitive consumers preoccupied with self-indulgent goals and trivia, and guaranteed not to concern themselves much with the appalling events taking place all around them.

Schools are obviously not there to Educate. The people who run them say they are, but a glance at their organisation and products ridicules the claim. But there is a much more powerful proof. If Education was a goal then whether or not it was taking place would be assessed, and it isn't. School children are assessed to death. They constantly sit tests and exams, receive grades, and worry about results, but this is only to do with whether they have remembered the facts and skills drilled into them. None of it is concerned to see whether any Educational goals have been achieved. No school or university attempts to assess whether their graduates think about Shakespeare or evolution or Spinoza in their spare time, or do maths problems for the fun of it, or read War and Peace again, or look at the world differently after having studied the French Revolution, or can think more clearly and critically now, or whether they love learning and hold it as a supreme concern in life. No such goals are even taken seriously enough to warrant checking whether any progress has been made towards them.

The ingrained institutionalized irrationality is evident in many unexamined practices, such as forcing kids to do sport, or anything, when they hate it. Consider the rationality of an examination situation where you are worried about what they will ask, or whether the stress and the lack of time will lead you to muck up your answer, or whether you learned the wrong material. If this happens then you are not in a situation where you are going to be able to show them what you know. Surely the point of examining should be to find out what you know. If the outcome can be influenced by factors such as chance, headaches, stress, and whether the question was on the material you crammed, then the examiners are hopelessly incompetent with respect to the logic of assessment. 'I studied hard and learned a lot about that topic, but I couldn't answer that particular question well. So there goes the career I'd hoped for.' Yet this is accepted, especially by the victims.

The comical part is that these practices are perpetuated by people who are supposed to be highly 'educated' and who one would therefore expect to be capable of identifying absurdly illogical and invalid practices. How is it that they never seem to ask, 'What will this question indicate about the candidate, what is the empirical evidence on its predictive validity for any variable that matters, what will my defence be if I am sued for using a measure when I can't demonstrate its validity for any selection process?'

Long ago Berg (1970) and others showed the monumental irrationality of allowing school achievement to have much influence in the selection for jobs or courses. Grades achieved at school simply do not correlate well with success at anything, and should therefore not be given much if any weight in selecting people. This has been clearly understood for decades, but ignored – because everyone wants things the way they are.

Among the many unexamined paradoxes and irrationalities are questions like, why is most 'education' given to those who need it least, the 'brightest'. Why is it assumed that forcing people to learn things will Educate them, when Education involves becoming more intrinsically interested in what is being studied? Why does 'education' involve studying about six 'subjects' at high school and maybe one in depth at university, when an Educated person is a generalist, interested in and informed about and able to converse on an extremely wide range of topics, and continually concerned to fill in the gaps? Why do people say 'I was educated at... ', as if their education was finished there and then although Education is a process that never ends. If the point of Education is to nurture interest in the world, in thinking, exploring, revising ideas, systematizing a world view, why is education cast in terms of punishment for deviance from authoritarian dictates, resistance, sin, and coercion and compulsion? Similarly why is it cast so nastily in terms of superiority and inferiority, and of teachers who know and pupils who are ignorant and must be instructed. What has the power to coerce and punish got to do with Educating? Can it have any other than damaging effects? Why is it taken for granted if children resist being forced to learn things that are of no interest or apparent relevance to them they can be treated as being at fault, unwise and ungrateful, and punished until they conform? All this makes sense if the point of the exercise is to condition recalcitrant recruits to the discipline of the factory, the office and a lifetime paying off the mortgage, but if the point is to Educate then it can only prevent the achievement of the goal.

It is my firm belief that the net effect of schools is the prevention of Education. A few come out of their school years more intrinsically interested in Shakespeare or maths or biology than when they went in, but most have their interest in the world and in learning and analyzing damaged or driven out. When they come in at the age of five they are very interested in the world and in learning, but where is the research showing that by their fifteenth birthday these dispositions have been enhanced?

Clearly schools are not there to Educate, or we'd see if that is what they do. They are there to reproduce consumer-capitalist society. That's what everyone wants them to do, and they do it well. That is why schools cannot be fixed. They cannot be reformed to not be riddled with authoritarian relations, learning masses of irrelevant and boring stuff, exams, credentials, failure and human rights abuse. If these features were eliminated then schools would not reproduce consumer-capitalist society. If you want schools without these characteristics you can only have them in a very different society, one which does not need schools designed to reproduce this society.

What if we wanted an Education system?

The following thoughts reflect my preferred conception of Education, although I think many would share it. This centres on goals such as developing personalities intensely interested in important issues, in learning about the world, thinking about social problems, what life's about, how one should live, the welfare of others, how we can make a better world, constantly inquiring, exploring, thinking, and in becoming a wiser, better person. There's probably no point in distinguishing between Education and personal growth.

In my view the basic cognitive notion in Education is Dewey's focus on enabling one to make more meaning of the experiences one has. When a geologist looks at a landscape he literally 'sees' more than most of us, because he understands the significance of observations which most of us would not recognize. He might note that the hills are very steep indicating that the valley is young. An Aborigine might notice a bent twig and scattered sand and 'see' that a lizard went that way this morning. This means that factual knowledge is only relevant to Education insofar as it enables interpretation of the world. Education is not primarily about learning facts and skills. It is about wanting to understand things better, and therefore realizing that at times it is useful to learn certain facts and theories for this purpose.

No goal of Education is more important than to foster a strong intrinsic desire to do this, to understand, make sense of, question, think about, interpret and find out more. The supreme goal of Education is therefore not cognitive; it is affective. It is to develop an intense and lasting intellectual curiosity which will motivate a ceaseless quest to understand the world, oneself, one's society... more adequately. There is therefore no such thing as an Educated person, as if the task could ever be completed, let alone by graduation day. The goal is a personality which derives deep intrinsic satisfaction from continually increasing the capacity to make sense of the world.

This conception includes the capacity and desire for clear and critical thinking, the readiness to debate, consider alternatives, evidence and argument, and the capacity to revise or drop unsatisfactory interpretations and theories. These ideas and dispositions must be deep, powerful and never-ending forces within personality, and sources of life satisfaction. Little or nothing of Educational significance has been achieved here if a person does not want to do these things, or if they are not primary drivers in the individual's life. For instance knowledge which is not held on the understanding that is for use in this quest is less than useless (as my remnant Latin testifies). What is important here is the capacity for intellectual enthusiasm, to be fascinated and inspired. To Bertrand Russell 'zest' was a major educational goal, and Einstein recognized the capacity to wonder at the nature of things as being extremely important. Dewey and the Progressive educators realized that interest must lead.

Many radical implications follow when mere training and schooling have been separated from Education The role of the Educator is to develop interest in topics, theories, fields and issues, to enchant and inspire, to create awe and wonder, and thereby to stimulate the desire to know more to understand more deeply. Education therefore cannot be boring. If there is boredom Education cannot be occurring. Authority, power over others and punishment have no place in Education. They can only interfere with the achievement of the goal. Ideally Educators are wise friends with a strong interest in helping others to see the significance of things, to become inspired and to become wiser.

The individual controls his or her 'curriculum'. Only the individual knows what he or she wants to understand. This does not mean that there is no place for guidance and advice from others. Sometimes more experienced people can see that if a person studied particular topics he would be more able to make sense of an area he is trying understand. Sometimes we can see that he would benefit if he studied something he is not currently interested in. The 'teacher's' task is to get him to see the desirability of studying these things. A trusted helpful friend whose advice has been found to be valuable in the past should have little difficulty doing this, but if he can't then there is nothing to be gained by force.

Education is about individuals constructing, elaborating and revising their own world view, because they want to do that. Our role as Educators is to facilitate these processes. There is not likely to be much difficulty getting young people to see that the things we think are important actually are and helping them to explore these before long. We would of course try hard to get them to explore the major conventional fields of study, and get to the stage where they wish to develop the thorough understanding that requires working through standard courses. Obviously exams, credentials, grading, graduation and compulsory attendance have nothing to do with any of this. There is a place for determining how well someone understands something, how coherent or sound his position on a topic is, or how well he can defend his views, and 'teachers' would help people do this evaluating, but exams, grades and credentials have no contribution to make. You would probably know how thorough your grasp of genetics or linguistics or black holes was.

When Education is the concern, teachers do most of the failing, not students. They are the ones who have to worry about what's the most effective book or experience to suggest, how effective they have been in stimulating interest and insight, whether they have contributed to Education.

A very important goal of Education, surely universally neglected, is to make sure young people grasp the concept of Education underlying this Chapter, to see the importance and intrinsic value of seeking to understand the world, to see this as a guiding principle for how they will go through life, and to regard this orientation as a major source of life satisfaction. Like friendship Education is not a means to anything – one either sees it as worthwhile in itself, or one does not. (No one told me. I had got through primary school, high school, a BA and many post graduate courses, and indeed through an Education II Hons. strand, before I figured any of this out for myself).

Values, dispositions – personality.

The preceding thoughts have been mostly to do with the cognitive dimension of Education. Probably even more important are the affective and volitional aspects. Education is a matter to total personality development. We therefore have to grapple with questions about what kinds of qualities we want to see people develop. There is no correct list; this discussion can only be about one's preferences. Following are some characteristics that I would argue for.

More important than all the others must be what we could loosely identify as compassion or social responsibility as discussed in Chapter 10, the readiness to think about and be concerned about the situation of others. This includes much more than the negative readiness to be disturbed when others are suffering. It includes the positive gaining of satisfaction from seeing others thrive, the desire to help, care and nurture. These are the necessary sources of the motivation to fix the world and of the collectivism without which a satisfactory society is impossible.

Another important dimension is to do with strength or resilience, the capacity to plod and grind when that's necessary, to stand firm or stand alone, to see it through, to get the job done, to be faithful to principles. Educative experience is not necessarily pleasant. Sometimes adversity and loss are powerful sources of personal growth.

'Discipline' is very important in Education, but it must be sharply distinguished from obedience. What we want is the capacity to apply oneself when one can see that is appropriate. Learning to knuckle down and do what you are told by a powerful authority figure is quite different.

Another very important affective element in Education is the capacity for appreciation, the ability to recognize and be grateful for life's gifts, for nature, one's own qualities and achievements, etc. This connects with simplicity and frugality, being content with enough, appreciating what one has and things that are free, being able to be rather than do. It connects with nurturance; the capacity to feel good when one sees others thriving. It also involves a strong aesthetic element, the capacity to see beauty in things, and to be uplifted by creating. This is where the arts, nature, architecture, great cooking etc. come in. Education increases the capacity of such things to inspire. Possibly the worst thing about schooling is the deadening effect it has on the spirit. All those years of grind, boring work, discipline and obedience narrow and deaden consciousness and spirit.

The Educational significance of The simpler Way

Education would thrive in our new communities. We would be living in a situation crammed with systems, machines, devices, organizations, farms, animals, events and processes that are interesting, and we would be surrounded by knowledgeable people eager to discuss their domain. We would be dependent on systems which we must organize and run well. We will therefore be continually confronted with a wide range of technical, theoretical, social and ecological issues, and would be continually in conversation with others about what's happening and what needs doing and how best to organize. We would have to study, research and learn about things of vital interest to ourselves. The more knowledge and skills one has the more valuable one would be as a citizen. It would be an intellectually stimulating atmosphere. We would be surrounded by people who were experts at electronics, play writing, pottery, cooking, blacksmithing, grafting, astronomy, philosophizing...

We would understand that our town could not function well without good citizens and as has been explained this will be a powerful Educational force, encouraging us to be responsible, careful, well-informed, and concerned with the public good. Then there would be all the creativity coming from maybe five days a week to give to art and craft, amid expert practitioners, and from the beautiful architecture and landscapes this would generate.

The average person would be a multi-skilled 'jack of all trades', although most would also specialize in some fields. In general credentials would be of no significance. All that would matter is whether one could design and make and fix things. We would still need engineers and doctors who have certificates to say they have the required competence to do the more technically sophisticated tasks, but most of the necessary production and maintenance would be carried out by ordinary, but quite skilled, citizens.

We would have whatever formal provisions for learning that make sense, but it is not likely that we'd have things resembling schools today. Most learning would take place as the work of running the town was being carried out, for instance as children accompanied older people on the working bees and at the committees and meetings. Courses would be organized and conducted as people felt the need. Some of these would run all the time but others would be organized irregularly as the need arose. For instance a group might ask the town's experts to run a course on lead light window making or greenhouse thermodynamics.

We would make sure each child (eventually) developed a sound grasp of the fields we think are important, keeping careful records, plotting how best to entice them into various areas. We would probably have some professional teachers or to organise these things, everyone in the town would be a teacher, conscious of the importance of us all learning and growing.

Training would of course be important. We need engineers and doctors and their training would surely include the basic processes we use now. We would need colleges and universities to produce technocrats and to conduct research. However it would be clearly understood that training is not Education and is nowhere near as important for the individual or for society. Universities could again become primarily concerned with Educating.

Another crucial Educational task is to do with the reinforcement of those ideas and values that contribute to cohesion, solidarity, pride and morale. We must be continually conscious of these factors, whereas in all previous societies they have not been attended to, or not even recognized. We will be conscious of the need to think about how well the festivals, celebrations, town meetings and working bees are reinforcing town morale and mutual concern, readiness to contribute, enjoyment of giving and involvement. We will think about and research the experiences and conditions which reinforce the necessary ideas, values and dispositions. These subtle and powerful learnings and re-learnings might take place mostly at the level of cultural activities, through the experience of town festivals, folklore, customs and myths. We would have committees constantly thinking about and monitoring such things, although if all is going well; there would probably be no need to make a fuss about them.

We will devote many resources to Education. We will have developed the committees, advisors, resources, 'curricula', experiences and situations that are most conducive to the above kinds of goals. Note again that we will all have most of the week to give to important concerns like this.

Once again we are confronted by the sharp contradiction between what happens in consumer-capitalist society and how things could be. Little Education can occur in the educational institutions of this society, because that is not their purpose and because the functions they perform are not compatible with Education. The educational institutions of consumer-capitalist society reproduce it very effectively. On the other hand, institutions and practices which Educated could only exist in a radically different society. The Simpler Way requires and enables Education.

Chapter 10

VALUES AND IDEAS: THE BIGGEST PROBLEM OF ALL?

The foregoing chapters have mostly been about this society's deeply flawed structures and systems. Underlying these are the ideas and values held by individuals, and this is an even more difficult area for anyone concerned to bring about significant social change.

There is not the slightest possibility that Australia would accept slavery or the sale of children. Once no one saw anything problematic about the public torture and murder of criminals, or bears. Once everyone accepted the dumping of human waste into the streets. Not very long ago all British people not only saw nothing wrong with having an empire, they were fiercely proud of it. The practice of cutting the heart out of a living person was once thought by everyone (in Aztec society) as not only OK, but of extreme importance. They had no doubt that if they failed to do this the gods might not send the rain. Such is the terrifying power of ideas and values. Humans are capable of getting things into their heads which then focus them or blind them or glue them to a tragically mistaken path.

Especially problematic is the human tendency to 'normalize', to come to see their situation as OK/every-day/routine/familiar, as distinct from remarkable, awe-inspiring or problematic. We take for granted. We tend not to question. We adopt a world view, a frame for interpreting, whereby incoming experience is given a familiar meaning. Sometimes we have a strong tendency to deal with disturbing information by ignoring or denying it and deluding ourselves, thereby maintaining a normal interpretation of the situation. Sometimes this leads us to not see the elephant in the room. We are very good at rationalizing in order to maintain equanimity. If you tell someone that much of the chocolate we buy is produced in West Africa by children who are kept as slaves they might be disturbed, but come back a week later and see if they have given up chocolate, and see how most if not all of them have dealt with the situation in ways that leave their familiar world view and behaviour intact.

These phenomena set the most difficult problems in the quest for transition to a sustainable and just world. We are kept firmly on the path to the precipice by particular ideas and values, which will be extremely difficult and perhaps impossible to shift. The pathological ideologies are at the core of Western culture. Working out how to bury 26 or 52 billion tones of CO_2 each year, or how to make nuclear fusion work is nowhere near as difficult as working out how to get 6.7 billion people to undertake the necessary radical shifts in their ideas and values. The paradox is that because ideas are the key, if we could just get the right ideas held we'd change the structures in no time. If many people saw the world as I do we might get most of the necessary structural changes through in months!

It is not at all difficult to identify the essential syndromes here. They are,

❑ The obsession with affluence.
❑ The commitment to competition, hierarchy, power dominance.
❑ The acceptance and endorsement of individualism and the lack of concern about collective values.
❑ The lack of social responsibility; the indifference to social issues, problems, faults and suffering, the political apathy, the lack of compassion and commitment to the common good.

Altering these dispositions will be immensely difficult. They cannot be replaced in consumer-capitalist society, because they define the basic culture that drives that kind of society. But what is in our favour is that there are much more satisfying alternatives to these values, and our hope has to be that the coming conditions will bring about recognition of this.

AFFLUENCE

The supreme, taken for granted value in our society is to do with being rich, possessing and being able to consume. Purchasing, buying, having and displaying many things, and many relatively expensive things, are seen as not just legitimate and morally unquestionable, but as deserved. If one can afford a luxurious car then there can be nothing in any way wrong about buying it. There is little or no sense of unease or guilt associated with buying and having and using up things, and no idea that this is the basic cause of the global predicament.

Of course the goal is not just to be wealthy, it is to become increasingly wealthy all the time without limit. In other words the supreme national goal is keeping the GDP rising. The 'standard of living' is defined as GDP per capita, and 'prosperity' and indeed 'progress' are identified with increasing the capacity to produce and consume things. Chapter 2 explained that the obsession with affluence and growth is the basic cause of the global predicament, but it is extremely difficult to get any serious attention given to the issue. Yes, over-consumption is generally understood to be a problem, but mostly a problem of crass taste and unwise lifestyle choices (e.g. Hamilton and Dennis, 2005) while its significance for sustainability and justice is ignored. If as is likely we crash, it will be mainly due to the refusal to question affluence.

Wealth and quality of life

The conventional assumption is that to raise the GDP is to increase welfare and to raise the quality of life. The staggering, generally ignored contradiction here is that for some thirty years it has been increasingly clear from many studies that raising the GDP in rich countries does not improve the quality of life.

The irrelevance of wealth

Monetary wealth is not important for a satisfying life. The things that are important include,
❑ Good health.
❑ Enough good food, shelter, clothes.
❑ Safety/security, from poverty, violence...
❑ Family, friends.

- ❏ Community.
- ❏ 'Work' that is enjoyable, valuable and valued, having a worthwhile livelihood.
- ❏ Having time, a relaxed pace.
- ❏ Having purpose; things to do.
- ❏ Creativity; arts, crafts, gardening, cooking...
- ❏ Being respected, for one's contribution.
- ❏ Personal growth; sense of becoming wiser better person as time goes by.
- ❏ Sense of control; participating in governing one's community.
- ❏ 'Spiritual' resources; sources of restoration and inspiration.
- ❏ Pride in one's society.
- ❏ Sense that the world is well, that others are not in difficulties. Thus at least some peace of mind.

These conditions do not require monetary wealth; all people could experience them in a society with very low GDP per person.

At the very least wealth distracts you from the things that matter. There are far more important things to devote precious life time to other than getting rich and purchasing. Wealth also interferes with identity. Your worth, status, the kind of person you are in your own eyes and those of others, should not depend on how much wealth you have or what brand you wear. It should depend on how nice, resilient, kind, thoughtful, generous... you are.

More importantly, wealth impoverishes! It is not good for your spiritual development! Wealth debauches and de-sensitises. The more one has and the more one can consume, the less one appreciates the value of things, especially simpler things. Consider Kerry Packer, an Australian billionaire who gambled millions of dollars at a single sitting. If that's what it takes to make you feel good...

Third, wealth is socially divisive. The sense of unity, solidarity, mutual respect and comradeship cannot be healthy in a society where some are far richer than others.

'... independent wealth, the most precious of personal goals in our society, tends to be highly suspect in preliterate societies.'

It seems that '... the wealthy individual is a sorcerer who has acquired his riches by a sinister compact with demonic powers.' The wealth so acquired'... is 'treasure', bewitched power concretised, stuff... theology weaves into Faustian legends. It... implies a denial of the most basic of all primordial rules, mutual obligation... ' (M. Bookchin, *The Ecology of Freedom*, Montreal, Black Rose, 1991, p.85).

It's worse than that. In a world where one billion people suffer dreadful deprivation, wealth is disturbing and disgusting. An expensive car or too-big house or luxurious handbag has used up scarce resources and skill and capital that could and should have been devoted to meeting life and death need somewhere in the world. Few in consumer-capitalist society think this way. The dominant view is, if I can afford it I have the right to consume it.

Why the obsession?

How can we explain this obsession with affluence and consuming? Part of the answer must be in terms of the astronomical effort made to reinforce it. The corporations spend $500 billion every year on advertising, i.e. persuading us to buy things we otherwise would not, and shaping our images of the world to accept luxury as normal and deserved.

Another part of the explanation must be that in this society wealth is necessary for security. It is an intensely individualistic society so our fate depends primarily on our own efforts. We don't have a tribe to look after us. Thus we have to buy insurance, superannuation, aged care, locks and alarms, in an increasingly uncertain and risky world. 'Primitives' don't have to do this, yet they are far more secure than we are.

But the most important causal factor would seem to be the sheer lack of alternative sources of satisfaction. As Ivan Illich pointed out, commerce and professionals have taken so many functions from families and communities that we have little incentive to make things, grow things, organize, repair, discuss or get together with our neighbours to care and create and run and develop things. The council fixes the park, the doctors fix our health, the supermarket organizes our food. There is not much more left for us to do than work, purchase and have fun. We are in other words passive, acquiescent, docile, stupefied consumers by default –– because there isn't much else to do other than consume goods and experiences provided by distant and centralised corporations, professionals and governments. The coming scarcity will fix that!

The important sources of wealth are public

In affluent consumer society an individual's capacity to have an enjoyable life depends primarily on the capacity to purchase and privately own or consume. In the new society a high quality of life for all will come mostly from public resources, such as the beautiful landscape with its rich variety of gardens, farms, little firms and forests, from the friendly community, the festivals, the free concerts and plays, the help and advice generously given, the institutions such as the community workshops, the working bees, the sharing, the art and artists, the leisurely conversations, and especially the cultural atmosphere of generosity and mutual care. These are the things that make a society rich, and that enrich the lives of its individual members. No individual can be rich enough to own all these things, but all can have access to them regardless of financial wealth. In The Simpler Way we will all be very conscious of the importance of contributing to our community and its public wealth, knowing that when we do this we are enriching ourselves as well as everyone else.

'My garden is one kilometre across. It is crammed with every imaginable kind of plant, with ornaments, waterfalls, dells, pagodas, giant forests, nooks, ponds, stonework, orchards, fountains, statues, bamboo thickets, urns, elves... It is kept in immaculate shape by a large team of fanatical expert gardeners, who think and plan and fuss and work harder than any slaves could. And a large part of their motivation is to create and maintain this beautiful landscape for me and others to enjoy. I can just walk through it any time and find so many things, fruit, vistas, flowers, that I can't recall ever seeing before, because I haven't been to that nook for ages. I don't own it. I could never afford to make or buy such a garden, but that's not important. I have it because it's my village.'

Poverty – A requirement for spiritual wealth?

It is not just that affluence is impossible for all, unnecessary, distracting and not good for you. There is an important sense in which 'poverty' is necessary for a high quality of life. I must immediately stress that this is not to recommend hardship or deprivation. The Simpler Way is about having perfectly sufficient levels of everything that matters, and in a sensibly organized society this would be easily done on an income and an expenditure that is well under the present rich world poverty line. But my central claim here is that living with a considerable degree of frugality, self sufficiency and inter-dependence is necessary if one is to have some of the most important experiences contributing to a high quality of life.

If you don't have abundance you are more likely to appreciate what you do have. If you are rich you tend to move, to travel, to relocate. If you live without spending much you tend to remain in the one place, and thus are more likely to become 'earth bonded'. You can't develop a sense of belonging to place if you move often. When you live frugally you are more dependent on others and on your locality, and that means you need to share and cooperate and help, and that gives you satisfactions and security that cannot be purchased.

No theme is more important in the entire discussion of the human predicament and the saving of ourselves and the planet than coming to see living in non-affluent and self-sufficient ways as deeply satisfying. The Simpler Way will not be adopted if it is seen as an unpleasant effort that must be made to save the planet. The goal is to see The Simpler Way as attractive and spiritually rewarding, indeed as being the point of life. There's our biggest (and probably impossible) problem – to get people to understand the rich satisfactions that can come from living in materially simple ways.

The Simpler Way replaces material affluence with much more rewarding sources of satisfaction. It involves one in a Rich World of making, growing, repairing, planning, designing, working with others on important projects, giving, sharing, nurturing, taking cooperative control of one's local situation. Therefore it involves purpose, creativity, experimentation, comradeship and enjoyment of nearby nature and community activities. Consumer society more or less eliminates and prohibits these sources of satisfaction as it increasingly drives people to live privately, make money and struggle against each other to survive in the rat race.

The Simpler Way is about liberating ourselves from unnecessary work in the factory mode of production and having most of our time to devote to art, governing, sharing, learning, helping and enjoying life.

THE COMPETITION/DOMINATION SYNDROME

Consumer-capitalist society is intensely competitive. We must compete for jobs, credentials at school, status, and resources from government. The economy is structured in terms of mortal competition between firms to sell things. Nations must compete fiercely for export sales, foreign investment, and geo-political advantage. Sport is about trying to beat others to be the winner. It is generally accepted by most people that an economy must be competitive to be efficient. Competition is regarded as natural, good and delightful, indeed intrinsic to human nature.

In my view all this is not just wrong, it is pathological. Only mentally unhealthy people like beating each other. Normal/nice people find it repugnant and refuse to engage in it if at all possible. For a start it's infantile. Only insecure people want to be the winner, the best. More importantly it's nasty. Winners take all, and their triumph humiliates losers. When you organize competitively only one person wins and everybody else loses. Winning therefore contradicts concern for the other and sharing; again the winner takes all, when others would like some too. In this society it is alright for some to be big winners, and many to be big losers. Winners deserve their booty – because they must be superior. What matters in this society is equality of opportunity, that is, the opportunity to be one of the winners, not equality of conditions, outcomes or life experience. Hence we have gladiatorial sport, celebrities, idolizing the hero, Olympics mania, the acceptance of astronomical CEO salaries... and the acceptance of the large numbers of losers.

The competitive syndrome includes many phenomena to do with domination, hierarchy, power, patriarchy and the authoritarian personality. There is an easy readiness to take and exercise power over others, and to accept the power of authorities. Our corporations, armies, bureaucracies and schools could not work without this orientation. But normal/nice people do not like one person or group forcing others to do things they do not want to do. Friends do not force each other to do anything. To normal/ nice people the important concerns are to give, help, empathise with the situation of equal others and to delight in seeing others healthy, happy and flourishing.

Even worse, the line between competition and thuggery is easily blurred. Our economy is predatory. Advertisers are out to deceive you. Caveat emptor. The seller doesn't tell you if the thing has a defect. The seller tries to get as much money as possible. Wherever possible markets are rigged one way or the other, for instance by artificial scarcity or misinformation. Even the basic market principle whereby price rises when items become scarce is predatory, but no one seems to see a moral problem. In some ancient economies, when goods became scarce the price did not rise. Various social rules determined how the scarce goods were allocated. Some societies have had a concept of a just price. However in our society when the supply of an item falls sellers see no problem charging more for it even if its cost to them has not changed. Thus one of our core economic principles is, take as much as you can. That's why doctors and dentists are rich. They could live well charging far less, but in this economy you charge as much as you can, even though this means many people can't afford health or dental care. That's taken for granted and not objected to. But it's not very friendly is it?

At the global level the predation kills tens of thousands every day. Food is taken by the rich countries. Drug companies make fabulous profits by charging outrageous prices, thus preventing millions from getting life-saving drugs. Corporations take oil and minerals from poor countries (by paying for them) knowing that poor masses are getting no benefit. The IMF and World Bank enforce literally deadly policies on Third World governments. None of this would be tolerated if the climate of opinion was not one of winner take all competition.

Ivan Illich (1973) represented all this well with the term 'convivial'. We should try to establish relations and institutions which manifest, encourage, require friendliness, where we try to persuade not force and where there is concern to maintain a pleasant and helpful attitude and where the focus is on giving as much as possible to others rather than getting as much as possible out of them.

So a good society would be based on the opposite of competition, i.e. on a desire to cooperate and nurture. People would be primarily concerned to see others flourishing, happy, growing, thriving. This is the outlook that prevails among friends of a good family. People do things for each other and derive satisfaction from seeing the other happy.

'But competition brings out the best in us!'

The problem with this almost universally accepted claim is that it is wrong. Yes competition gets some or many people to strive hard, and in the business world it is a powerful stimulus to efficiency and innovation. But are you sure cooperation can't motivate effort? In a good society where cooperation yielded obvious and abundant benefits it would be a much more powerful motivator.

Have you ever experienced the surge of energy that comes when a group of friends come together to work for a cause they all enjoy and see as important. The synergism is miraculous. People 'work' harder than they ever would for money, or to beat someone. The good feeling multiplies efficiency as people try to help each other, think about better ways, and inspire each other. All our work could be like this. In a sane world all the jobs that need to be done could be organized as enjoyable 'work' in gardens and firms producing cooperatively to enrich the lives of local people, with no need for anyone to have power over others or for anyone to try to beat anyone else.

The point on which most people are most sadly mistaken is the belief that competition maximizes efficiency. If the goal is better performance then competition is actually about the worst way to organize things! A heap of evidence shows this, in a wide range of human activities, including the performance of staff within a business, and the performance of students within schools. Kohn's review for instance (1993) concludes that if you want kids to do well at school, or executives to work well for the firm, then do not pit them in competition against each other. If you do, then half their minds will be on their rivals rather than on the job.

A competitive economy involves extreme inefficiencies and wastage. Consider the $500 billion spent each year on

214

SOURCES OF SATISFACTION HOMESTEADERS AND COMMUNARDS KNOW WELL.

Firstly there is the sense of being able to provide. We can make, grow, build and repair. We have our 'oikos' (household economy) in good shape. We can produce carrots, firewood, songs, sandals, advice, water... We make and repair our systems, fences, tanks, socks. We experience control and responsibility; if we don't fix the gate or the chicken pen properly they will breakdown and we'll be sorry. How can we make it or fix it using a minimum of resources from the recycling racks in the shed, and ensure that will be strong and long lasting? Making do – what's good enough to do the job solidly but without unnecessary use of materials and time. Using up the leftovers. The satisfaction from dismantling the old one and putting the oiled bolts back in the boxes for reuse.

The faithful old tools, chipped and worn but tough and reliable, and with a history. Grandpa used that one. The gradual modification and improvement of our systems. Designing, planning, experimenting, trying out, reviewing, developing good devices and ways. Making the place beautiful. Where to plant what, where to put the tea house, the fish pond, the tomato seedlings?

The breakfast ramble with the porridge pot to the chickens and ducks, enjoying the bird song, admiring yesterday's digging, noting things that need attention. The managerial achievement, prioritizing the jobs, organising things well, monitoring and noting what is to be done next. Painting the shed roof before the rust gets going. I can decide what to do next, when to change, how to do the job. Enjoying the perfect food we grew, at no cost in global resources. The satisfaction that comes from all that time spent gardening, painting, writing, playing the guitar, in the pottery. The satisfaction that comes from being a jack-of-all-trades, able to fix and make many things. The many craft skills – I can make sandals, paper, lead light windows, cement pots, houses... None of these experiences is possible when things are bought. If there's a serious problem in homesteading it's that there are always too many (enjoyable) things to do.

The sharing and the gifts. The cooperation and camaraderie. Who can I give the surplus nectarines to? If we could afford a bulldozer to do the job we'd miss out on all the enjoyment on the working bees. If we could hire an electrician and carpenter we wouldn't experience the solidarity and appreciation that comes when we do things for each other, or get so many cups of tea scones and conversations. If you could buy alll the goods and services you want you'd miss out on the generosity that comes when people give and help and share, and the climate of mutual concern and solidarity would not be reinforced.

215

advertising, much of it intended to shift consumers from Coke to Pepsi. Competing for the tourist dollar generates negative benefit, because it is essentially about persuading people to go here rather than there for their holidays, and uses money, resources and talent in the process. Add the waste involved in bankruptcies, refitting the shops, the social wreckage and the taxes needed to deal with it. Also consider the waste of that perhaps two-thirds of all work done that we would not need to do in a sane economy.

Most importantly, competition is nasty. To encourage it is to choose not to bring out the best in people. It's bad for personality development. Nice people don't try to beat each other and don't get a kick out of being the winner or the greatest. What the world needs desperately right now is concern to help others rather than to beat them, and the readiness to give rather than take. Sensible cooperative solutions to problems such as global warming cannot be achieved without the willingness to give up or forgo privileges, such as exorbitant energy and CO_2 rates. The last thing we need is to reinforce the opposite dispositions and these are what competition is about.

The Eco-feminist view

The Eco-feminists discuss this syndrome in terms of 'patriarchy' and they have given valuable analyses of history, science and capitalism from this perspective. Benholdt-Thomsen and Mies (1999, see also Mies and Shiva, 1993) for instance argue that because of their role in reproduction females have done most of the caring and their productive activity has been about subsistence, providing directly for the needs of family and clan. When the agricultural era began and wealth was accumulated enabling warfare, males made tools, especially weapons, moving towards separation from nature and manipulation of nature. Whereas tribal people see themselves as part of nature and appreciate the benevolence of the earth-mother, and thus do not exploit nature, 'civilization' has been about seeing human culture as separate from and superior to nature, and about controlling and exploiting nature.

Ecofeminists see the rise of science as especially significant in the history of patriarchy, focusing on the separation of humans

216

from nature, forcing nature to reveal her secrets, manipulating her and making her produce. Once Nature was regarded as a living being, and there were taboos against digging holes in the earth, i.e. mining. Some tribes still see Nature as a unified living being, and see themselves as part of it. The separation of man from nature also allows us to see nature as a machine whose pieces can be taken apart to be studied. Bacon spoke of torturing nature to get her to reveal her secrets. Civilisation came to be seen as contradicting and transcending mere nature and the 'primitive realm, in which women and colonized people came to be placed. Similarly Bookchin sees domination as our greatest fault and as the source of the environmental problem. Because we dominate each other so readily we dominate nature. Eisler (1990) distinguishes between 'dominator' and 'participant' cultures, and believes we are slowly moving towards the latter.

The Ecofeminists are therefore dealing with a core fault in Western Culture. Clearly a good society must emphasise care and nurturance, not competition. However, in my view, the Ecofeminists put insufficient emphasis on the problem of over-consumption).

The Simpler Way.

Little needs to be said about the obviously cooperative nature of The Simpler Way. When people are very rich they can be independent, purchasing everything they want. They have little need to get together, share or help each other. But in the coming era of intense scarcity we will not survive, let alone live well, unless we develop highly collective ways. Unless we cooperate, share and focus on the welfare of the town then the systems we depend on will not work well; e.g. the working bees and concerts will not be well attended. The situation will make us depend on each other and on our local society and ecological systems and it will make us work together. But we will not cooperate reluctantly; we will find that living as friends working together and caring for each other and our town is a far more enjoyable way.

INDIVIDUALISM

In Chapter 4 the economy was discussed in terms of the excessive freedom it gives individuals to buy, produce, trade and invest as they wish. In the wider cultural realm life for most people is now predominantly about the pursuit of individual self interest, and this typically takes the form of extravagantly wasteful self-indulgence. As long as the law is respected and taxes are paid one can focus on travel, property, having fun, status, and shopping. The desire to serve or contribute to the welfare of others (beyond family and friends) is either weak or non-existent.

Self interest and competition go together. If one's primary concern is to maximize one's own welfare then one is inevitably in competition with others similarly motivated. As has been noted, take this to its end point and there is no society, because society is constituted by the values and dispositions that transcend self-interest. The greenhouse problem cannot be solved unless there is willingness to forego self-interest, to make huge sacrifices in energy use for the good of the whole. Our economy makes this extremely unlikely since it casts us all as individuals in competition. In our individualistic culture we are unaccustomed to foregoing privileges for the sake of others or the collective good.

One of the ways we pay a high price here is in the individualizing of failure. In consumer-capitalist society a very few do most of the winning, yet the losers see the situation as legitimate. They think they have no right to complain because in a competitive society we all had our chance, the best have won and therefore deserve more than the rest of us. The poor and unemployed are inclined to say they would not be in their situation if they had worked harder at school or had more talent. In other words they are strongly inclined to blame themselves, not society. They are not inclined to say a society that inflicts unemployment on anyone is a bad society.

It is of course in the interests of the rich for us all to take for granted a society made up of individuals struggling against each other for their own advantage. Such isolated people are not likely to get together to share information, develop critical perspectives or take control over their situation. They are likely not to question life being about coping as best one can in a world organized by a powerful few. They are strongly inclined to conclude that the winners deserve their privileges, because they must have been superior individuals.

In consumer-capitalist society contradictions between individual and society are felt strongly, such as when the payment of tax is resented. In The Simpler Way this is much less likely to be the case. Individuals are more likely to realize that contributing to society will directly and visibly benefit themselves, and yield satisfaction from making that contribution. To enhance the public good is to increase the wealth of your town which you draw on. This is evident when paying one's taxes takes the form of joining working bees building the pond we can all paddle on and fish in.

At the very least in The Simpler Way tensions between individual interests and the good of society are likely to be much reduced, and it is conceivable that they would be negligible. The collectivism required would seem to be nothing more sinister than a strong desire to see one's community flourishing and happy. It obviously need have nothing to do with obedience to the state, deference to party edicts or self-sacrifice for the good of the Father land. Nor need it imply conformity. A highly collectivist village can contain a wild diversity of individual and indeed conflicting artistic, literary, religious, sporting etc. orientations. When paying tax is a matter of enjoying a working bee and the associated picnic a conflict between what's good for the individual and what's good for society is not likely to be felt.

SOCIAL RESPONSIBILITY

Why is there so little concern with social issues, with the state of the world, and so little dissent or effort to change things? How can there be such apathy, complacency and indifference? How is it that we are faced with terrible events and conditions in the world, including alarming challenges to our own existence, yet most people seem to show little or no serious interest in any of these? If they cared we'd solve the problems very quickly.

This I believe reveals the most serious and probably fatal flaw in the human mind. It is not aggression or greed that is most likely to destroy us, but indifference. The factor we lack here begins with empathy, the capacity to see and feel from the position of the other, but it goes much further, even beyond sympathy and indeed compassion. Humans tend to be moved by face to face confrontation with the suffering of others, or of animals and even forests. But that's not enough. We now need the capacity to be moved by statistics, by cold information on distant effects, especially the effects our flawed systems have. If most people were sufficiently concerned about unemployment or poverty or hunger then the necessary remedial action would soon be taken. There is, in other words, little social responsibility. The fate of the planet hangs on whether it can be suddenly and dramatically increased. Following are some thoughts on this crucial but puzzling phenomenon. (These themes have previously been explored in Trainer, 2005).

> In the BBC documentary 'Bolivia; The Tin Mountain' we meet Cesar who seems to be about thirty. He has worked every day for thirteen years drilling for tin, with his cheeks puffed out by coca leaves to numb the mind from the boredom and the hunger. Where does the tin go? To make the tin cans on our supermarket shelves. Cesar is lucky because he has a job. When the video was made the mine was killing one person a day, mostly from the dust which causes silicosis TB. It killed Cesar's father, and he now has it. It is fatal. He is weak and has difficulty walking. But if he does not work his family will be evicted from their company house and literally destitute. He should be in a sanitarium but there he is in the truck on his way up to the mine again. He is totally and inescapably trapped and he will die in that trap and he knows it. How do you feel about that?

The appropriate emotional response a normal human would have to any of the terrible things happening in the world today would be to feel for/with the victim and to feel an intense outrage and anger and desperate panic-like urge to do something to end the situation immediately. If your car were to roll onto your dog or your baby daughter, how would you respond? To put it mildly you would feel extremely distressed and you would leap into action because every microsecond would count. If you were there, beside someone who is malnourished, or one of the thousands of children who lose their sight each year because of a vitamin A deficiency that could be remedied for a few cents, what would you feel? There is no doubt whatsoever that you would be very disturbed. In fact any normal person would probably never get over such an experience. And you would feel a powerful drive to do something to get rid of the problem as quickly as possible. Well then, how can we explain that typical people, as distinct from normal people, don't?

Even more puzzling and annoying than indifference to the plight of others is the failure of people to respond appropriately to social problems which directly impact on their own welfare. Take for example the deterioration in health services that has occurred in Australia in the last twenty years as governments have cut spending. I have just been listening to an account on ABC Background Briefing on the crisis now set by the many nurses who are leaving their profession because of the stress caused by insufficient resources. A patient interviewed was a bystander injured in a bar room brawl and in need of surgery. He had been sitting in a waiting room for 12 hours. In another case an elderly man was left unattended on a trolley for a long time, fell off and broke a hip. In 1999 a report estimated that every year possibly 18,000 Australians are killed by mistakes made in Australian hospitals. (Metherell, 2007). A 2009 report put the figure at 4,000, still 11 people every day... but in neither case was there any outrage. There was in fact almost no comment. People simply accept all this even though they themselves suffer the consequences. They apparently do not care even though many of them will end up in those waiting rooms every day.

A 'normal' human being cannot but be wounded and feel pain by exposure to another who is suffering serious harm, or to a social issue where there are grossly unsatisfactory effects. (Of course the reference here is not to statistically normal, i.e. typical humans). The problem of social responsibility is that there are very few normal people. Everyone is crystal clear about the fact that terrible things are happening in the world all the time, on an incomprehensible scale – billions suffer appalling and avoidable conditions, ecosystems are being shredded, governments do disgusting things, yet for all intents and purposes most people simply could not care less and focus their minds on utter trivia and self-indulgence. If they cared situations would be instantly fixed. If they cared they would think and inquire and soon find that chief among the forces causing most of the wreckage are the processes providing their own 'living standards'.

It would seem therefore we must accept that most people are brutal zombie monsters. Zombies are dead. They are not conscious of their surroundings. They do not feel and they do not grasp what is going on around them. Only monsters can be in the presence of extreme injustice, suffering or destruction without being emotionally shattered. Our problem seems to be that for mysterious reasons most people most of the time are zombie monsters.

The proximity to the suffering is not crucial here. Just to know that somewhere in the world a child is hungry should evoke profoundly disturbing compassion in any 'normal' human. The research task is to understand the forces and conditions that block such a response. Is distance in time any more significant? Should the Irish Potato Famine evoke within us a different response to a current famine?

Somehow we humans seem to develop an emotionally protective cocoon, a shell which ensures that the emotional significance of things we know about does not get through. There is a powerful numbing force. When we hear on the news of a murder or a famine it usually has little or no emotional impact. Occasionally the emotional significance of something does break through and we get a shock. I was sitting on a quiet railway station recently, daydreaming, when a train I had not heard approaching suddenly thundered through jolting me into fear at the sense of tremendous noise and power and violence, and how puny a human body would be if something like that ran off the rails. My mind raced to what it must be like to be in a grass hut on the Bangladesh floodplain when a cyclone comes through hurling palm tree logs like straw. It made me feel how absolutely terrifying it would be if a tank ran over your mud hovel. How immeasurably important it is to make sure that things like that never ever happen to anyone. Yet on that same day I probably heard of many violent deaths on the radio news without being moved.

At times normal people do focus on the situation of the distant other, and are momentarily impacted by the frightening horror of what it would really be like. Whatever that situation is you could multiply it by millions. To contemplate this is disturbing, so we don't. We (have to) deny, push out of mind and get back to the familiar, normal orientation. The numbness, the amnesia has to be restored. So we must do the very thing that in effect ensures that the problems endure, i.e. turn away and ignore them. Central in the problem of social responsibility is this emotional shell that inhibits empathy, sympathy, compassion and action, yet the dreadful paradox is evident. Obviously to respond emotionally to all such information would be totally debilitating, but to not respond emotionally at all is perhaps our greatest global problem.

Maybe we should just focus first on the biological observation rather than on the moral implications. We are dealing with a being that is capable of brutal and callous indifference to the situation of others. Sometimes in some situations humans are intensely moved, but most of the bad things happening in the world do not affect most of them much, or at all. Several million years living in small tribal bands on the plains of Africa seem to have built into us powerful tendencies to see and respond effectively to immediate threats to ourselves and to our small band, but these conditions did not prepare us to attend to distant or future threats. It certainly didn't sensitise us to threats evident only in reports and statistics and requiring critical thought about taken for granted assumptions, systems and structures.

How many wars would not have happened had there been just a little more social responsibility? How many appalling bungles on the part of kings and politicians too arrogant to back down or to question their prejudices or listen would not have led to armed conflict if publics had had even a little more sensitivity, let alone had they demanded to be given a full, clear and convincing account of the situation and why this or that policy was appropriate. For a start World War I could not have happened (20 million dead), which ended in a way that set up World War II (another 50 million dead), which ended in a way that set up the Cold War and the nuclear arms race (nearly another 5 billion dead from nuclear war; see the film Thirteen Days).

Of course if we had any significant level of social responsibility then wars would never occur in the first place. The time to end a war is several years before it breaks out. If and when it comes to blows then you have failed abysmally to do the sensible thing, i.e. to see trouble coming, to work out accurately what is causing it, and to face up to the fact that often it is our own greed and previous thuggery that has been the major causal factor.

It is true that surveys indicate sometimes even majority concern about the deterioration of society and excess materialism. (See Eckersley's review, 2004). The trouble is however that it is hardly ever significant concern, anywhere near sufficient strength to prompt action.

The power of the masses.

Usually it would only take the most miniscule response on the part of the mass of people to quickly remedy a problem. For at least thousands of years millions of people have suffered social and political conditions that were somewhere between bad and appalling. Although some societies seem to have been remarkably satisfactory, especially many tribal societies, in most a few thugs and manipulators have arrogated themselves into a ruling class and dominated the rest. They have bossed and bullied, and hogged most of the wealth and privileges and sat around in luxury while others had to work to provide for them and often have had to fear for their lives. How could this be?

Consider the global predicament again. In the world today there is an enormous and increasing problem of domination. A tiny few are taking most of the wealth and running the world in their own interests. In America the richest 1% have more than half of all the capital and more wealth than 90% of people. In the world as a whole the rich manage to keep in place systems in which the majority of people increasingly work mostly for the benefit of the few while billions get relatively little in return, or are totally 'excluded'. The present global economy probably only works well for less than 10% of the world's people. (Fotopolous, 1997). Inequality is rapidly increasing as globalisation gives the corporate super rich the freedom and the right to take even more and to condemn more people to miserable conditions. Even the Rich World's middle classes are being driven off the levels of affluence and comfort they have become accustomed to as the super-rich 1% rocket to obscene wealth. But remarkably few people seem to see any problem with these phenomena or the domination they experience.

All this could be thrown off very quickly if there was only a small amount of concern about social problems and conditions and their causes. The many tyrants and bullies and plundering ruling classes that have made life a misery for countless people throughout history could have been tipped out at any time had a significant proportion of their victims said 'Enough! Get out! From here on people around here will run things in everyone's interests.'

Brecher (2000) says, 'The ultimate source of power is not the command of those at the top, but the acquiescence of those at the bottom.'

Chomsky puts it in terms of Hume's paradox; '...in any society the population submits to the rulers even though force is always in the hands of the governed... the rulers can only rule if they control opinion – no matter how many guns they have.' (Chomsky, 1986-92, p.81).

Regarding colonial India Gandhi put it more colourfully noting that if all Indians merely spat the British would drown.

Of course a few do respond appropriately, but very very few. At the peak of the Peace Movement, when the Cuban missile crisis brought us close to nuclear war, less than 1% of Australians marched on the main protest day.

Now who is the problem? Rarely is power taken and exercised against the will of the oppressed. Mostly power is given or permitted. Legitimacy is about acquiescence. The problem therefore is not the few who the situation benefits, it is the many who accept a situation which disadvantages themselves. Yet the focus of dissenting thought and action has usually been on the dominators and scarce energy and resources have typically gone solely into (usually self-destructive) struggle against them – when they are not the crucial element. The key is the consciousness of the dominated. If only a small proportion of them came to see the situation differently, as illegitimate, as outrageous, then the dominators would be immediately dumped, probably in non-violent ways, perhaps simply by being ignored from thereon.

Of course, the persistence of unsatisfactory social conditions is usually due in large part to the fact that a few have far more capacity than others to influence ideas and decisions and therefore to keep in place the arrangements that suit themselves. But again if many people objected those arrangements would be rejected. Sometimes it takes remarkably little public outcry or action to get things changed. Publics are like large and fierce dogs that sleep most of the time allowing a few sneaky mice to get away with what they want, but if they are roused and angered just a little the mice have to flee. In 2001 the very powerful drug corporations moved to stop the South African government from producing anti-Aids drugs at a price Africans could afford, below the prices the obscenely rich drug corporations wanted to charge. Drug companies have got away with these kinds of actions for years, including refusing to develop the drugs that would do most good in the world, i.e. drugs for the diseases that afflict Third World people, while focusing on the high priced and often trivial lines that sell well in rich countries. (For instance only 1% of new drugs developed are for tropical diseases). Somehow the tiny groups working against the drug companies in the South African case managed to stir up enough public attention, not much really, but enough to panic the drug companies into giving up. The space in our newspapers given to this issue at its peak would have been about 0.1% of that given to sport, but that relatively minute amount of public interest and discontent was enough.

The anthropologist Maybury-Lewis (1992) reports a member of a desert tribe saying, 'A poor man among us would shame us all.' Consider the enormity of that statement in the light of the Western mentality of selfishness, competition, greed, acceptance of vicious inequality, predation, and the readiness to condemn those who fail. (The term 'loser' says it all). The right response to the existence of a poor man is indeed shame and disgust that we have allowed this to happen. If your dog messed in the living room and trampled it all through the house would you clean it up? Would you be content to leave a smelly shambles for others to see? Would you not be ashamed to think that people might judge you to be the sort of person who would tolerate squalor and not want to fix it up? I cannot see much different between this and being a member of a society that is grossly ugly and disgusting. One cannot but be deeply ashamed of Australian society which has allowed 200,000 young people to become heroin addicts, 100,000 to be homeless, and many young people to become so disenchanted and hopeless that they take their own lives. It is a mark of lack of civilisation that we do not feel intense shame that there are poor among us. Similarly only barbaric, callous and primitive societies tolerate unemployment. Many societies do not. One cannot but be ashamed to be part of a society that refuses to make any realistic effort to get rid of it.

For how many milliseconds would any outrageous situation last if just a tiny proportion of people in general became appropriately aware of it and annoyed about it. Thus we again see the relevance of the basic Anarchist theme running through much of this book. The outlook of people in general is everything. If their world view was as it was in Spain in the 1930s, people would 'spontaneously' get together and perform miracles, with no need for top-down leadership. They will probably get rid of oppressive systems and regimes in the nicest possible way, just by ignoring them and building good alternative systems. If the awareness is not there, then there's little or nothing to be gained by force or by grabbing for state power. You just have to get on with building that awareness. This point is crucial in the debate between Marxists and Anarchists and in the discussion of strategy in Chapter 12.

The unseen empire.

No aspect of the phenomenon is more puzzling, disturbing and infuriating than the failure/refusal to recognize the empire. Chapters 3 and 5 sketched some of the appallingly thuggish things our governments do to make sure they control countries, resources, markets, and Third World governments, take their resources and deprive the poor majority of their fair share of the wealth beneath their feet. We who go to supermarkets are beneficiaries of the economic and foreign policies which deprive billions of people and routinely kill large numbers, indirectly through the imposition of the market system and directly by the military activity. Despite a huge literature documenting what goes on and the tireless efforts of people like Pilger and Chomsky to raise awareness, it seems that only the tiniest proportion of people know or care. Everyday life in the rich countries remains totally unaffected and everyday thinking never considers that we could not live so well if we didn't control and loot our empire. The empire is not recognized let alone thought about. The media never discuss what is going on. Politicians never discuss it. Most ordinary people would react with indignation if you suggested that we have an empire.

'Post Modern' society; The stupefying cultural conditions.

The numbness and apathy are essential features of Post Modern society and a glance at the concept throws some light on the problematic dispositions, the conditions producing them and the daunting task before us.

Most people spend most of their time doing or thinking about things that are of no importance whatsoever in view of the global situation we are in. All around us there are serious, skilled, intelligent, conscientious people who actually think it is important who wins the next cricket test match, or that it is important to write yet another cookbook, or dictionary, or buy that album, or make a career move, or work for years to win a gold medal or shave 0.1 sec of their PB. Turn on the radio and imagine what a visitor from Mars would conclude about our mentality. He would get no clue that one-fifth of us are hungry, or that petrol supply will probably peak soon bringing on a collapse of industrial civilization that might kill off two or three billion of us.

A central theme in Post Modern society is the mindless preoccupation with utterly trivial and self-indulgent concerns. Consider the fleeting, exciting, fun, spectacular and superficial nature of sport, computer games, pop music, crime dramas, quiz shows, soap operas, lifestyle, celebrities, throw-away cultural products, fashion, scandals, the next momentary thrill, fantasy and transitory relations. It is a culture of the shallow and fleeting, and of the absence of seriousness and responsibility.

What distinguishes a culture are the things people are preoccupied with, what they think about. In Post Modern society a great deal of attention is given to mindless, distracting trivia. Americans are said to be watching an average of 4 hours TV every day, and it is reported that electronic games are overtaking TV as sources of 'entertainment'.

The media must take much of the responsibility. A few centralized agencies dominate thought and action and have an interest in perpetuating the distracting superficiality. They have great power to shape consciousness. We can only form a view of the world in terms of very selected images and simulations presented to us by the media. It is in their interests to reinforce consumer values and the legitimacy of capitalist power, seducing attention with huge quantities of mostly irrelevant, spectacular and violent entertainment. There is little critical analyses of crucial social issues, and fundamental criticism, e.g. of the market system, hardly ever appears. The broadsheet newspapers most able to provide discussion in depth are dying out, in favour of the electronic media which are by nature more suited to superficial bites. Adverts and movies set ideals, norms and models which can't be achieved unless expensive products are purchased; beauty aids, furniture, cars. High rates of consumption are portrayed as normal. Style, image and identity are everything and underlying substance or meaning doesn't matter. Violence and destruction are normal, exciting and attractive and legitimate means for resolving conflict. It is in the interests of the media to screen out, exaggerate, distort, trivialize and sanitise. They reinforce the impression that life is about acquiring possessions and having a good time. The terrible plight of many is invisible, sanitized or interpreted in ways that conceal what is happening. Portraying nasty realities would scare away the advertisers.

So there is virtually no dissent. The many extremely serious social problems confronting us evoke little complaint or protest. There is discontent, but it is predominantly with the experience of the isolated individual. Many are quite depressed and anxious... about their personal circumstances, not the system.

The large numbers impoverished and 'excluded' accept their situation without a whimper. Occasionally they grumble about their misfortune but they do not question the legitimacy of the rules that have inflicted it. Indeed they are among the most enthusiastic participants in consumer society; they happily devour the pacifying spectacles, sport, soap operas, trash products, gambling, and shopping mall experience. Thus little effort is now needed to ensure that the system is regarded as legitimate or to keep people in line. In the distant past grizzly public executions were necessary to keep order. Decades ago the police and the army had to be sent in to quell protest. Not now. The masses have been seduced by affluence and trivia into willing, docile acquiescence. Whenever they do become discontented they go shopping.

Authority numbs and infantilises.
Like Bookchin Illich points to the way the very presence of bureaucratic and professional 'authority' deadens responsibility, simply by taking functions away from us. Once, if the village well failed we would all have to go and fix it. Now it's the responsibility of the ministry or some professional to fix whatever goes wrong,

and of the doctor to fix our health and the counsellor to fix our relationships, and of the government to fix unemployment. If there is a flood or a bushfire the police, the firemen and the army take charge. In fact then we the people become part of the problem to be managed. (Once when a bushfire was about to devour my house I was threatened with arrest if I didn't obey an order to leave). Illich's essential critique of modern society is in terms of this loss of autonomy, the taking of control by corporations, professionals and governments, and the resulting passivity.

Remarkably when disaster impacts the stupefaction can be blown away and people can quickly become human beings again. Foote (2009) discusses what typically happens when a hurricane hits and the authorities are not around. People immediately leap into sensible, compassionate, cooperative, effective and selfless action. They help, and organise and give generously – then the army arrives and takes charge and herds them out. After all authorities know best and people really can't be trusted to run things. Foote says, '... disasters give rise to small, temporary utopias in which the best of human nature emerges and a remarkable spirit of generosity and cooperation takes over. 'Disaster' is when... the shackles of conventional belief and role fall away.' She argues that capitalism focuses people on competitive, selfish struggle and the general result is bored, alienated and unhappy shoppers. Yet our 'natural state', as Kropotkin argued, is tribal and communal, and '... a disaster returns us temporarily to that state of grace... '

This confirms the Anarchist belief in 'spontaneity', the capacity of ordinary people to come together and take responsibility and care and run things, when the stultifying forces are removed.

Intellectuals.

Most annoying is the default on the part of the 'intellectual' ranks in society, the teachers, writers, journalists, professionals and especially the academics. These are the people who are most highly 'educated' and are supposed to be the critical thinkers, analysers and enlighteners. They have the intelligence, skills, position, security, comfort and time to at least draw attention to the problems. Their cleverness enables space travel, computers and atom splitting, yet historically the intellectual ranks have mostly failed to think critically about their society and their role has mainly been to serve the privileged classes. Today only a very small proportion of them ever attend to the critical issues now confronting us, let alone call for transition to a better society.

Most academics even within the 'humanities' devote themselves to studying and teaching about topics that are of the utmost triviality given the situation we are in. We do not really need another translation of Ovid or treatise on Medieval poetry or dictionary of Australian slang, certainly not while 850 million are hungry. Indeed right now we do not need any activity in many entire fields of academic inquiry, such as Linguistics, English Literature, or Astronomy (… a keen hobby interest of mine). What is going on here? Don't these people understand the situation? Don't they know the 2030 spike is coming. Don't' they know a good case can be made that billions will perish before 2050? Have they not thought what might happen to their own privileges and comfort if oil becomes scarce? How then can anyone opt to devote their scarce and expensively trained intellectual skills to looking for life in space? Let us get back to such things later if we can after we have saved the planet from collapse and made sure no one is hungry.

Reflect on the unfathomable state of mind that allows the thousands of lecturers in banking and finance who clearly understand the farcical money creation system to make no effort to expose or change it. As was explained in Chapter 3, because the trading banks are allowed to create money and lend it for interest each Australian pays about $1000 p.a. to them via taxes the government uses to pay interest on its loans from the banks, let alone how much more we pay out on all the other money borrowed. There are large numbers of academics who understand all this in detail, yet make no effort to do anything about it. How many thousands of academics clearly understand the imperial nature of international relations or the way IMF policies shred whole economies and help to kill thousands of people every day yet make no effort to alter the dominant indifference? How can such behaviour be explained?

Academics spend many years learning their field and how to research it, but their training allocates no time to the question,

'To what kinds of problems ought I apply my skills?' Evidently it never occurs to most of them that there might be serious moral problems to do with whether they should devote their talents to trying to do something about the situations large numbers of people endure and indeed about the forces now threatening their own fate. Most enjoy extremely privileged work conditions, with great freedom to decide what topics they will work on. Most exhibit immense self-indulgence, often following unimportant obsessions without thought about relevance or misapplication of scarce resources. These dispositions are glowing tributes to the twenty years of 'education' invested in them. What a strange and difficult animal we are dealing with. Have they not heard, 'The Buddha cannot be happy if one being is suffering.'

Similarly distressing is the smug complacency of the 'educated' upper middle classes. They devote time, attention and talent to self-indulgence, jet away to unnecessary holidays and conferences, renovate, and watch their property values and investments. They quietly enjoy what Galbraith referred to as the 'the culture of contentment' and they have little interest in questioning the systems which deliver their privileges. They are strongly inclined to see their wealth and comfort as just rewards for their hard work and superior abilities and to see poor people as deserving their fate in view of their lack of application and talent.

Citizenship.

The social responsibility problem can be put in terms of the lack of citizenship. There have been societies in which there would seem to have been a remarkable amount of it. In ancient Greece high priority was put on the discussion of public affairs and participation in government. (The word they used for anyone who did not do this much is said to translate into English as 'idiot'). Unlike in our society, the individual was trusted with making decisions concerning the welfare of society and was therefore conscious of the responsibility and of the importance of helping to sort out issues effectively and to find the right answer. There were issues which the Greeks failed to question, most obviously the use of slaves and the exclusion of women from public affairs, but in a world where the norm since the tribal period seems to have been unquestioning obedience to thuggish kings and ruling elites the Greeks stand out for the remarkable extent to which people were citizens concerned with social issues.

Bookchin describes a similar situation in Medieval towns and in the early towns of New England USA. Ordinary people carried out the governing via highly participatory democratic procedures and were therefore very involved in the discussion of social issues. In both cases the conditions people experienced would have provided powerful incentives because small isolated communities without a state to provide for them knew they had to take responsibility for their own fate. The Israeli Kibbutz settlements also involved remarkable levels of social responsibility on the part of ordinary citizens.

The overriding significance of citizenship for the issue of government has been emphasized. A satisfactory society cannot involve the government of people by governors. It must involve the government of the people by the people, directly through participatory democracy. For 10,000 year since we left tribal societies we have allowed a few to rule, and in recent times when states have grown to enormous size 'order' has required dictatorship by a tiny number of (usually elected) authorities, and mostly by a single person. Now as in late Roman times, large more or less apathetic and stupefied masses distracted by trivia and myth are ruled by 'leaders' who by and large do not rule in the interests of all, and do not rule wisely. But the solution is emphatically not to find good rulers; the solution involves getting rid of rulers. As Chapter 6 argued, human political 'evolution' will not have reached maturity until we take responsibility for governing ourselves. That is not possible without good citizens, and it is not likely before the era of scarcity impacts.

A society's level of civilization, nobility, robustness etc. does not depend on the sophistication of technology, the power of its military machine, the brilliance of its leaders, or the size of its GDP. It depends on the level of social responsibility among people in general. That's also where its security lies. These are the things that get you into wars or keep you out of them. Appalling national policies are adopted because people in general want them, or do not object to them. It is a mistake to see Australia's recent grubby treatment of refugees as the work of its Prime Minister or his government. It was what the majority of Australians wanted, or would not object to.

This is the core problem that will determine our fate in the decades ahead, the failure to think critically and compassionately about fundamental cherished assumptions, faiths and delusions. Thus myths such as the desirability of economic growth go on, not thought about let alone challenged. Social responsibility involves the readiness to think critically about fundamental assumptions and commitments, the readiness, the will, the discipline to examine and cut through the comforting delusions in an effort to sort it out, get it right, face up to the situation. The delusions are close to finishing us off, so it is not too much to claim that whether or not we make it will depend on the extent to which citizenship and social responsibility can rise to the challenge in the coming era.

Rationality.

Post-Modern social theorists ridicule the Enlightenment belief in the power of reason to understand and control the world and guide emancipation. Reason, they argue, has led to the Twentieth Century wars and death camps, atomic weapons and corporate rule. I think the criticism is mistaken.

It is indisputable that our global predicament raises disturbing questions about the collective rationality of homo sapiens. Consider the incredible, meticulous rationality evident in the design and construction of a pencil, or a wrist watch, let alone a battleship or space shuttle. Reflect on the vast amount of careful, patient, logically sound thinking, the R and D, the planning, the system development, the discipline, hard work and organisation involved in the production of pencils. Now consider the staggering, incomprehensible, imbecilic lack of rationality evident in, for instance the prison system, or the war on drugs, or an economy which must have growth or any one of countless other examples that could be given. The Easter Islanders cut down all the trees and thereby destroyed their society. We are doing much the same, running down a suicidal path driven by insanely irrational ideas and beliefs and values, with virtually no recognition that the problems can't be solved by the present economy or culture or political system.

The greenhouse problem cannot be solved without an enormous reduction in the amount of producing and consuming going on, and a vast shift to a very different conception of development, one that does not convince the Chinese that they need a new power station every ten days. What can you say about rationality when more than 6.7 billion people seem to have no understanding whatsoever of such things?

Clearly social responsibility is a problem of rationality. It is irrational in the extreme to fail to attend to fundamental critiques of cherished values and systems, but that that is what we do. As Hume pointed out, reason is only about means. What matters most are the ends to which reason is put and our most daunting problem is that in consumer-capitalist society the ends are wrong and that most people couldn't care less.

How can the syndrome be transcended?

It can't – in consumer capitalist society. The four problematic factors discussed in this chapter constitute a large part of Western culture. Take them away and you don't have much of Western culture left. There are of course other elements in that culture, some of them of immense value, especially the Enlightenment achievements such as the hard won liberties (Grayling, 2007), the concern for reason, the emancipation from superstition, and the notions of rights, democracy and the rule of law. But the overwhelming focus in the everyday life of most people, and in national policy, is the individualistic, competitive pursuit of limitless wealth. Consumer-capitalist society would not be possible if people were not driven by these values and ideas. If they focused on the alternatives argued in this Chapter, there would not be a consumer-capitalist society. What then could possibly shift the syndrome?

The coming scarcity, that's what? Soon it will render the old syndrome worthless and push us towards the more sensible orientation. It is by no means inevitable that this transition will be achieved, given how deeply entrenched the old ideas and values are. Nor is it being assumed here that the change in outlook will tend to occur automatically as scarcity impacts. A great deal of slow and painstaking work has to be undertaken, and the last chapter discusses this task.

The Simpler Way requires and rewards responsibility.

It seems that social responsibility does not come easily to us, and that in consumer-capitalist society powerful forces militate against it. Back on the plains of Africa where we began lack of citizenship didn't matter much. Now how much of it we can muster will probably determine whether we survive as a species. The main task before us is therefore to establish firstly the necessary personal dispositions, and secondly the social conditions that will prompt, encourage and reward social responsibility. Like community, social responsibility cannot be grafted on or applied as a patch over a flaw, or treated as a missing ingredient that can be added. It can only come from, be evoked and rewarded by, be integral to, the normal thriving of a good society. It is pointless trying to artificially stimulate social responsibility in a society that does not need it, does not reward it and works through processes which cannot do so, such as having everyone compete against each other with many losing and being dumped, and having all important decisions and provisions come from centralised massive corporations and governments.

It should be obvious that The Simpler Way a) requires social responsibility; it cannot work without energetic citizenship, and b) rewards it. This way cannot function unless there is enthusiastic willingness to contribute to the committees, working bees and town meetings. Because there will be extreme dependence on local ecosystems and social systems and because these must be kept in good order, people will have a strong incentive to cooperate and to think about social decisions and problems and to get the right answer for the town. If they don't do it, no one else will do it for them. This dependence will radically transform politics to be mostly about, not individuals and groups competing for favours from central authority but about the quest by local citizens to find what's best for the community.

One's quality of life will derive primarily from the many public sources of welfare, rather from private wealth, effort or talent. Access to commons, community workshops, free goods, artists and crafts people, festivals, a supportive community and mutual aid will be the important determinants. Any individual will therefore be acutely aware of the fact that his or her own welfare depends heavily on the welfare of the community and its ecosystems, and will therefore be aware of the importance of everyone taking responsibility to keep these systems in good shape.

However the rewards for social responsibility which The Simpler Way can deliver are even more significant than the requirements. The localism and smallness of scale will give individuals a sense of being able to make a difference in the decisions that affect them. Participation in the development, maintenance and governing of one's community will be empowering and satisfying. Contributing to working bees, committees and town meetings will be enjoyable. All individuals will feel, know, that they are important, that they are partners and equals in running their town and developing it into something to be proud of. These will be major source of self-esteem, enjoyment and life purpose.

Thus the conditions which The Simpler Way will locate us within are likely to get rid of the mindless self-indulgence and numbness, the vacuum that fills with trivial concerns. Attention will mostly be given to things that matter. Most important however is the distinction between positive and negative motivation. Good citizenship and mutuality and care will not come primarily from duty, discipline and compassion, from the sense that socially required actions ought to be undertaken, e.g. to care for the underdog. They will be the outcomes of a desire to see things working well and to see people happy and fulfilled. Compassion for the less fortunate is not the essence of what we are after. What we want is delight in seeing the other flourishing, desire to nurture and to provide for.

Is this to ask for saints? It is only to ask for the way parents regard their children, or people regard their friends or pets. A number of strands within psychology and sociology, such as Maslow's self-actualisation theory, take it for granted that these dispositions are the essence of humanity and that they would predominate if we could get rid of the circumstances and institutions which drive them out and distort and corrupt and numb. Central among these is an economy, a political system and a culture which condemn us to ceaseless competition against each other for impossible goals. If we could liberate ourselves from all that we would surely explode into an era of self and social actualization. Just imagine if one-tenth of the time now going into the production and consumption of rubbish could go into the creation of beautiful landscapes or happy artists or convivial conversation.

Another powerful strand in our cultural origins is a miserable conception of human nature, the assumption that humans are fallible, sinful and weak, requiring ceaseless discipline, guilt, grind and struggle against our impulses. Christianity points to a 'fallen' nature, Freud to the anti-social impulses inevitably setting up the irremediable 'discontents' of civilisation. Hence the priority on control, especially self-control, the acceptance of Puritanical schooling, factory work and a lifetime paying off the mortgage, and the discipline and toil that has build industrial civilization... at a crippling cost to spontaneity and spiritual growth and wisdom. Many have noted the pathological nature of the personality industrial-consumer-capitalist society requires and produces. People who love beating other people, or want more than they need, or seek to assert their superior status or boss others around, are not psychologically well.

In addition to the informal conditions conducive to desirable dispositions, our new towns and villages would have many deliberately planned systems and structures designed to facilitate the continual critical monitoring and reflecting on our society. There would be voluntary committees, information feedback systems and review processes to watch the way things were working, look for ways to improve, study what other towns were doing, set up trials, etc. One of the main functions for the remnant central state government would be to promote research and education on community self-government and the experienced quality of life and to facilitate the communication of such information. Again there would be plenty of time for this given that the average individual's paid-work week would be short.

Chapter 11

SUMMING UP

Part 2 has attempted to elaborate the case for the basic perspective outlined in Chapter 1. The first of the two claims argued was that the big global problems we are running into are in general not well understood. There is a great deal of discussion and many books on sustainability, but almost all of it proceeds on the assumption that sustainability can be achieved by adjustments which leave intact a society that is fundamentally about the pursuit of ever-rising living standards and economic growth. In my view the case for concluding that this assumption is totally wrong is overwhelming and irrefutable. Consumer-capitalist society is based on levels of resource consumption and environmental destruction that cannot be up for much longer and could never be extended to all people, and on a grossly unjust global economy that delivers to the rich few far more than our fair share. We could not get that share if we did not possess, oppress and loot an empire.

The generally unrecognised basic fact underlying this perspective is that the era of abundance is over and we are now plunging into an era of intense and permanent scarcity. The few in rich countries will not be able to go on taking most of the resource wealth, firstly because it is dwindling, and secondly because the Indians and Chinese will take it first.

The fundamental conclusion is that this society cannot be fixed. The overshoot is far too great for plausible technical advance to redress. More importantly it is a society built on mechanisms and values that are logically incapable of attending to needs, rights or justice. The market delivers most wealth to the rich, gears the resources and productive capacity of the poor majority to the rich, and cannot do otherwise. Underlying the flawed systems and mechanisms are the values and ideas defining and driving consumer society, the individualistic, competitive acquisitiveness. A good society cannot be built on such foundations.

If these conclusions are sound then the nature of a satisfactory society is more or less given and obvious. Although some of the detail suggested in Part 2 might be mistaken, the general form of the alternative way we must pursue is beyond dispute. It has to be a Simpler Way characterised by frugality, self-sufficiency, localism, cooperation, economies geared to need and under participatory control, and nice values. But the argument is not that we must make a grim and unpleasant transition in order to save the planet and ourselves. The argument is that the transition advocated would be a delightful liberation. The following list details this claim.

The benefits of The Simpler Way.

The most important goal of this book is to convince that there is an alternative that is not just workable but is an inspiring vision to work for. It is not just a way that would defuse the problems threatening to annihilate us. It is the way to a far higher quality of life than most have in even the richest countries today. Consider the following benefits.

❏ Living within a strong community; living close to many friendly people with whom you work and play and who will help you out if you have problems.

❏ Having a lot of free time, because you would probably only have to work for money about two days a week. Thus you would have much time for arts, crafts, gardening, home-making, learning and personal development.

❏ Living close to nature, in a green landscape, with wilderness, farms, forests close by.

❏ Having excellent food, fresh, grown nearby, diverse, without preservatives, perfect taste and nutritional value

❏ A relaxed pace. Little or no pressure or stress.

❏ Work that is varied enjoyable, and worthwhile, under your

control, not competitive, and fulfilling, contributing to your learning and development as a person. You could do many different things in a day if you wish, and you could see your work benefiting your community. Everyone has a livelihood. Few if any gigantic corporations, meaning many can enjoy running their own little firm or farm.

❑ Being secure, from poverty, unemployment, isolation, boredom or lack of purpose, adversity in old age. Being secure from the threat of violence. Being totally secure from the erratic and treacherous global economy.

❑ Having access to many skilled people, thus being able to observe and learn many skills. Living close to many artists and craftspeople and having time to devote to these activities.

❑ Being healthier, because of access to high quality food, clean air and water, more exercise in a more labour-intensive lifestyle, and especially because of less stress and insecurity, and access to community support and purposeful activity.

❑ Having cheap, well designed, repairable, durable items, e.g. furniture, radios, appliances, houses, bikes...

❑ The satisfaction that comes from running a household economy well; growing, organizing, cooking, repairing, having things in good order.

❑ Being involved in self-government, i.e. in participatory democracy, whereby local meetings make the important decisions about local development and functioning. Being a good citizen. Satisfaction from the sense of empowerment and competence associated with helping to run a good society.

❑ Living in a beautiful and leisure-rich landscape; having around you many animals, firms, farms, forests, commons, ponds, community facilities, artists, projects. Living in a magic landscape full of gardens, unique architecture, inspiring public works, shrines, caves, fountains, ponds and lakes, adventure trails, all created by us and overseen by the leisure and culture committee.

❑ Being in control of your collective fate; running a thriving and robust local economy with the people who live there.

❑ Having a sense of pride in your admirable society; i.e. a society that cares for all, is civilized, friendly, does not allow anyone to be poor or unemployed, has high standards, does not waste, is cultured, makes good decisions, looks after its ecosystems, takes responsibility for itself... being proud of being part of and contributing to a beautiful and noble society.

❏ A 'spiritually' rich life; having meaning, purpose, hope, inspiring surroundings and friends, and the stimulation to reflect and learn and grow. Circumstances which ennoble and bring out the best in people.

❏ Being respected for one's contribution, no matter how humble. Status according to one's contribution to enriching the community, not from wealth or power.

❏ Many festivals, celebrations, rituals, ceremonies, focused on local events, traditions, folklore.

❏ Enjoying helping others, giving, contributing to working bees, being convivial. Enjoying cooperating, reinforcing solidarity and cohesion and social wealth. Satisfaction in helping others thrive.

❏ The peace of mind that comes from knowing that you are not living in ways that create serious global problems.

Analyses by other critics and utopians.

There is now a voluminous literature on the problems confronting our world and on desirable changes. I want to argue briefly that although many works are very valuable in documenting the problems, almost none of them gets the overall picture right.

Most of the literature deals with the ecological, economic and social consequences of the consumer-capitalist way, and presents indisputably valid and convincing analyses. However when it comes to solutions almost all of this literature and the associated campaigns seek only to make the existing system work more satisfactorily, as distinct from recognising that it cannot be fixed and must be replaced. The discussion is, in other words, almost solely reformist.

It is remarkable that most of these authors fail to see the radical implications of their own meticulous documentations. There is a general failure to grasp the insurmountable magnitude of the unsustainability problem, to realise the significance of the scarcity problem, to see that the present market economy cannot be made just, to see that growth and affluence are absurd and suicidal goals, or that core values in Western culture are incompatible with a satisfactory society. Almost none of the literature acknowledges that the solution has to be some kind of Simpler Way. This is an extremely disappointing state of affairs. Despite so much recognition that consumer society is intensely problem-ridden hardly any draw what seem to me to be the inescapable and glaringly obvious conclusions. Following are brief illustrations of this claim with respect to some of the best known authors and movements. (The selection is for illustrative purposes and many valuable contributors are not mentioned).

For many years Lester Brown and the Worldwatch Institute (for instance 2006) have drawn attention to sustainability and limits issues, providing valuable data and summaries, and abundant warnings regarding the trends. However they never question the capacity to solve the problems within consumer-capitalist society. Nor do any other of the high profile green agencies, such as Greenpeace, Friends of the Earth, the World Wide Fund for Nature, or the Australian Conservation Foundation.

Much the same can be said of Hazel Henderson (2006) and David Korten (1999), again both providing valuable discussions of the problems, but both actually endorsing a (reformed) market system, and neither recognising any need to abandon the quest for affluence and growth. Similarly for years Peter Newman (Newman and Jennings, 2008, Newman, Beatley and Boyer, 2009) has contributed valuable analyses of urban sustainability problems but does not call for the scrapping of the market or the quest for growth or affluence. Like most within this camp his underlying assumption is that sufficient adjustments can be made within the present kind of society, by adopting better planning and technology. (For instance he believes solar energy can meet all needs. See ABC Occams' Razor, Dec., 2008).

Tim Flannery (2006), James Lovelock, Gustaf Speth (2001) and George Monbiot (2006) can also be grouped here. All provide highly valuable critical analyses of the dire global situation we are in, and the urgency of the need for change, yet all of them assume that some kind of affluent consumer capitalist system can solve the problems, and none indicates the slightest interest in anything like a Simpler Way. Monbiot says in effect that any move in that direction would condemn the Third World to mass starvation, thereby revealing an inability to think of development in other than the conventional uni-dimensional terms.

Most commentators on sustainability focus only on how to cope with the (ever-accelerating) supply problem and thus fail to see that the solution can only come through system changes which enable demand to be cut severely. Thus Lovelock embraces nuclear energy as a desperate move to solve the greenhouse problem, with no thought whatsoever about the possibility that we could live well on a tiny fraction of present Rich World per capita energy demand. Flannery is so confident that renewable energy sources can sustain affluence for all that in The Weather Makers (2006) he sees no need to provide any serious support for this faith. I have made attempts to engage with all these people via personal communications regarding their challengeable assumptions, but without response.

Almost all Green groups are firmly within the reformist camp, including the Green political parties and the conservation and wildlife etc. agencies. Almost none see that affluence or growth are problems. For many years I and some colleagues (notably ex-Senator John Coulter) have laboured to get the Australian Conservation Foundation to oppose economic growth. As well as failing in this quest I have received instruction from the chief executive officer that I am mistaken on this issue; growth is actually both possible and desirable.

Much the same can be said about almost all Third World aid and development agencies, including the fair traders, micro-credit enthusiasts and Tobin taxers. These people do valuable work assisting Third World people but all of them think solely within the conventional development paradigm, taking it for granted that development can only be capitalist development and revealing no understanding whatsoever that scarcity makes this impossible, or of what appropriate development might mean.

The anti-globalisation camp and the World Social Forum have been remarkably successful in drawing attention to the unacceptable nature of the global economy, yet most of the solutions they put forward are also depressingly reformist. They are typically concerned to establish more controls, more justice, more ecologically defensible ways, within basically the same old market and profit and growth-led system. Again there is little recognition that affluence for all is impossible, that markets cannot be just or meet needs, that growth is an absurd goal, that radical scarcity is now the central defining issue... or that only a Simpler Way can solve the problems. (However there is concern for localism and to allow different cultures to pursue non-conventional development paths).

There is now considerable recognition that the solution has to involve localism and smallness of scale. Here we owe much to people like Colin Hines (2000), Helena Norberg-Hodge (1991), Richard Douthwaite (1992, 1996), and the 'small is beautiful' team including Fritz Schumacher (1999), Lopold Khor (1957) and John Papworth (1995, 2006). However small scale and local systems are far from sufficient. They can fit comfortably within growth economies and market systems, so have to be seen as (very important) parts of the whole solution.

Chapters 3, 4 and 5 above show that a basically Marxist critique of the global economic system is absolutely crucial. However the Left typically fails to comprehend scarcity and its implications and remains steadfastly determined to achieve affluence for all, via industrialisation, centralisation and globalisation, and indeed what was explained in Chapter 6 to be the conventional capitalist conception of development. If the global situation is to be understood satisfactorily a Marxist approach must be taken, because the situation is primarily due to the dynamics of a capitalist system, but this book argues that when it comes to solutions, and how to get to them Marx is not helpful. (See in more detail Chapter 12).

There is a large literature critical of consumerism but its focus is largely on the syndrome as a mistaken life choice which cuts off more satisfying paths for middle class workaholics. Some authors point out that the stress and depression associated with climbing the company ladder can be avoided by 'downshifting' to the slow lane. Some are disgusted at the crassness of conspicuous consumption, as when Hamilton (rightly) exposes the $7,000 barbeque. But remarkably Hamilton's influential works, (e.g. Hamilton and Dennis, 2007) identify over-consumption as a problem of alienation. In his view our biggest problem is the hollowness of a life obsessed with material wealth. If only! We could be within a few decades of a three billion die-off (if you think that's implausible, take a look at Joseph Smith's, *The Coming Colapse of Civilization*, 2010 or Google the term) yet Hamilton thinks our biggest problem is the boredom of people with more money than sense. Neither book stresses the fact that the over-riding problem we have is that the looming die-off is being brought on by over-consumption.

Bookchin and others identify 'domination' as the core fault in our society. He believes that where humans have gone wrong is in moving from the equalitarian values that characterised tribal societies to obsession with gaining power and advantage over others. At first this emerged with respect to age; i.e. it was the older members of the tribe who began to dominate younger members. Domination then became embedded in religious practices, privileging the priests, and more recently it has been built into military and class structures. The cultural foundations of Western civilisation now take for granted hierarchical and authoritarian relations, top-down control, competition, the importance of winning, royalty, privileges for superiors and the legitimacy of inequality. Bookchin sees this syndrome as explaining the environment problem. That is, because we humans so readily dominate each other we also dominate the environment.

Eisler's *The Chalice and the Blade* (1990) also focuses on the problem of domination, although she believes we are slowly moving to 'participator' culture. She provides an inspiring account of the Old European culture which thrived in the Eastern Mediterranean for 1500 years without violence and with high levels of equity and participation, showing that humans are capable of building a good society.

It would seem to be beyond dispute that Bookchin and these related theorists are making valid and important points about the source of our problems. The readiness to dominate is indisputably a serious problem within the Western mentality. Much of our malaise is due to the fact that people tolerate domination by tiny super-rich elite classes. Fotopolous (1997) and Chomsky should also be credited for arguing valuable critiques centred on elite domination. However the limits to growth analysis shows that domination is only part of our problem. Our most alarming and urgent problem is not domination and justice, but sustainability.

Let us assume that everyone in the world suddenly lost all interest in dominating, competing, winning and bossing others around, but continued to be as obsessed as they are at present with affluent living standards and economic growth. The basic global problems would remain about as serious as they are now, because people could not live affluently without taking more than their fair share of the world's wealth and therefore without depleting its resources and ecosystems and depriving the majority. The world has suffered eras and regimes of extreme domination for long periods in the past without threatening ecological collapse.

Those who see that reduction is inevitable.

Relatively few have focussed on the notion of a coming major and unavoidable decline due to over-consumption and the depletion of resources and environments. The classic early works by Paul Ehrlich (notably *Population, Resources and Environment*, 1972) and by Meadows, Meadows and Randers (*The Limits to Growth*,1972) were extremely valuable and influential in warning that the binge could not go on for ever. More recently those I am aware of who have independently put forward perspectives which best align with the analysis of our situation argued in this book are Howard Odum (2000), Richard Heinberg (2003,), Pat Murphy (2008), James Kunstler (2005) and Joseph Smith (e.g. 2010). Unlike most they see that the magnitude of the sustainability problem means huge and probably catastrophic 'de-development' is coming, that technical wizardry can't save us, and thus that radical lifestyle and structural changes must be embraced. The more optimistic of them focus on localism in supply and government, greatly reduced economic throughput, the need to accept much lower 'living standards', and the need for new visions and values. Some of these people have been remarkably energetic and successful in raising awareness (for instance through the videos made on Cuba's achievements in sustainable urban agriculture: 'The Power of Community'). The more pessimistic of them are in the Die-Off camp, believing that massive collapse is unavoidable.

Where this book differs from these end-of-the-road theorists is mostly with respect to the detail it offers regarding the possible nature and functioning of the new society, and with respect to optimism regarding its positive and liberatory potential. If there is one goal above all others that I hope this book achieves it is to inspire with a vision of the marvellous alternative we could easily build, if we wanted to.

Few endorse frugality, self-sufficiency and subsistence.

This is the issue that sorts them out. Very few among those grappling with the global predicament argue for simplicity as an intrinsic good. Many accept that consumption has to be reduced, but do so reluctantly. The Voluntary Simplicity movement, and associated groups such as those advocating Slow Food, point to the personal lifestyle benefits of dropping the pace. This initiative has been remarkably effective, as surveys seem to indicate that Voluntary Simplicity ideals are now endorsed at least to some extent by tens of millions of Americans. However, as with Hamilton's 'down-shifters' Voluntary Simplicity is mostly discussed as a lifestyle option individuals might choose within existing society and there is no reference to the need for collective solutions and radical changes in settlement, political, economic and cultural structures and systems.

'Subsistence' is the concept we should attend to here. The overwhelming dominance of capitalist development theory and practice ensure that 'subsistence' is seen as a primitive and erroneous path which has to be eliminated because it blocks progress. This is what Marx thought. The Simpler Way strenuously contradicts this assumption.

Unfortunately discussions of subsistence are usually obscure and misleading. The term tends to be used to imply a peasant family barely surviving through the consumption of all that it can produce for itself. As I see it the basic theme is production for direct use by the individual, family and nearby community, as distinct from production of commodities for sale in wider national and global markets in order to accumulate money, with which to purchase necessities from those wider markets. Thus a subsistence economy can involve sale for money but the use of money is only to facilitate local exchange of goods intended to meet needs. It can involve some selling of exports out of the locality, to earn sufficient export income to import a relatively few necessities. It does not involve putting all one's productive effort into selling into the big distant market in order to accumulate money with which to purchase necessities from that market. Subsistence also implies production and exchange governed primarily by other than market considerations such as traditions, social forces and needs.

Few theorists endorse or advocate subsistence but it is the defining element in the notion of development accepted by many Third World movements, such as the Chiapas in Mexico. Samana (1988) argued for it with respect to PNG. Vandana Shiva (2005) defends the right of peasants to remain in such economies, working out their own notion of 'development'. The International Society for Ecology and Culture (2009) is explicitly working to reinforce the appreciation of Third World people for their own traditions and ways and not to be seduced by the Western way.

However it is not clear in at least some of these instances whether subsistence is seen primarily as a defensive strategy in the face of globalisation, or whether it is seen as in principle valuable and preferable. If the poor were not being devastated by globalisation would they still recommend subsistence? There is usually no indication that the polar distinction between conventional and Appropriate development argued in Chapter 6 above is clearly and strongly held, nor that subsistence is recognised as socially and spiritually superior.

Perhaps the most extended and explicit advocacy of subsistence comes from Benholdt-Thomsen and Mies (1999), although their concern is primarily with the role of women in the history of development. Endorsement of simpler and more self-sufficient ways is evident in the writings of Tolstoy, Thoreau, Prudohn, Bakunin, Kropotkin, Bookchin and Leopold Khor. Tolstoy is notable for his respect for the ways of the peasant, his suspicion of specialisation, and the value he put on the village, family and manual labour. Thoreau valued simplicity and living close to nature, and argued against competition and obsession with owning property. Many of these themes are embedded in Christian philosophy, especially the concern with the rejection of material wealth (although one would hardly realise this from the behaviour of most Christians today).

It is therefore encouraging that there are strands endorsing subsistence and simplicity in our cultural heritage. However they are overwhelmed by the mainstream's preoccupation with big, complex, centralised and globalised systems, and the neglect of the simplicity theme in the vast literature on the global situation indicates the magnitude of the task we face. Part 3 takes up the question, how then might we best proceed.

Part 3

HOW DO WE GET THERE?

This book's final purpose is to put forward a practical action strategy which is convincingly derived from a fairly detailed examination of our situation and the changes we have to make. The strategy is offered in the next Chapter. The present Chapter examines a number of common ideas and theories about social change in the light of the conclusions arrived at in Part 2. Most of these are rejected because they are no longer relevant or helpful given the situation we find ourselves in. The extensive and diverse literature on social change and social action has in general not taken into account the significance of the severe scarcity we now confront, the limits analysis of our situation, the impossibility of fixing consumer-capitalist society, the kind of alternative we must develop and the impossibility of progress as it has previously been conceived. This review of major theoretical positions derives the principles for Chapter 13. It concludes that the classical Anarchists have the most valuable ideas for us.

Chapter 12

A CRITICAL LOOK AT ACTION PHILOSOPHIES AND STRATEGIES

This Chapter considers a number of common ideas about the way significant social change can be brought about, in order to clear the ground for putting forward a strategy in Chapter 13.

Change your lifestyle.

If the general limits to growth perspective on consumer-capitalist society seems convincing there is a strong tendency to conclude that one ought to simplify one's own personal lifestyle. This is of course appropriate and desirable but it is far from the most important response. It can't make much difference to the problems. In the first place it is not at all easy for most people to change their personal lifestyles significantly while they are living within a consumer society. Most people have no choice but to drive a car, buy food that has been transported a long way and use flush toilets. The structures and systems within which we are trapped condemn most of us to doing a lot of consuming and polluting. We can with effort change some things about our lifestyles, e.g. many of us could grow more food and wear out old clothes. But we can't bring about the huge social transformations needed, such as establishing a zero-growth economy, through individuals resolving to change their personal lifestyles.

The sustainability problem is mostly to do with faulty social structures and systems. Individual decisions to live more simply will not contribute much to getting those local economies established or to digging up many city roads and planting edible landscape beside the railway tracks or eliminating sewers or the advertising industry. These structural changes will only take place on a large scale when many more people understand the need for them and become willing to support the political action that might achieve them. This will not happen before a great deal of educational work has been carried out. Deciding to make one's personal lifestyle more ecologically pure will make little or no contribution to achieving these public educational goals. Moreover, to cast the problem as changing one's lifestyle reinforces individualism and obscures the need for collective responses or structural changes.

Of course personal change can be important for one's own morale or sense of consistency or capacity to influence. One is not likely to be a very effective advocate of simpler ways if one's lifestyle is materially extravagant. 'Down-sizing' one's consumption or joining a bush regeneration group can also be important in enabling a feeling of having taken a crucial step in the right direction or having made a significant commitment. This is especially important with students who often need to take some action in the short term. Even actions which are not very relevant to structural change can be worth undertaking for this reason. Many tree planting, recycling and conservation projects fall into this category and there's nothing wrong with undertaking them, as long as it is understood that such actions can't make much difference to the big picture and it is understood what actions can.

The extreme 'change your lifestyle' response is to shift to an alternative rural commune or Eco-village. This can be a valuable contribution to transition if it puts one in a position to have a significant educational impact, e.g. by working with a group setting up a demonstration or educational site. But merely to increase by one the number of people living in alternative ways out of sight is of little value, and it could even be of negative value if it means there is one less person in a position to work on what most needs doing. A sustainable society will not come into existence simply through a process of more and more people individually opting out of the mainstream in search of a nicer or more ecologically acceptable life experience for themselves. This will not change the general level of public awareness regarding limits to growth and it will not change the faulty systems and structures. (The value of the Eco-village movement is discussed in more detail below).

Thus the relative unimportance of the 'down-shifting' Hamilton advocates is evident. Of course reduction in the amount of work and consuming an individual does is crucial and Hamilton's works have helped to increase awareness of the quality of life benefits 'down-shifting' can bring. But again this is a minor element in what's required, can't make much difference on its own, and will not lead to the big structural changes required. Down-shifting within the conditions consumer-capitalist society enforces on us cannot involve anywhere near a sufficient reduction in consumption, resource use, carbon emissions or footprint. A very keen down-shifter might cut his or her personal or household per capita rates by 30% or more but the target has to be in the region of 90%, and 100% on some dimensions such as carbon emissions. And these must be reductions in national consumption. An individual's down-shifting does not affect national military spending, advertising, trade or fridge production much if at all. Downshifting is only about dropping from the level of the workaholic and mindlessly rampant consumer to a more modest but comfortable Prius-owning and more discriminating supermarket consumer... still living on a footprint maybe seven times one that will be possible for all.

Hamilton does not consider the fact that while a few can downshift without much trouble, if many do this economy will collapse. It cannot tolerate significant reduction in production and consumption. Before all could downshift we would have to not only scrap the growth economy but design one that functioned on a small proportion of the present GDP, when just about every economist and politician on the planet is working feverishly to increase the GDP.

So what is at stake is far more than lifestyle change, although this is essential. The most important task is to help more people to understand the need for system transition to The Simpler Way, and to see it as satisfactory and attractive. The core question then is, what should I do in order to help achieve that goal?

Work for green agencies and parties via normal channels?

At present and in the foreseeable future there is no possibility of achieving or even contributing to the kinds of radical changes outlined in the Part 2 by working within governments and existing official systems. Virtually all governments and associated bureaucracies are run by people who believe in affluent 'living standards', industrialisation and free markets, and hold economic growth and the promotion of consumer society as their top priorities. Very few have any awareness of or interest in the possibility that there might be a problem with the pursuit of affluence and growth. Anyway if they didn't proceed that way the vast weight of public, media, academic and corporate wrath would descend on them.

Green agencies and political parties do heroic work and can be highly effective in getting 'light green' policies adopted, such as strengthening recycling laws, saving forests and creating more national parks. But the argument in Part 2 was that the required huge structural changes cannot be made until most people understand and accept radically new ideas and values. For example there is no possibility of getting laws through in the near future that will enable special zonings to locate many market gardens in cities, or allow many city roads to be dug up, or to form Community Development Coops that will eliminate unemployment... let alone laws to phase out growth. These structural changes will become possible only when most people can see why they are desirable. The question is therefore how likely is it that working to save whales or to have green party candidates elected will increase the public awareness of the need for such radical change... when that need is actually almost totally unrecognised even within green parties and agencies?

Most of the energy of a green politician or party is inevitably drawn into fighting immediate threats to the environment. A great deal of grass roots political educational work will need to be done over decades before there will be any chance of having built the level of public support that will enable the necessary laws to be put through legislatures. The original German Greens split and the faction that wanted to put the emphasis on raising awareness about the need for radical system change, the 'Fundis', has since died away. As Fotopoulos (2001, 477) says, '... the Green movement has abdicated any anti-systemic or liberatory role and today is directly or indirectly reformist', i.e. not concerned with change from the system to another but only working for change within it.

The same points apply to working for the many environmental, aid and social justice organisations that exist, such as the Australian Conservation Foundation. These do extremely valuable work saving threatened bits of the environment. But it is no exaggeration to say that most of them are making no contribution whatsoever to eliminating the basic systemic causes of the problems they deal with. They bandaid the problems, and it can be very important to do that, but in general they are not concerned with radical change from the features of consumer-capitalist society that are causing the problems. The vast bulk and often all of the literature, media statements and work of these kinds of organisations makes no reference to any of the fundamental system faults and required changes discussed in Part 2.

The environmental problem is caused by commitment to levels of production and consumption that are grossly unsustainable, and to limitless growth in these, but 'peak' environmental agencies do not challenge these commitments. They never say, let alone stress that saving the environment is totally impossible unless we abandon the quest for high 'living standards' and economic growth. To work for such organisations as they are at present might be to contribute significantly to saving another species or another forest, but it will make no contribution to transition to a socio-economic system which does not cause and require massive and accelerating environmental destruction.

Supporting light green organisations carrying out good works in environmental, Third World, peace and justice areas can actually be counter-productive. These organisations give the impression that band-aiding and reform-within-the-system is all that is needed, and that there is no need to scrap some of our fundamental social systems. Their strategies imply that all we need is more aid, recycling, energy conservation, national parks and conservation law etc.

'Environmentally Sustainable Development' and 'Ecological Economics'.

In view of the argument in Part 2, little needs to be said about the significance of engaging in discourses on 'Ecologically Sustainable Development' and 'Ecological Economics' or working with groups advocating these concepts. Most pronouncements under these headings are thinly disguised reassurances that the same old goals of maximising production, consumption and profits within the market system can continue to be pursued because greater effort and technical advance can and will reduce the resulting environmental impacts to sustainable levels.

'Environmentally Sustainable Development' is most often conceived in the terms the Brundtland Commission (1987) used, whereby the goal is development that does not endanger the living standards of future generations. But advocates then typically proceed as if this is quite possible without reducing living standards or economic output. In fact reference is frequently made to the comical oxymoron, 'Environmentally Sustainable Growth'. After giving a valuable account of the global predicament the Brundtland Commission itself went straight on to recommend rapid growth. To speak of 'Environmentally Sustainable Growth' is logically about the same as saying, 'Heavy smoking is quite safe so long as you don't endanger your health doing it.' The statement is perfectly valid, and perfectly useless as a guide to action. Just as smoking heavily is incompatible with health, growth is totally incompatible with ecological sustainability.

The discussion of multiples in Chapter 2 made it clear that we are already many times beyond sustainable levels of production and consumption. Rich world resource use, production, investment, sales etc. per capita must be cut to a small fraction of their present volumes before a sustainable world order becomes possible. People who talk about ESD usually have not the faintest grasp that it can only be achieved if most of the factories in the rich countries are closed and most of its capital is written off.

The Anti-Globalisation, Fair Trade etc. movements.

The remarkable outburst of protest over globalisation in the last few years, evident in the Seattle demonstrations and the meetings of the World Social Forum, have been extremely encouraging. In the one or two decades since Neo-liberalism became the unquestioned orthodoxy dissent seemed to have disappeared. The econorats were able to quickly carry out a revolutionary scrapping of Keynesian and equity principles and to refocus official doctrine and policy on freeing capital to maximise profits. Remarkably the attempt by the corporate rich to push the Multilateral Agreement on Investment through seems to have been just a little too brazen and arrogant a grab to be tolerated, provoking a sufficient outburst of revulsion and anger to at least stall the campaign. Anti-Globalisation resistance subsequently swelled to generate a huge movement, including the now vast literature documenting the evil effects of globalisation.

It is of course extremely desirable that the Anti-Globalisation movement should gain in strength, but its nature and prospects are problematic and it is not the most important cause before us. It is primarily a movement of opposition, striving to stave off further catastrophic damage, and it is not at all clear or unified about any alternative vision. For many within the movement the goal is only a re-regulated consumer-capitalist society, a tamed, humanised globalised economy, in which for example there is a tax on speculative capital flows, there is greater control over corporations, the World Bank is no longer allowed to inflict Structural Adjustment Packages on the Third World, and there is 'fair' trade rather than free trade. But Part 2 showed that in a sustainable world there can be little international trade, and only a small international economy, and that welfare must depend primarily on the local economy not on earnings from trade. Campaigns such as Fair Trade, the Tobin Tax and debt relief are about pleading for existing systems and authorities to operate or allocate somewhat differently, and the argument in Part 2 was that no version of existing systems can solve the problems.

Especially important is the fact that the Anti Globalisation movement is not informed by any clear conception of a positive alternative, let alone by a notion of a Simpler Way. The movement does contain a strong re-localisation strand, but in general it seems to be for the standard goals of higher incomes for the poor, better distribution and more responsible governments providing more jobs and welfare services.

What about left theory and strategy?

Though there is a strong tendency to assume that Marx is irrelevant now, many of the central questions to do with the theory and practice of change are questions Marx raised and it is valuable to begin considering several important issues from a Marxist perspective.

First it should be noted that this realm, to do with change theory, is distinct from that to do with understanding the problems facing the planet. For this latter purpose Marxist analysis is absolutely crucial. As Part 2 argued, the problems we face are largely consequences of the condition the capitalist economy has developed into, led by the ceaseless drive to accumulate more capital and therefore to gain access to more and more resources, markets and profitable investment outlets for capital. As time goes by the dynamics built into capitalism lead to increasingly serious contradictions, polarisation and social and ecological destruction. Most of the suffering, social breakdown, conflict and ecological damage evidence on the global scene is directly due to the fact that there is an enormous contradiction between doing what is most profitable to capital and doing what is most needed. These obvious aspects of our situation are points Marx made regarding the nature and inevitable working of capitalism.

However in my firm view Marxist theory is far from a sufficient base from which to understand our situation and how to get out of it satisfactorily. We must add the key resource and ecological insights into our global situation deriving from the limits to growth analysis. I think there are a number of ways in which these limits themes show contemporary Marxist thought about our situation, the good society and the way to get to it to be insufficient or mistaken.

Before going into these issues the outstanding merit of Marx's vision of the good society must be acknowledged. Although he said little about its form he did endorse the ideal distributional principle 'From each according to his abilities, to each according to his needs'. The wisdom and the virtue of this principle are profound. That's how a good family works, or a good club, and how the Spanish Anarchist collectives worked. It is difficult to see how anyone could dispute the value of this principle, although

259

there are others one might wish to add, such as 'Care for each other'. But now to the difficulties.

The good society cannot be an affluent-industrial society.

It can be argued that the limits to growth analysis shows that capitalism is not the fundamental problem confronting the planet. Clearly we cannot develop a sustainable and acceptable world order while we have a consumer-capitalist economy, but we must do much more than transcend capitalism. If we eliminated capitalism and implemented 'socialism' everywhere but remained committed to affluent living standards and ceaseless increase in the volume of production and consumption, then we would inevitably have just about the same range of global problems we have now. The Rich World would have to go on grabbing most of the scarce resources because there aren't enough for all to be as rich as we are, and more and more Third World productive capacity would have to be geared to Rich World consumption. More environmental damage would accumulate, regardless of how effectively a socialist economy eliminated waste, corruption, advertising and inefficiency. (Remember, present levels of production and consumption are quite unsustainable, and current growth rates will multiply these many times within 70 years, and no realistic assumptions about pollution control or a rational socialist economy can reconcile such multiples with planetary resource limits).

The fundamental point here has been emphasised in Chapter 4. It is that a good, post-capitalist, society cannot be an affluent, industrialised or consumer society. Marx was wrong in assuming that a good society is not possible before the productive forces reach high levels of development. Many 'primitive' societies and presently functioning alternative communities show that only very low material living standards and levels of industrialisation and technology are necessary for a high quality of life. The Kalahari bushmen don't begin work until they are about 23 years old and then, like many tribes-people, they work only about 19 hours a week. They have a satisfying life and many reach an old age. Long ago Sahlins (1972) reported on how rich 'primitive' tribes were, lacking almost nothing they needed for a good life. Benholdt-Thomsen and Mies (1990) discuss the virtues of the 'subsistence'

260

way evident in peasant life and they strongly reject conventional development. Monetary wealth is not only largely irrelevant in the societies they discuss, but it detracts from and damages the social relations within a 'moral' economy that ensure security and welfare for all. (Hyde makes the point in *The Gift*, 1979).

Many homesteaders and members of Eco-villages live idyllic lives in peasant ways, using little more than hand tools and natural materials such as earth, wood and leather, and being secure within cooperative social arrangements. I know these things at first hand from the way I live. Apart from a very few items such as medicines, my lifestyle would be easily achieved without sophisticated technology, international trade or mass production. Most of any modern technology I'd use, such as corrugated iron, seeds, shoes, cement, paint and radios, could have been produced with pre-1950s technology. The good life and the good society depend primarily on values and expectations, on having purpose and worthwhile work, on the richness of community and culture, and on the collective capacity to organise sensibly. They do not depend much on material goods, income, modern technology or the GDP. The world and indeed most Third World countries are far beyond the levels of technical sophistication necessary for a good society.

So, sorry Old Left but 'socialism' does not require a high level of 'development of the productive forces.' Indeed simplicity in everyday lifestyles and technology is important for a good life in a good society (although there is a place for some sophisticated R and D and technology).

An inevitable, painful long march through capitalism?

In Chapter 5 the largely unrecognised distinction between capitalist development and appropriate development was discussed. Unfortunately Marx assumed without question the capitalist conception of development. He, like almost all Western development theorists and practitioners before or since, saw development as movement down a uni-dimensional path to industrial-affluent society, driven by the increasing capacity to invest capital and purchase goods. The advent of socialism as Marxists conceive it today would continue the process, but with the capital in society's control not in private hands, and with the redistribution that would make everyone more able to purchase. Most importantly they think development can't occur without the investment of capital. The 'subsistence' characteristic of cultures unaccustomed to the Western way of cities, bureaucracies, centralisation, factories etc. was seen as primitive and to be eliminated.

It has been explained that Appropriate Development flatly contradicts these assumptions. The limits to growth perspective reveals much of Marx's taken-for-granted goal to have been mistaken, making it clear that the good society cannot now be defined in terms of affluent or industrialised society, and that frugality, subsistence and localism are essential. The argument following is that these points also have profound implications for process. We must go to a very different place to that which Marx envisaged, and we must get there by a very different path to that which he argued.

The Marxist is confronted by the dreadful task of fighting and defeating capitalism, a campaign which after 150 years is a very long way from success. More importantly, followers of Marx's 'laws of history' are strongly inclined to believe that capitalism has to mature before its contradictions will bring about its self-destruction. Warren (1980) for instance argued this regarding the possibility of emancipation for the Third World and various gurus and organizations have refused to support revolutionary movements on the grounds that their societies were not far enough down the path to capitalism.

Later in this chapter it will be argued that we do not have to wait for capitalism to self-destruct, and we do not have to fight it and defeat it. Essential to The Simpler Way strategy is the Anarchist approach, i.e. to begin here and now to build the radically new systems. (The classic Marxist dismissal of this is of course that if we manage to become a threat the monster will crush us. It will be argued that this will not be possible this time, because of scarcity).

It is remarkable that late in his life Marx came to think about the possibility of a quicker and more direct route to post-capitalist society, a route which did not involve first defeating capitalism in mortal combat. He toyed with the possibility that the Russians might build socialism on the existing model of the

Mir, the traditional peasant collective village, without having to fight capitalism head-on and defeat it. (See Shannin, 1995, Bideleux,1985 and Kitching, 1989).

The significance of the issue for Marxist theory and practice could not be exaggerated because what Marx was contemplating contradicts the essential elements in the approach to revolution taken by his theory and by subsequent Marxist revolutionaries. The possibility that the new society might be achieved by helping peasants to build on their traditional collective village practices jettisons the 'the laws of history' which decreed the need to suffer the maturation of capitalism, the need for a vanguard party, the inevitability of violent class struggle, violent revolution and the taking of state power.

The conflict over this issue between Marxists and Anarchists became so serious that it split an international conference and led to violence between the two within the Spanish Civil War, contributing significantly to Franco's victory. It remains as a source of serious conflict between them.

The important point for us seems clear. Where revolution is only a matter of changing the class controlling a society in which masses lack the necessary class consciousness, a society which is then going to continue to pursue greater income within centralised industrial systems etc., then it might make sense for the revolution to be led by an authoritarian, centralised vanguard and to involve violence. However the argument in this Chapter is that the new situation of scarcity we are entering totally disqualifies this approach. This revolution cannot be led by a centralised, authoritarian vanguard – scarcity and the need for local self-sufficiency rule that out.

The 'Mode of Production'.

Central in the Marxist account it is the focus on the mode of production. The fundamental fault in capitalism is seen in the fact that it is a productive system in which a small class owns capital while most people make up the large class which must sell its labour to capitalists, and the working class is exploited because it does not receive the full value it creates in the capitalist's factories. To a Marxist progress is to do with the transition to 'a more advanced mode of production.'

It is not that the limits to growth perspective shows this analysis to be mistaken or unimportant. However attending to the mode of production does not focus attention on what is now the most important problem, which could be labelled the mode of consumption. Marxists do not question this factor.

Again let us assume that we abandoned the capitalist mode of production and put production entirely under social control. As has been explained, this in itself could make little or no difference to the global ecological predicament if the rich countries remained determined to consume as they do now. They would have to go on taking most of the resources, thereby depriving the Third World and generating unsustainable resource and ecological consequences. Again fundamental change to an ecologically sustainable world order is not possible without dramatic change to the more advanced mode of consumption that The Simpler Way represents.

Of course much of the detail in Part 2 above is in fact to do with a new mode of production, but not one that is more technically complex or sophisticated than that characteristic of capitalist society. It is in many respects a more 'primitive' technology, involving crafts, hand tools and labour-intensive gardening, and closer to the despised ways of the peasant than those of the industrial worker. (However the 'relations of production' would not be primitive, but would be close to those Marx envisaged, i.e. there would be democratic control of the means of production and no class domination).

We could put it this way. The Marxist threat to capitalism is the strike, i.e. the threat to withhold labour. The Simpler Way raises a far more dreadful threat; the threat to withhold our shopping!

The role of force and power

It is axiomatically assumed by Marxists that fundamental system change will inevitably involve force, the exercise of power, and overt, intense and violent conflict. People on the left tend to embrace conflict, on the grounds that the ruling class will not voluntarily step aside and it will have to be pushed. The Simpler Way takes a completely different orientation to the significance of force and power, seeing them as having little relevance. This is not a matter of moral or aesthetic preference. The fact is that given the situation we are in and the goals of our movement, force and power are of no value. They are not means that can help us to build what we have to build.

There are two issues here. One is the possible role of force in getting rid of capitalism, which will be taken up later. The other is the need to force people to follow the new ways after state power has been taken. Regarding the second, consider again the logic of the situation. We cannot have thriving local economies unless people in general willingly adopt the new ways and make them work because they understand why such arrangements are necessary, and more importantly, because they find those ways of living satisfying. The Simpler Way cannot work without a motivation whereby people in general find strong intrinsic values and rewards in living simply, cooperatively and self-sufficiently and living in the knowledge that only by following The Simpler Way can we enable a satisfactory life for all other people. Now force, power and confrontation can make no contribution to achieving this goal.

You cannot force people to eagerly and conscientiously pitch into building and running their own frugal household economies and local cooperative economies. This can only be done by people who are keen to get their local economies into good shape because they can see the global significance of doing that, because they know their quality of life depends on contributing enthusiastically, and because they enjoy doing it. Either they will want to do the crucial things primarily for the satisfaction these activities yield or those things will not be done.

Therefore the essential revolutionary work we have to do is to help people in their towns and neighbourhoods come to this vision and to the necessary skills and intentions. That will be a complex and bumbling learning process and will at best take a long time. The people in your neighbouhood will have to come to see that it must become a local economy, that they must run it, that they must work out how best to do this in the light of their unique circumstances. They will have to find and learn the necessary skills and develop the sense of competence and empowerment and confidence. None of this has anything to do with force, conflict or power conventionally defined.

Take state power?

Certainly The Simpler Way vision has little or no role for state power. To Marxists it is essential to eventually seize and use state power. But state power cannot make our new villages work! It does not matter how much control lies in the hands of the state or its secret police, this would be of no value whatsoever in getting people to contribute willingly, conscientiously and happily to the new neighbourhood and town socio-economic systems, or to work out how to run our unique local economy well. These cannot function effectively without a great deal of care, thought, cooperation, sharing, initiative, voluntary contribution and concern for the common good. Negative motivation cannot produce these dispositions. The state cannot force the new social arrangements into existence or force them to work satisfactorily. That's what Pol Pot tried to do but even a thoroughly benign state could not do it for us. A distant state simply cannot work out what are the best ways for each little locality with its own indiosyncratic set of values, conditions and problems, and it cannot make us want to find and practise those ways. What our town needs is not to be told what to do – it needs the desire to work out for itself what to do.

This can be put in terms of the irrelevance of top-down 'leadership'. In Fotopoulos' terms Marxists believe the required changes can be got through while only a few have the right consciousness. (2001, p.454). This may be so where the change is in effect a coup, a change in top management of the same old industrialised, authoritarian, centralised system, but in our case the changes cannot occur unless people in general understand and opt for them, meaning that they cannot be carried out or pushed through by a vanguard.

So the ordinary people of the neighbourhood will have to do the job and what is to be done by activists now certainly does not include working to eventually seize state power. Yes our long term goal is to have largely eliminated state power, along with capitalism and several other nasty things, but the way we are going to do it will not and cannot involve taking over the state, using it to bring in the necessary changes, and then eventually demolishing it.

However in the immediate future it is possible that we could get considerable assistance from governments, e.g. via the grants, land and resources that they might be persuaded to provide. Councils are willing to support local initiatives, and as the problems become more serious this readiness will increase. However they will baulk when we start taking control of our local affairs and doing things contrary to free enterprise and market principles. So we will have to do most of the job on our own.

Ideally your town would be able to tap into a global movement for guidance and support and tried and tested strategies and plans. It is not that each little community would have to work everything out for itself from scratch, but it would have to develop its own version of the general approach, adapted to its conditions and preferences. The hope that the Transition Towns movement will be the global movement we can work within and learn from is discussed later in this Chapter. Thus we are talking about a global political movement, but not one that is out to take state power.

Perhaps most important is the fact that our new politics must be primarily consensual, concerned to reach agreement about what's best for all. In such a situation force and power are of little relevance. Government will no longer be primarily about the power to force decisions through against the wishes of many. In large centralised and competitive social systems there is often a need to build a freeway or locate a new airport, inflicting great hardship on many who are opposed to it. Because governments have the problem of getting these things through against the resistance, great power is necessary and often great damage must be done to minorities. But in the new landscape, much of which will probably have approximately one village per kilometre, one small town every five kilometres and one small city every one-hundred kilometres, and no growth, there will be no need for more freeways and international airports to be built, nor therefore for the power to inflict them. In a zero-growth economy there will not be a frenzied struggle to get development approvals through.

Because it will be obvious to all people in a region that the welfare of all will depend on the health of their local social, economic, cultural and ecological systems we can confidently expect the focus not to be on their individual wealth but on what would be best for the town. (This point is illustrated by the cases discussed in Bernard and Young, 1997). Whereas at present politics is largely about individuals and groups competing to get what suits their conflicting self-interests, often in the new situation all will have strong common interests in maintaining the systems that provide for all people in their region. You will realise that your welfare depends on a thriving town and therefore the power to force your desires on others will simply be of little use or relevance.

So it follows that there is no place for a ruthless vanguard party before this revolution, or for a dictatorship of the proletariat after it. Again these are not moral choices; the fact is that these would be of no use to us in doing what needs to be done, which is essentially to get people to understand why The Simpler Way makes sense and to want to follow it. We can't be saved against our will, which has been the task in previous revolutions requiring a vanguard.

On the concept of power

These differences suggest that the concept of power needs to be reconsidered. The Simpler Way is best thought of as involving an uncommon or at least wider conception of power. The dominant idea of power, notably associated with Max Weber, centres on the capacity to impose one's will on others. This is a negative and conflict-ridden conception of power, with at best zero-sum and usually destructive implications. It is quite different to the positive and liberatory conception of power that is evident in my power to walk, or write, or play football or share, or tell a joke or explain things well. Because I have learned to write I now have the power to enjoy doing many things I otherwise would not be able to do. Skills are powers. Power in this sense is much the same as 'freedom to', for example, walk, understand, achieve, create, grow, enjoy. When we refer to 'computing power' we have no notion of any capacity to impose will. We have only the idea of capacity to do things.

The most important thing about positive power is its 'synergistic' potential, i.e. the tendency for the use of such power to facilitate and to multiply the occurrence of desirable effects. The more power I have to chair a meeting well or teach well or tell a good joke the more capacity I have to bring benefits to others, to stimulate positive contributions from them and so to cause beneficial multiplier effects. On the other hand mere power to coerce tends to have zero-sum effects at best. In fact its use is likely to reduce the readiness of others to contribute to the general good.

Power in the Weberian sense is not of much use to us in this revolution, but power conceived as capacity to stimulate, organise, inspire, lead, release potential and facilitate socially beneficial processes is crucial. Without this our new communities will not work very well. It is both necessary for and a product of the revolution. The more we succeed in establishing the new ways the more that the readiness to cooperate and facilitate and bring out the best in others will flourish, because these will be experienced as enjoyable. Our new neighbourhood economies will be largely fuelled by the satisfaction that comes from being able to do things that benefit other individuals, the community and the local ecosystems. The more power people have to do these things, the stronger citizenship will be and the more satisfaction people will derive from being a good citizen. As the stories in The Ecology of Hope (Bernard and Young, 1997) demonstrate so well, when people do become conscious of their dependence on their local ecosystems these common values dramatically change the nature of politics to a consensual as distinct from an adversarial form.

The Simpler Way is likely to greatly increase the average quality of life largely because of the much greater positive powers it will give to all, i.e. the greater capacity to do things that are enjoyable and beneficial to others. We would for example be in a position to experience, and enable others to experience, the satisfactions that can come from giving, helping, and joining in working bees and making our locality thrive.

Is the working class crucial?

The old left has a fundamental faith in the importance and the role of the working class. To Marxists it is axiomatic that change will come through the revolutionary action that class will take. As Wood says, '...the working class, strategically situated at the heart of capitalism, is still the only social force with the capacity to transform it.' (Wood, 1998, p.33).

There would be little argument that the working class is at present of little and of diminishing revolutionary significance. Union membership has undergone dramatic long term falls, and is still declining. Workers rights and conditions are being driven back. Globalisation has undermined the conditions necessary for unionism, especially in creating many mobile, technocratic elite workers with an international focus and able to bargain individually with employers, and with interests aligned with capital. Meanwhile the Rich World workforce has become much more casualised and therefore less able to organise resistance. The working class vote ensures the election of governments determined to push through more and more vicious free market policies. The official organised 'labour' parties commonly endorse globalisation, privatisation and the liberalisation of trade as enthusiastically as the Neo-liberals.

Unfortunately the class interests of 'workers' clash with The Simpler Way. They are for bigger pay cheques and more consumption, more jobs and production, more trade, a greater role for the state in running things, redistribution of wealth and provision of better 'welfare' by the state. The working class is strongly in favour of economic growth. Higher 'living standards', better health, education and pensions, and especially more jobs are seen to depend directly on how rapidly business turnover and GDP can be increased. Unions, socialist organisations and working class people in general are quite hostile to any suggestion that there is a problem of affluence, industrialisation or over-development or that the solution has to involve reduced per capita levels of consumption and a shift to simpler lifestyles. This is immediately seen as condemning those struggling to survive to even lower living standards.

At a more profound level there are problems to do with the psychology of the working class. Bookchin (1973) points out that the industrial worker is intensely disciplined by the factory mode of production to acceptance of authoritarian conditions, to doing what he is told and of not seeking autonomy or imagining a post-industrial world. His experience does not include co-operating with others to take charge of his own situation, plan, organise, and run things. He is a specialist, without the multi-skilled 'jack of all trades' orientation that the peasant or homesteader must have. The small farmer or businessman or homesteader must be autonomous and responsible, planning, fixing, adjusting, monitoring, deciding all the time. Workers tend not to be very interested in the self-sufficient outlook of the homesteader or in the business of collectively running their own economy. They tend to be more interested in a good wage, a good car, a good supermarket, and a good plasma TV. The missing traits are those of the Anarchist. Perhaps most significant is Bookchin's claim that the worker is not inclined to utopianism, to imagining a new and better society.

As Bookchin also points out, to Marx the industrial worker's revolutionary role is to revolt against one set of authoritarian rulers, and then submit to the next lot. He also points out that Marx didn't think this problem of personality was important; it could be attended to long after the revolution. For decades before their revolution The Anarchists in Spain had worked hard on this task of developing what they called the 'integral personality' and their success in the 1930s was largely due to the resulting initiative, responsibility and autonomy at the grass roots level.

Clearly The Simpler Way cannot function and cannot come into existence unless ideas, values and dispositions quite different to those of the industrial (or office) worker prevail. To add insult to injury, the required traits are to a considerable degree those of the peasant. This too is evident in the case of the Spanish revolution, where the rural co-operatives thrived more impressively than those in the urban industrial regions, because of the strong collectivist traditions and the dispositions peasant life produce. In our era the practicality, responsibility and initiative of the peasant-homesteader, family farmer and small businessman probably best represent what we need, and what is not found in abundance in the urban worker, consumer, official or academic.

Finally, the working class's record is not encouraging. Lack-Newinsky (2009) documents 'The Many Deaths of Socialism' over the last 150 years, the many times dissent rose but the chance was bungled, most tragically when the European anti-war movements before World War 1 collapsed and workers turned on each other in support of king and empire. This history testifies to the centrality of the problem of ideology and the

Left's failure to raise working class consciousness to sufficient levels.

It is therefore now difficult to sustain faith that the working class is going to contribute to the removal of the capitalist system, let alone be willing to contribute to the transition to The Simpler Way. If we get to it, the working class will just be among the many classes that have helped to build it, and they are not likely to be in the front ranks.

We are confronting the old Left here with the ultimate heresy, the possible irrelevance of class in this revolution. It will not be a working class movement. There is of course a mortal conflict of class interests at stake in this revolution. After all it is about whether or not capitalism survives. But the revolutionary process will not be about overt conflict nor about conflict in which classes confront each other, let alone a conflict in which the working class leads. (This will be explained further below).

Another cherished assumption largely unquestioned by the Left is that after rule by the capitalist class ceases workers will run things. But what about pensioners, artists, children and disabled people – why can't they do some ruling too? Again the foregoing discussion seems to help us settle the issue. In The Simpler Way the basic political forms and processes must be intensely inclusive and participatory, involving all people in town self-government, formal and informal committees, referenda and public discussions. Otherwise the town will not work satisfactorily. It will therefore make no sense to exclude any group from full participation or to privilege any one group such as workers. To put it mildly, Marx did not reinforce the desirability of rule by citizens, and it is not so surprising that 'Marxism' has come to be so strongly identified with rule by authoritarian elites.

These themes connect with Marx's contempt for the peasant. His theory of development was quite conventional and more or less the same as 'modernisation' theory in our era. He saw development as being about the increasing replacement of primitive/tribal and peasant ways by capitalist ways. The peasantry must become an industrialised proletariat before revolution is possible. 'Indeed the sooner the village decayed the better.' (Bookchin, 1994). Thus many Marxists, including Stalin in the case of the Spanish

Civil War, have refused to support liberation movements on the grounds that they do not conform to the orthodox theory whereby capitalism has to mature through the industrialisation stage to the point where revolution can occur. For example Warren (1980) argued that capitalist development in the Third World is good because it moves poor countries closer to the point where revolution becomes possible. This doctrine has helped to keep billions in misery for decades, ruling out any thought of trying to move directly and immediately to Appropriate development. It does not align very well with the fact that the major revolutions have all occurred in peasant societies and none have occurred in industrialised societies or been led by the working class.

Socialise the means of production?

A related issue is the Marxist axiomatic insistence on transferring the means of production to public control. This might be a good idea in some circumstances, such as those that prevailed in Spain in the 1930s where cooperative control seems to have greatly improved the performance of factories and farms and the conditions of those who worked in them. But in the coming conditions it is not likely to be necessary or desirable. Certainly it will makes no sense for enterprises that have to be large, such as steel works, to remain privately owned and controlled. These should be run as they were in Spain, as public services controlled by participatory democratic means. But in an economy that will be made up mostly of family enterprises, small firms and co-ops there is no need for these means of production to be owned by society. The need is only to make sure they serve society rather than seek to maximise profit in the market, etc.

It can be very enjoyable to run your own 'enterprise', whether it be a household economy or a farm or small business. There would obviously be no sense in society telling you how to run your own vegetable garden, and if it did this it would seriously jeopardise your productivity, as well as your gardening enjoyment. The Simpler Way is about releasing and encouraging enthusiasm, energy, good will and contributions, and these goals are significantly served by making sure people are as free as possible to do their own thing. All that matters is that they keep within the (easy-going) guidelines, e.g. gear their activity to meeting local needs, do not exploit labour or attempt to dominate the market. (The Spanish Anarchists allowed people to operate private family businesses and farms outside their collectives, and treated them well, at times giving them access to benefits, loans and surpluses on equal terms with members, but they set guidelines).

Whether or not the private ownership of the means of production is socially undesirable depends entirely on the attitude of the owners, providing it is not an economy which obliges them to behave in anti-social ways as the present economy does. It's the same with guns or drugs; there would be no need to ban them if people had my attitude to them. In a satisfactory society there would be powerful psychological forces leading owners of private small firms and farms to behave in socially positive ways.

What comes first, the revolution or the world-view change?

Marxists believe that after the revolutionary seizure of state power there would have to be a long period of dictatorship of the proletariat during which new habits, ideas and values would be established among people in general. Then a cooperative and rational society would be able to function without the need for a coercive state. At the time of the revolution the vanguard party would be clear about the required new values but the masses to be liberated would probably still be a long way from holding the necessary understandings and ideals for a communist society. Therefore it might be necessary to force them to comply, for some time. In Fotopoulos' terms Marxists believe the required changes can be got through while only a few have the right consciousness. (2001, p.454).

Again, if the revolution is seen only as a matter of changing the ruling class from capitalists to Bolshevic or some other vanguard party, which will then run the old industrial system from the centre still in authoritarian ways, then maybe it doesn't matter much what the masses think so long as they will support the revolt.

Previous sections have made clear that whereas many kinds of new orders can be enforced on unwitting or resistant masses, The Simpler Way can't be, because it is by definition a way that involves aware, willing participants. It cannot work unless people see that it makes sense and see it as inspiring. Thus our revolutionary task is primarily about developing the consciousness without which the transition cannot take place.

This crucial point was glaringly evident in the Spanish Anarchist revolution. In some regions the effective reorganization of economies was carried out very quickly. For instance within a few days of the end of the fighting in Barcelona the tramway workers had cleared the lines and started running services. These things would not have been remotely achievable had there not been widespread and deeply held ideas and values to do with collectivism and autonomy. They knew that effective self-management could only take place if ordinary workers held ideas, values and dispositions to do with self-management, responsibility and initiative. Our supreme problem now is how to develop among people in general the world view that will lead to fundamental system change and enable the new ways to be implemented at the grass roots level.

Despite the centrality of 'Working Class consciousness' and 'ideology' in Marxist analysis, the Left has been surprisingly weak on these themes. In my view they have not written much that is of any value to us on these topics, and have not put much energy into studying and describing the way ordinary people see the world and the delusions and myths that trap them. The working class has consistently failed to see that situations are not in their own interests, have failed to seize the many opportunities they have had for system change, has turned its back on peace movements and flocked to fight for nation, king and empire, and in the richest societies shows no interest in fundamental change from the systems that disadvantage them. (Lach-Newinsky, 2009). All this is about ideology; the failure to grasp that arrangements are not in one's interests. THE problem for anyone who wants to help solve the big problems is, how can one best contribute to developing the necessary consciousness for radical system change.

The Spanish Anarchists got the opportunity to implement ideas and values that had been strongly held by millions of people for fifty years. Our situation will be quite different. For us it will not be a matter of developing the dispositions and then implementing them when the chance arises, because they can't be widely developed while consumer-capitalism still appears to be thriving. Our task will be to develop the necessary ideas and values as the changes attending the breakdown of consumer-capitalist society take place. The structural changes and the ideological changes will occur concurrently. Our task is to work on both aspects of the problem.

Means must be consistent with the ends.

To followers of Gandhi and many others it is a matter of principle that means should not involve practices that clash with those that will characterise the society being worked for. Unfortunately there are many situations in which people have no choice but to adopt means which contradict the ends they are intended to achieve. Often in dreadful Third World situations there seems to be little choice but to use violence in an attempt to get rid of murderous regimes as the first step towards establishing a non-violent society. However, in getting to The Simpler Way there is no option but to adopt means which are consistent with ends.

Consider centralisation. The Marxist view of the revolutionary process, and of immediately post-revolutionary society, assumes highly centralised systems where top-down control is essential. However The Simpler Way involves mostly small scale decentralised productive and organisational systems, under the control of local people. These can only be established by decentralised practices.

It is not that we opt for the decentralised principle when we might not have, or opt for cooperative, non-authoritarian and non-violent means when their opposites could have been employed. There is no choice here. The transition will be a process of learning by practice, e.g. how to cooperatively run meetings, look after our old people, eliminate unemployment, make sure enough bread is produced around here, and it is impossible to learn via authoritarian means how to do things in non-authoritarian ways. The strategy must involve finding and practising right now the ways that will characterise post-revolutionary society, therefore any notion of behaving in authoritarian, centralised or violent ways as means to the ultimate goal is logically and empirically nonsensical.

A major tactical principle; Do not confront capitalism!

It is understandable that when confronted by a monster that is out to dominate us the temptation is to turn to face it and fight it strenuously. This describes just about all previous liberatory movements and revolutions, and there are situations in which it can't be avoided. But this is not how we are going to proceed. We are not going to confront the consumer-capitalist monster. What we are going to do is in effect to ignore capitalism to death.

Capitalism cannot survive if people do not continue to purchase, consume and throw away at an accelerating rate. Our aim is to gradually build the alternative practices and systems which will enable more and more people to move out of the mainstream, to shun consumer society, and to secure more and more of their material and social needs from the alternative systems and sources emerging within their neighbourhoods and towns. This revolution is without doubt about the death of capitalism yet it could be a peaceful and non-violent revolution, whereby new local, small scale and participatory systems slowly develop within and replace the old systems. At first sight this will probably not seem very plausible, especially to people on the Marxist Left, but consider the following.

Appfel-Marglin describes the large scale Andean peasant movement as a grass roots non-confrontational phenomenon of direct alternative (re)building. There is a '... withdrawing from and creating alternatives to the dominant system, rather than challenging it directly.' (1998, p.39). These groups do not seek recognition of their territory by the state; that would be to acknowledge that the state had authority. He notes that they regard themselves not as anti-citizens, but as non-citizens. The Relocalise site (2009) says, 'As the industrial system spins towards exhaustion... people at the base are not revolting in order to take the power that the elite have but are revolting to take power over their own lives.'

The Zapatistas in Mexico seem to give us a paradigm example. They are not out to defeat the Mexican state, take power from it and then build a new society. They are simply building their own society, although from time to time they have to fight to defend what they are building. This is how we will get to The Simpler Way, just by starting to create it in the ways open to us, here and now where we live. Vandana Shiva and Maria Mies point to possibly thousands of villages in Asia and Latin America taking much the same approach.

Korten holds open the hope that we can 'starve capitalism to death' (1999, p.262). Rude says, 'The goal is no longer to overthrow world capitalism in an anti-capitalist revolution as in the traditional Marxist model, as much as it is to leave capitalism behind by slowly creating a new post-capitalist culture and economy in capitalism's place... ' (1998, p.53). Quinn says, 'To overthrow hierarchy is pointless; we just want to leave it behind. (1999, p.95). Buckminister Fuller put it this way, 'You never change things by fighting the existing reality. To change something, build a new model that makes the existing model obsolete.' (Quoted by Quinn, 1999, p.137).

The standard Marxist retort here is of course that you must fight the monster because if you begin to become a significant threat it will crush you. Ah, but in the coming era of scarcity, will it be able to? We have now entered an era in which forces undermining the legitimacy of consumer capitalist society are gaining strength. Legitimacy is fed by comfort and complacency. Consumer capitalist society is safe as long as it keeps the supermarket shelves stocked and holds the lack of cohesion and the unemployment and injustice to ignorable levels. But scarcity is going to shatter all that. There have already been increased rumblings in the most comfortable countries about the failure of the system to deliver quality of life and cohesion and about the obscene inequality. The 2008 financial crisis was a blow to the taken for granted infallible correctness of free markets. But these effects will be nothing compared with what's coming. Just wait until we slam into the '2030 Spike', the coincidence of huge and insoluble shortages of oil, water, food, land, phosphorous and several basic minerals... accompanied by rising population, greenhouse effects and accelerating social breakdown. We are likely to see collapses in the supply systems stocking the supermarket shelves within the next 20 years. This multifaceted global catastrophy will eliminate the power of the super-rich to run things at all, let alone run them in their own interests. The system will have no capacity to deal with these events. It will therefore be in no position to stop people voting with their feet.

It cannot run big governments, secret police forces or armies without lots of oil. It cannot undertake surveillance and intervene in every town and neighbourhood to stop us planting carrots and oganising our co-ops.

Never before will revolutionaries have had such an opportunity, such a vacuum to walk into. Throughout the previous 200 years revolutionaries have been up against increasingly powerful industrial, bureaucratic and military systems, capable of turning guns against dissenters. But our enemy will have great difficulty finding the resources to organise anything at all and will confront a foe that is everywhere, with enormous capacity to do its own local thing and ignore bamboozled authorities and elites.

Time is therefore very much on our side. Before long circumstances will jolt people into the realisation that consumer-capitalist society will not provide for them. Our crucial task is to get the alternative ways up and running well enough in the time that's available so that people will be able to see that there are great alternatives, and come across to join us.

The worry is that the coming crises for consumer-capitalist society will come too quickly and be too severe for a more or less orderly transition. If the breakdowns are too disruptive we will not be able to get The Simpler Way going well-enough in time and our situation could quickly descend to the chaotic conditions in some Central African regions today. We in the alternative movement therefore must work as hard as we can to get the alternative up and running to be seen as the lifeboat.

Let us step back for a moment and consider this theme from a more philosophical and historical perspective. Sometimes profoundly radical change occurs without overt conflict. Sometimes it is more like the fading out of a once-dominant paradigm, to be replaced by a newly popular one. This is in fact the norm at the level of big paradigm change in science (on Kuhn see Barker, 2006), and in many cultural realms such as art, pop music, style, manners and fashion. A particular view or theory or form is dominant for a time, but then people more or less lose interest in it and move to another one. In science a dominant paradigm is rarely if ever dropped because it has been shown to be wrong. It will not be that the Psychoanalytic approach to psychology will some day disprove or defeat the Behaviourist one, or the other way around. What will happen, if anything, is that over time most psychologists will come to prefer one or the other, or a third position. If one 'wins out in the long run' it will not be as the result of a process well described as overt struggle whereby one vanquishes the other. It will be a matter of the waxing and waning of support.

Some of the biggest revolutionary changes of the twentieth century seem to have occurred in this way, most notably the collapses of the Soviet Union, the apartheid regime in South Africa, and the fall of the Berlin Wall. All seem to have been characterised not by set-piece, head to head, violent confrontations in which one side was driven off the field, but mostly by people 'voting with their feet' and ceasing to support, after a long period of growing disenchantment and increasing awareness of the desirability of other ways. These revolutionary changes seem to be much better described as collapses due to increasing internal failure to perform or to sheer disenchantment, rather than as defeats in mortal combat with superior opposing powers. In the end the vast military, bureaucratic and economic power of the ruling establishments counted for nothing in the face of a withdrawal of support, a loss of legitimacy.

Think about getting rid of the most powerful imperial monarchy the world has ever known, one which controlled most of the globe after fighting some seventy wars to establish its empire. Could such a brutal monster be defeated and got rid of without cataclysmic confrontation? Well, that's what we did to the British Empire. If we just wait a little longer the British royal family will have faded to little more than a minor element within the entertainment industry. It will have gone simply because people in general ceased to take any notice of it. Sixty years ago Britain and the Dominions fought World War 2 to defend the British Empire. Australia took it for granted that this was of enormous importance. (Freudenberg, 2008). But now the British Empire is found only in the history books and just about no one has the slightest interest in it, let alone in defending it.

If it's really broken, don't fix it!

This vision sweeps away mountains of problems and toil. At present many people are working hard on each of the many separate faults in consumer-capitalist society. Some are trying to provide better care for old people, some are trying to get more resources for homeless children, some are trying to raise more money for refugees... ad infinitem. This implies that we can't have a good society until we manage to fix each and every one of these myriad problems one at a time. It's like an old house where most things don't work any more, the roof's sagging, the pipes leak, white-ants in the floor... Well sometimes the best thing to do is not to fix the house, but to bulldoze it away and build a quite different one, that doesn't have or create those problems. If we build The Simpler Way we will not have to fix unemployment, homelessness, the environment, poverty, the traffic, peace or many other problems... because we will have scrapped the system that creates them.

So what is the most intensely subversive and revolutionary thing one can do? Train as a guerrilla for the day we storm parliament? Learn how to make suicide bombs? Plot to expose corporate power? No, it is to turn away, ignore consumer-capitalist society, and come and help us start building the new ways here and now.

Governments cannot solve the problems.

There is not the slightest possibility that the required changes can be made by governments or global institutions. The problems are far too big. They involve the transition to economic, political, social, geographical and cultural ways that contradict present ways, and the changes must be made quickly. They represent a contradiction of hundreds of years of thinking about the nature of the good society, progress, and human technical potential. No change in history comes anywhere near what is on our agenda. Reference is sometimes made to the way the US jumped into action when it entered World War II. There is no comparison. That was a response just about everyone agreed was needed, and it was a response that didn't involve any challenge to existing procedures, assumptions, systems or values. It was also a response that was a delight to business, kicking the economy into its biggest ever boom.

We have political systems which make significant change extremely difficult. Consider the US health insurance situation.

There are huge snouts in the trough and any suggested change that might threaten any of their interests is met with squeals of outrage. Because they have refused to move over the system has remained a moral outrage for decades. Governments must not upset many people, especially powerful sectors or they will lose the next election. The greenhouse problem provides an even more depressing example. It can't be solved unless many huge interest groups including coal miners and electricity consumers accept painful change and indeed major reductions and losses. The entire coal industry has to be phased out, entire countries have to shred previous 'development' policies, the amount of production, industry, investment, mining and industrial farming has to be cut right down. Every one of them will fight any suggestion that they should make any sacrifice, and they must fight or in this winner-take-all system they will go down. Already we have seen industries and countries adamantly refuse to consider slowing their CO_2 emissions growth, let alone halting it, let alone cutting it drastically (e.g. when the Chinese and Indians sabotaged Copenhagen).

So at this level of staggeringly big change Governments and international agencies cannot do more than dither and splutter rhetoric and come up with token initiatives and great-sounding proposals that can't be achieved or won't make any difference. They will not and cannot solve these problems. The only way the required changes can be made is by people moving to The Simpler Way as the problems get worse and the effects start to impact at the level of the supermarket and the petrol station. It does not need to be pointed out that the chances of this happening smoothly, or at all, are not good. It should not need to be pointed out that working hard to make it happen should be our top priority.

So the anarchists are right!

The first part of this book testifies to the importance of Marx's analysis of the nature and functioning of capitalism. If one does not think in his terms one will have a quite inadequate grasp of the situation, how we got where we are, where we are heading, and why the global problems we confront have emerged. However, much of this Chapter has argued that Marxist ideas on the kind of alternative society we need and on how we might get to it are in general of little value to us (although it has been useful to approach the issue of transition via Marxist ideas).

The argument in this Chapter has in effect been for a basically Anarchist approach to transition. The coming of the era of scarcity has invalidated most of the ideas and campaigns to do with social change that have been on the agenda for centuries. The sustainable and just society must be very simple and self-sufficient and participatory, and it has to be built by ordinary people as we learn our way, without direction from authorities (but with assistance from our global movement), in a very cooperative manner, focussed on collective need at the small and local level. What's more, we can and must begin the building now, before the old system has gone. We must, as the anarchists say, 'prefigure' the new, build those aspects of it that we can now, within the old society, with a view to attracting others and elaborating our construction until it fully replaces the old.

Bakunin said the revolutionary must '...try to build the structures of the future society within the present society'. (Rai, 1995, p.99). Pepper says, '...the way to create a desired society is to start living it out – thinking it and doing it --here and now in the society you want to replace.' (Pepper,1996, pp. 36, 305). Bookchin advocates building instances of the new society now. (1980, p.263). The Eco-village movement literature makes clear that this is the transition strategy many of its members explicitly hold. (Global Eco-village Network, 2001). It is also at least implicit in the Transition Towns movement (below).

Reflect again on the astounding achievements of the Spanish Anarchist Collectives during the 1930s. In a period of about three years, under conditions of war and privation with many away at the front, people just took control of the factories and farms and not only ran the economy, but evidently did so far more effectively than had been the case when it was in private hands. They insisted on running things without authorities giving the orders and without a paid bureaucracy. Assemblies of all people involved met and made the decisions. Add the fact that in the frugal and zero-growth conditions of The Simpler Way economic and political tasks will be even less complex than they were in the industrialised regions of Spain in the 1930s.

This would seem to leave no doubt that ordinary people can get together and organise their own affairs satisfactorily.

The Anarchists are also right about the importance of the consciousness of people in general. The achievements of the 1930s came from strongly held ideas and values. Our most important and difficult task will be to develop the necessary outlook on consumer-capitalist society and The Simpler Way in the short time available. Without this consciousness The Simpler Way cannot be.

The Marxists' rejection of the Anarchist way is based on the highly plausible belief that people in general are not presently capable of autonomy, do not have the necessary consciousness, and will not push the revolution though without the leadership of a strong and if necessary ruthless vanguard party. The history of revolution would seem to validate this gloomy view. However if the revolution is to establish communities capable of running their own affairs, then there is no point taking state power and the supreme goal must be to develop a well-informed, cooperative, responsible citizenry which can be autonomous.

This is the position argued by some of the best known Anarchists of the past, including Tolstoy and Kropotkin. If you had given them state power on a plate they would have turned away knowing that it is of no use. It can't be used to create autonomous citizens who will govern their own villages well. They urged revolutionaries simply to get on with the task of moving their communities towards the awareness that will motivate self-government. If people don't rise to the opportunity to take control of their own affairs this means there is a lot of consciousness-raising work still to be done, so get on with it. Don't waste your time trying to confront the ruling class head on or take control of the state from them because that can make no contribution to raising the crucial awareness. When the job has been well-enough done there will be no need to confront or fight; people will just vote with their feet and ignore the old ways and build the new ones.

Build Eco-villages?

I have been (understandably) ridiculed for saying, 'Would it be an exaggeration to claim that the emergence of the Eco-village movement is the most significant event in the 20th century? I don't think so.' (Jackson, 2000). But in my view, if anyone is around to write the history of the 21st century they will agree with my seemingly reckless claim. Unless we take The Simpler Way there probably won't be anyone writing the history of the 21st century, and if we do take it I think it will be recognised that the emergence of the Eco-village movement around 1980 was the beginning of our salvation. It was the first significant attempt to build settlements that are ecologically, socially and spiritually satisfactory (... the three principles the Eco-villagers emphasise).. There have been many inspiring utopian initiatives in the past but it would seem that only late in the Twentieth century did some of them come to be based primarily on considerations of environmental sustainability as well as community support and solidarity, and liberation for personal growth.

The Eco-village movement now includes thousands of intentional communities, that is, mostly small groups of people who have deliberately come together to plan and build communities that rate high on ecological, community and spiritual dimensions. The Global Eco-village Network wesite (2009) gives an impressive picture of how extensive and well organised the movement has become. Many of the settlements have state of the art environmental architecture and renewable energy systems, built-in industries and farms, often with a considerable educational emphasis. Indeed education broadly conceived is a major purpose of the movement and it has developed elaborate materials and courses. Some eco-villages host visits from students in mainstream institutions, as parts of regular university and college courses.

Eco-villages vary considerably. Some are large, most are small, some are intensely collective with common ownership, but probably most involve private property and incomes. Yet all are highly communal and collectivist in various ways. The ecological focus is evident in the widespread adoption of Permaculture design principles in village planning, organic agriculture, solar passive housing and alternative energy technologies.

Perhaps the movement's greatest strengths are to do with the community and spiritual dimensions. Eco-villages guarantee abundant access to friends, emotional support, common purposes, mutually beneficial arrangements and activities, ideas and opportunities to enjoy and grow with others.

So for thirty years now the Eco-village movement has been pioneering, building and illustrating ways that are more or less contrary to those of consumer-capitalist society. However I wish to restate the following (friendly) concerns I have previously offered from time to time.

Firstly, there is not enough emphasis on living simply. Much of the movement is too affluent and in general a footprint measure would show that we have to go much further than the typical Eco-village. A study of UK settlements found that they had cut their footprint to about 50% of the national average. (Dawson, 2007). Liz Walker (2005, p.174) reports 4.7 per capita ha for the well-established Eco-village at Ithica, USA.

Part 2 above argued that we must develop and run highly self-sufficient integrated regional economies, as well as town or neighbourhood economies. Most of the goods we can't produce in the town, such as radios, fridges, stoves and bikes must be produced within say 10 km radius. The establishment of Eco-villages does not contribute to the development of these regional economies, let alone to taking control of them.

Another concern is to do with the extent to which the eco-village movement is driven by the hope of saving the planet, vs. a desire to escape to a haven within consumer-capitalist society. I would like to have seen far more anger at the way the world works and a clear and explicit connection between this and the Eco-village project. The movement is indisputably about working for a better society, but the primary motivation of most participants seems to be to attain this for themselves, similar to the motivation of down-shifters, rather than as a means to solving global problems.

This feeling is reinforced by the Global Eco-village Network literature. It is in my view quite inspiring in the images it gives of the idyllic experience Eco-villagers are saying we can all have, but for me there could be much more sense of mission. (These are generalisations; some within the movement are making heroic efforts).

More important is the question to be taken up below regarding the strategic significance of just building and demonstrating alternative ways. I'll argue that establishing examples of admirable new ways is crucial, but in itself will actually achieve nothing of significance. This is essentially a problem of clarity regarding goals. Most green initiatives reveal the assumption that the task is to reform consumer-capitalism, by adding more things like Permaculture gardens. If however you see the goal as replacing that society, then you must do much more than add gardens to it. If that's all you do the alternatives will only attract the few who find them interesting, and few will realise why everyone ought to take them up. What matters is increasing the understanding as to why the alternatives must be taken up. (The issue is discussed in more detail below).

The Left in general either doesn't take any notice of the Eco-villagers, or dismisses them as irrelevant and incapable of having any revolutionary significance. In either case they are seen as self-indulgent, relatively privileged escapees failing to help fight the system, and continuing to benefit from the empire. They see Eco-villages as easily accommodated within capitalist society, indeed assisting it by defusing potential discontent. My firm beliefs are firstly that the movement is of great potential revolutionary potential if only because it demonstrates many of the ways we will have to adopt, but secondly that it could very easily come to nothing. As with the Transition Towns movement it depends on whether the Eco-village movement can come to be informed and driven by a radically critical global vision.

The main practical limitation for the movement is that very few people can join or set up Eco-villages. They are quite difficult to create, involving years of dedicated planning, meetings, fund raising and getting plans through councils. Planning authorities are making it more difficult to establish Eco-villages. Appropriate land is scarce and expensive and few ordinary people can afford to become involved. It is not surprising that the movement seems to have slowed down significantly in recent years, with some of its advocates recognising its increasing difficulties. (Dawson, 2007).

For these reasons it seems that the planet will not be saved by the construction of Eco-villages in the sense of new green-field intentional communities. The Eco-village has performed heroically for the cause through pioneering and publicising many of the principles of the required way. Although this contribution will continue, from here on the transition will be mainly via a different process, that of the Transition Towns. The essential difference is not in goals but in means. The Transition Towns initiative involves beginning with existing towns and working to convert them into Ecovillages.

As has been explained, and cannot be stressed too much, the core problem in this revolution is not the actual building of new ways, it is the development of the consciousness that will lead people to want to build the new ways. People who join Eco-villages already have (at least some of) the necessary consciousness before they join. What we need is a process that will help more ordinary people to develop the necessary world view and desires. The Transition Town movement has by far the best potential formula here, because it enables us to work with and influence people unfamiliar with our vision and goals.

The Transition Towns Movement.

The Transition Towns movement has virtually exploded onto the scene since 2005. By early 2009 the website referred to 80 initiatives in the UK alone, and more in the US, New Zealand and Australia.

The movement emerged primarily because people in a number of English towns suddenly realised that a serious, terminal and insoluble shortage of petroleum is probably coming up fast. They grasped with alarm what this could mean and saw the urgent need to think about how their towns could be made more resilient, self-sufficient and independent of petroleum. (Hopkins, 2009).

The movement is drawing on many previously existing ideas and practices to do with local economic and social self-sufficiency. The potential list includes Community Supported Agriculture, farmers' markets, community gardens, LETSystems (to enable trade between people who have no money), town banks and business incubators, Permaculture, school gardens, the Slow Food movement, alternative technology groups, arts and crafts groups, mutual loan and insurance funds, and housing co-ops.

The great virtue of the Movement is that it can take advantage of and build on all the existing physical, economic and social structures that already exist in a town, whereas new Eco-villages would have to create these from scratch. That's years of effort saved. There are also pre-existing familiarity, community, mutuality, local knowledge, and people in familiar and stable circumstances. The people there know the place, the human and physical resources and they know what can and can't be done in view of the history, the locals and the conditions. The town also has lots of unused resources already there, vacant blocks, parks, sheds, backyards, surplus fruit trees, retired and unemployed people, and grandmas who know how to knit and bake dinners. Most of the world's people live in towns and suburbs so the task is to harness up and refocus the structures they already have.

In my very firm view this is, in general, the only way we can get to a satisfactory world. If we manage to get through the next fifty years to a tolerable world, then it will have been through some kind of grass roots Transition Towns process. (I have argued this for quite some time now, see for instance Trainer, 1985, 1995).

However I have serious concerns about the present Transition Towns movement and I fear that it could easily end up having made little contribution to the solution of global problems. Transitioners would probably be surprised and disappointed to hear this. Following is a brief indication of the thoughts first circulated in 2009.

Goals? Reform vs revolution?

As with Eco-villages, the main problem the movement sets is to do with what its goals are and ought to be. At this early stage it is perfectly understandable and inevitable that its goals are overwhelmingly reformist. The defining goal is to do with making towns more 'resilient', i.e. more able to withstand the onslaught of dwindling petroleum supply. The literature contains little or no reference to radical structural change of towns let alone of the national or the global economy. It does contain references to discontent with consumer society but the movement is not explicitly about replacing it. Some of its participants would probably say it is but a glance at the literature, the websites and at what is actually being done settles the argument. Participants are doing things like developing community supported agriculture and farmers' markets, planting community nut plantations and running courses on homecraft, activities, all of which are easily accommodated by consumer-capitalist society and are no potential threat to it... and cannot lead to its replacement.

Again, it is inevitable that as people begin to become concerned about difficulties in consumer society they will seek to deal with them by exploring minor and achievable immediate adjustments they can make within the existing society, such as setting up recycling and gardening groups. They will not at this early stage be thinking about goals like scrapping the economy. Thus the goals first taken on will inevitably be reforms achievable within consumer society, very distinct from major structural changes that would mean its replacement. So the question is will the movement someday shift from the present kinds of goals to those at the system replacement level, and what can and should we do to enable that shift?

This gets us into territory that most nice green people, and most transitioners find distinctly uncomfortable. Anyone who wants to talk in terms of reform vs revolution, and what the goals of the movement ought to be is sure to appear naïve, dated and doctrinaire (as feedback to me from people within the Transition Towns movement testifies!) I'm sorry, but as I see it the discussion in Part 2 supports some very confident assertions about the changes required, and they are not reforms. Consider again,

❑ Sustainability is not possible unless there is a zero growth economy, so the present economy has to be replaced.

❑ Sustainability requires shifting to very low levels of per capita consumption in an economy that has no growth, and this is impossible in the present economic system.

❑ Therefore a good society cannot be an affluent society, and this contradicts a consumer society.

❑ An economy that focuses on need, rights, justice, especially with respect to the Third World, and ecological sustainability cannot possibly be driven by market forces.

❑ The conditions of severe scarcity we are entering leave no choice but to shift to mostly small, highly self-sufficient local economies run by participatory procedures, and this contradicts present centralised and globalised political and economic paradigms.

❏ The more the individual competition within the market is allowed to determine what happens the more that social cohesion, community, collectivism and solidarity will be driven out.

❏ The basic values driving a good society cannot be individualism, competition and acquisitiveness.

At present the Green movement as a whole, and the Transition Towns movement in particular, reveals little or no recognition of these contradictions and is clearly not geared to the associated goals. If we ask what would we have to do in order to eventually achieve such huge and radical changes the answer goes far beyond the things that green and transition people are doing now.

Many people within the green movement assume that if we just work at establishing more and more of things like community gardens then in time this will have created the new society. This is seriously mistaken. It is the 'just do something/anything green' rationale. Just set up a community garden here, a nut tree plantation there, and eventually we will have built a satisfactory society. No need to think hard about ultimate goals. As Steffan (2009) has said '... just go ahead and do something, anything... All over the world, groups of people with graduate degrees, affluence, decades of work experience, varieties of advanced training and technological capacities beyond the imagining of our great-grandparents are coming together, looking into the face of apocalypse... and deciding to start a seed exchange or a kids clothing swap.'

If your goal was to build the kind of radically different society that Part 2 argued we must have you would very definitely not think it was sufficient or appropriate just to encourage a thousand flowers to bloom. You would think very carefully about what projects were most important to achieve that goal, you would realise that this must involve things like eventually scrapping a growth economy and taking collective control over the local economy, and you would recognise that some sub-goals would be much more likely than others to lead to such outcomes.

How could building more community gardens and recycling arrangements lead to the implementation of a zero-growth economy? There is no possibility of achieving such a goal unless at some point in time it becomes explicitly and strongly held by many people, and a great deal of work goes into moving from the present economy to such an economy. Just adding more community gardens etc. to the present consumer-capitalist society will only result in a consumer-capitalist society with more community gardens in it.

The goals evident within the present Transition Towns movement are easily accommodated within consumer-capitalist society and are no threat to it. They are more or less the lifestyle choices and hobby interests of a relatively few people and they will appeal to only that minority potentially interested in composting or organic food or Peraculture etc. Large numbers will not come to them unless they understand and accept the world view argued in Part 2, and just establishing more community gardens and recycling centres does little or nothing to increase that understanding.

If the movement does not go on to embrace the system-changing goals it is very likely to be only a NIMBY phenomenon, an attempt to insulate our town against the coming petroleum problem. Clearly 'resilience' is much too limited a goal, and it reveals the need for deeper thought about what's wrong with the world. The ultimate goal should be to build the kind of settlement, and wider economy, that would enable all the world's people to have a satisfactory life.

The prominent people within the Transition Towns movement seem to be very keen to avoid imposing their goals on it. They seem to see their role as facilitating it in going wherever it wants to go and not attempting to influence that direction. This politeness has been an attractive feature of the movement, but I think it reveals confusion about the state of things and what has to be done. There is of course no sense in trying to impose goals, but if Part 2 of this book is more or less valid then it is very important for those of us who see things that way to try to persuade transitioners to our view. It seems pretty clear that few within the movement at present do hold that view, because if they did they would not be happy just to see the movement go where the winds might take it and they would want to persuade participants to (eventually) adopt fundamental system change goals.

How do you make a town more 'resilient' anyway? The lack of guidance.

This general lack of any felt obligation to think about and choose between goals also feeds into the lack of guidance the Transition Towns literature offers for those who want to do something. The website, the handbook (Hopkins, 2009) and especially the Twelve Steps document are valuable, but they are predominantly about how to organise the movement (e.g. 'Awareness raising', 'Form subgroups', 'Build a bridge to local government'). It is remarkably difficult to find clear guidance as to what the sub-goals are, i.e. what to actually change in your town. People coming to the Movement will find little help in answering questions like, 'What projects should we plunge into because these will make our town more resilient? What should come first? What should we avoid? What projects have been found to be most effective? It is especially important that we can be shown the causal links, so we can see why setting up this venture will have the effect of creating greater town resilience. Without guidance of this kind the movement has been rightly criticised as simply encouraging anyone to do anything that takes their fancy. The only relevant reference in the current literature is the Twelfth Step in the much-celebrated list, which simply says 'Create an energy descent plan' without any indication of how we might do that or what it might involve.

The worry therefore is that the many people now flocking into Transition Towns initiatives will jump into all manner of projects without making much difference to the town's resilience, and in a few years there will be widespread disenchantment and drop off. If this happens it will be difficult to get anything resembling a Transition Towns movement going again.

What should be the near-term goal? Build a new economy, and run it!

In my view the focal concern of the movement should not be energy and its coming scarcity. Yes that sets the scene and the imperative, but the solution is not primarily to do with energy. It is to do with developing town economic self-sufficiency. As argued in previous chapters the top goal should be to build a radically new economy within our town, and to run it to meet our needs. It is not oil that sets your greatest insecurity; it is the global economy. This kind of vision and goal is not evident in the Transition Towns literature. It is the focal issue in the next Chapter.

If we focus on the goal of a local economy developed and run by us to meet our needs we realise we must somehow set up mechanisms which enable us to work out and operate a plan. It will not be ideal if we proclaim the importance of town self-sufficiency and then all run off as individuals to set up a bakery here and a garden there. This means that from the early stages we should set up some kind of Community Development Co-operative, and processes whereby we can come together regularly to discuss and think about a coordinated and unified town plan and our progress towards achieving it. It does not need to be elaborate or rigid, but we do need some agreement about priorities. We should think out what are our most urgent needs and what are our long term goals. What will the early working bees do? What co-ops do we need? Our most important projects will be collective, public works which provide crucial services for the town and these need to be formed by public processes.

Use of local currencies.

I have serious concerns about the schemes for creating local currencies being adopted by the Transition Towns movement and I do not think the initiatives I am aware of are going to have desirable effects. It is not evident that they are based on rationales that make sense and enable one to see why they will have desirable effects. Most seem to do no more than substitute new notes for old money.

The main point of introducing new currencies is to increase the amount of desirable economic activity, especially to enable the many people who are not able to produce or purchase or otherwise obtain necessities to start doing so. Just enabling those with money to swap some of it for notes we have printed cannot do this. Chapter 14 offers a strategy whereby the local currency helps to get neglected productive capacity to work to meet neglected needs.

Conclusions.

The Transition Towns movement is characterised by a remarkable burst of enthusiasm and energy. This seems to reflect a long pent up disenchantment with consumer-capitalist society and a desire for something better. This book argues that the inexorable logic evident in our situation means that the only way out of the alarming global predicament we are in has to be via a Transition Towns movement of some kind. To our great good fortune one has burst on the scene. But the worry is that it could very easily fail to make a significant difference and could end up wasting our one and only chance. My great hope is that this book will help to take the movement beyond its present goals and to gear it to a much more radical vision.

It should be noted that the kind of movement I think we need is not likely to develop quickly. The next Chapter offers considerable detail regarding what we might do, but this should be seen as an agenda it might take us twenty years to get going well. At first and for a long time we might not be able to do much more than take small and humble steps, but that doesn't matter so long as we have clearly in mind where they are heading.

'But setting examples, exhortations and lifestyle changes will not produce revolution.'

The transition strategy being advocated is easily misunderstood. It has been criticised as essentially being only about setting examples and hoping they will be followed, or about exhorting people to change their lifestyles. Thus some people dismiss the Eco-Village and Transition Towns movements as incapable of revolutionary potential. This general claim about the insufficiency of examples and exhortation is in my view quite correct --- but it does not apply to The Simpler Way strategy.

The revolution will not be a matter of simply setting examples that will automatically attract people to follow and that will thereby eventually accumulate into the revolutionary change of the whole society. As I have stressed several times the core problem is one of ideology or consciousness. Vast and radical system change is not possible unless people in general come to think and value in very different ways to those dominant in this society. Its intrinsic and inescapable injustice and lack of sustainability must come to be clearly understood and regarded as totally unacceptable. This cannot come to be the case without a great deal of educational and political work. At the core of The Simpler Way strategy is the conviction that by far the best base from which to do this awareness raising work will be our involvement in building living examples of the required alternative settlements and institutions. By working side by side with our neighbours in the gardens and co-ops we will be in the best position to communicate our vision, i.e. to explain the huge structural changes necessary and how they can be approached through the things we are doing in the gardens and co-ops we are working within.

The coalition enlistment task.

There are at present millions of people all around the world working for good causes which I have argued are mistakenly geared only to the reform of consumer-capitalist society, and are incapable of solving the problems. The implication is not that we should dismiss these initiatives or refuse to work with them. What we should do is try to bring them all into a huge broad coalition concerned with many distinct aspects of the overall problem but united under a shared vision which recognises that bandaids are not enough and that they cannot achieve their many sub-goals unless and until we move to some kind of Simpler Way. The aim is for us all to see our groups and movements as working in our separate domains and on our particular campaigns in order to advance the general vision. Often this would involve a broadening and extending of the present goals of the various movements, a coming to see how their goals can be part of a much bigger picture.

The (exhasperating) Men's Shed Movement.

The Men' Shed Movement is a marvellous initiative providing many mostly older men with a source of activity, purpose and company, especially those retired, divorced or isolated. It is extremely valuable in the psychological support, leisure, creativity, community and mentoring it enables. It must be saving state budgets huge sums.

But look at what else they could be doing! Why not go out and tackle some projects in the locality, identifying some needs and organising to deal with them. How about connecting with teenagers and working out how to get them into making things, or door knocking to find out whether elderly people might come down for a regular cuppa at the shed and a sharing of their skills, or planting a community orchard, or setting up some fish tanks, or starting a repair and recycling operation...

Similarly what about all the churches with land, premises, people, money and time that could be put into such initiatives. Could they assist local poor and homeless people more effectively than by setting up community gardens and workshops so people could enjoy producing some of the things they need?

In other words, think bigger, go out into the community and start throwing your weight around, identify needs and take action... and start taking some control over local affairs. That'll give you a sense of purpose and power!

The Simpler Way strategy; A summary of principles.

Chapter 13 will offer the practical steps in the strategy this book has been building towards. This chapter has prepared the way by arguing the following points regarding the theory and philosophy of social change relevant to our situation.

❑ The coming era of scarcity will impose conditions that rule out most of the theoretical options previously assumed regarding getting to post-capitalist society.

❑ A sustainable and just society has to be conceived primarily in terms of localised economies under the participatory control of local people, using local resources to meet needs. This has profound implications for how we can transition to it.

❑ The Simpler Way cannot be given nor imposed by force. It is about institutions, processes and skills which the people in a town have developed, which suit their social and ecological conditions, and which draw out conscientiousness and energetic and enjoyed contributions. Without this good will and satisfaction The Simpler Way will not work. States cannot create or enforce these ways. In any case states function in the interests of the dominant classes and can not be expected to facilitate the replacement of consumer-capitalist society.

❑ It is a mistake to think that the old ways must be eliminated before we can start to build the new ways.

- ❏ There are many possible action strategies that can be seen to be mistaken in view of the situation explained in Part 2.
- ❏ The most important concern must be world view or consciousness. What matters more than anything else is getting people to see and feel strongly about a) the fact that consumer-capitalist society is extremely unsustainable, unjust, and socially unacceptable, and b) that there is a much better way. If this outlook is held people will build the necessary structures and ways. If it is not then no amount of state power or force by a vanguard party can get us to where we need to go. Everything therefore depends on whether we can develop that outlook.
- ❏ The conclusions derived in previous chapters confirm a basically Anarchist transition philosophy.
- ❏ We must therefore start now building those aspects of the new way we can in the places where we live. This is because a) we need to have the new ways established as extensively as we can by the time consumer-capitalist society starts to fail seriously, so that people can see the alternatives and start moving across to them, and more importantly, b) because the building will give us the best possible opportunities to do the awareness raising work among our neighbours.
- ❏ The transition process can only take the form of existing communities moving to take control over their own affairs, slowly learning how to do it well in the ways that suit them. No other way is possible. Governments can't organise or give the new structures or force us to adopt them.
- ❏ There is now a Transition Towns movement heading more or less in the right direction and it will greatly accelerate as consumer-capitalist society increasingly fails to provide. This is the most effective arena in which to work.
- ❏ However at this stage the Transition Towns movement is (understandably) not geared to the goals that matter most.
- ❏ There will be no significant or large scale change while the supermarket shelves remain well stocked. Only when people are jolted hard by something like a major petroleum shortfall will they realise that the old system will not provide for them and that they must start thinking seriously about The Simpler Way.

❏ The magnitude of the change could not be exaggerated. It is about vast, radical and historically unprecedented change in economic, political, social, and cultural systems, and in the geography of settlements. Therefore governments cannot make the changes required; they are far too big for our political systems to cope with. They can only come through communities taking control of their own affairs as they start to feel the need.

❏ It could be a thoroughly peaceful revolution, even though it is about intense class conflict and the end of capitalism. It could be essentially a turning away from the consumer way to take up the frugal, self-sufficient, local, communal and participatory ways which will obviously be the best options.

❏ Our chances of success are not at all good. However there are some important factors in our favour. Firstly people will be forced by the coming scarcity to give up the old ways and to move in the general direction of localism. The conditions we will experience will tend to require and reward good values and behaviours, especially involvement, conscientiousness, cooperation, mutual aid, responsibility and enthusiasm.

❏ The window of opportunity will be short given the approach of the 2030 spike. Scarcity could hit too suddenly for sensible responses and descent into conflict and squalor are quite possible, given the present lamentable state of awareness.

❏ Therefore the task for people concerned about the fate of the planet is clearly set. We must plunge into getting those local systems going, with a view to using them to develop the crucial global consciousness.

What is the strategic implication for those many activists presently saving whales and forests and establishing community gardens? It is to go on doing what you are doing... but with the big picture in mind so that you do those things in order to be in the best position to raise the critical global consciousness of the people you are working beside. In other words, go on working hard to set up the gardens and recycling centres in order to do the consciousness raising work. Right now building the new institutions is not the main goal, important though it is. What matters most is helping others see that it is crucial to build them because we have to replace consumer-capitalist society.

So we must watch for opportunities to start setting up those crucial local collectivist institutions presently not being established, or even considered, the mechanisms whereby we can start coming together to take control of our local economic fate and start building our Economy B. This might take the form of calling meetings just to discuss the town's problems and needs and what we might collectively try do about some of them. Can we for instance set up a community garden to enable unemployed and homeless people to produce some of the things they need? Can we try voluntary working bees to help meet some of the needs of aged or young people around here, or give free labour to struggling little firms the town needs but are being squeezed by the supermarkets, or set up a tiny market that will enable some people to sell small amounts of home-produced items...

Everything depends on vision, goals and consciousness. If most people saw the need for The Simpler Way and wanted to establish it, we'd get this revolution through in a matter of months! We are however highly unlikely to avoid catastrophic global breakdown, because the mainstream remains obsessed with growth and affluence despite decades of effort many have made to expose those delusions. Clearly our top priority must be to work at changing this distressing lack of awareness, vision and concern. There's not much point establishing nice green things unless we are doing so in order to develop the necessary critical global awareness. There's nothing more important to do, and it can be done via the projects that green and sustainability people are working on, just by making the awareness raising the main purpose of their work.

My question to all who want to see a better society is, if you agree with the arguments in Parts 1 and 2 above, then how could there be any better arena and strategy for working on the consciousness raising task than the local community initiatives emerging? My plea addressed to all good people in green and red organisations, and those in between, is please think carefully about whether there is any more effective activity to put your scarce energies into. What we need most urgently now is not another book or academic paper, or campaign to save the whale, or green politician, or compost heap, or Prius. What could be more important than coming over to help us begin here and now to build inspiring elements of the new society – primarily in order to influence the thinking of one's co-workers. That is by far the most effective and subversive thing you can do.

There could not be a more safe and enjoyable revolution to join! No need to risk anything. No need to learn how to use an AK-47. No need to give up your career. No need to fight anyone head on. No need to fear arrest. No need to make any sacrifice at all. And no need to struggle for decades before you have any chance of enjoying some of the experiences the revolution is for, such as the building, the camaraderie, the good food, the concerts, the supportive community, the beautiful landscapes... and the greater peace of mind.

What if we fail?

But let's assume that we will inevitably fail – then we should nevertheless strive to build The Simple Way now. Why? Because it is most important to have established the alternative ways in the cultural memory, to have got these ideas into as many minds and records and libraries as possible. If and when people struggle out of the rubble after the collapse of growth and greed society then the chances of them not going down that path again will be greater the more successful we are now in establishing the sensible ways. Chances like this are extremely rare. Lenin got the opportunity but took the industrial consumer path with no consideration of any other possibility. Gandhi managed to get the right path on the agenda, an India of simpler ways in self-sufficient villages, but Nehru took India down the industrial path. Such monumental choices will not go the right way unless there is widespread understanding of what the right way is. The achievements of the Spanish Anarchists were made possible by the prevalence of strong and deep ideas and values which had been developed over many previous decades. Although tragically faded in memories and literatures, those achievements have left a trace in our intellectual history. They showed that ordinary people can do miracles, and this is remembered, faintly but significantly. If we now try again and fail we can at least hope that we will have added a little to the accumulating human understanding of what has to be The Way.

Chapter 13

A PRACTICAL STRATEGY

This chapter sets out the kind of action strategy I think will be the most effective for those who wish to help save the planet. It is built on the argument elaborated through the previous 12 Chapters. I believe they constitute a weighty case against most previous thinking about how to bring about social change and against most of the planet-saving effort presently being made. The argument has been that these ground-clearing considerations point to one and only one general approach. Its theoretical form has been offered in Chapter 13. This Chapter translates those conclusions into practical steps.

So there you are, living in a typical suburb within consumer society, and surrounded by people who only know the consumer way and are unaware of the need to shift the world to very different ways, quickly. What on earth should you do?

The following sequence of practical steps is set out as if a small group is starting from scratch, the only ones in the town who have the vision, and as if they are without any assistance from official bodies. Often conditions will be much more favourable than this. Sometimes local councils will be eager to help with many of our proposals and many local people will be interested in or already doing some of the things suggested.

I have argued this general strategy for a long time (e.g. see Trainer, 1985, 1995). It is most encouraging that in recent years the Transition Towns movement has taken off more or less in this general direction (although I doubt that's due to any influence I have had). There are some significant differences between what is happening in the movement and the ideas in this Chapter, and my hope is that in time the movement will take up the ideas offered here.

1. Form a Community Development Cooperative.

A small group of people simply begins meeting as an embryonic Community Development Cooperative (hereafter CDC). This will eventually develop into the institution which organises and 'runs' the town's new economic, political, ecological and social systems, but at first it would be tiny with very humble goals.

The CDC will think about the town's many unmet needs and its many unused productive resources. Any neighbourhood has unemployed people, all that time spent watching TV, unused backyards and nature strips and school yards, retired people, skills and the immense untapped good will and energy that people could give to the cause. The town also has vast unmet needs, including the need for more basic food, furniture, entertainment, etc., the need for livelihoods and for the sense of making a valued contribution, for community, solidarity, friendship, comradeship, worthwhile activities for young people and a sense of having some power over the control of local affairs. So our task is to harness and connect and organise, to begin applying some of that unused productive capacity to producing to meet some of those unsatisfied needs.

2. Set up a community garden and workshop.

The ideal project to begin with is the establishment of a cooperative garden and workshop. Even if only on a very small scale this quickly gives the capacity to grow and make many important things participants need. While it might be decided to also enable individuals to garden their own private plots, the central function must be to organise a cooperative 'firm" whereby people can work together to produce things they all need. This enables working bees to get the site into shape and to share the thinking, the expertise and research, and to share the produce. It also means that if only one person knows how to grow good vegies, we can all have good vegies.

Now we have the means to begin providing for those many people dumped by the conventional economy. We make it possible for local people who are unemployed, homeless, convalescent or retired. to join us in productive activity, working to start producing vegetable, repairs, toys, for ourselves and each other.

We will record time inputs to the cooperative firm with a view to sharing output in proportion to these contributions. Thus someone who can only come along occasionally can be part of the team. (What we have done here is create a new currency, i.e. 'print' our own money. The significance of this will be elaborated below).

Every carrot we produce represents a saving of scarce money participants do not have to spend at the supermarket. More importantly we have begun to create livelihoods, purposes, community and cooperative skills, leisure resources and a cooperative climate... and a new economy.

3. What else can we do?

The CDC would then look for other activities to take up. What else could we produce for ourselves, cooperatively and without much capital? Bread is an obvious possibility. We could research and build an earth oven, buy a bag of flour, and organise a weekly bake-up to churn out stacks of irresistible hot bread, pizzas, biscuits and cakes. Baking day would then become the beginning of the weekly community working bee, business meeting, banquet and concert.

Of course all the way we will be publicising and recruiting, knocking on doors to explain what's going on and to invite people to join us. Remember our primary objective is not to build things, it is to develop in people the consciousness that will lead them to build eagerly.

Our working bees will build the benches, seats and shade houses, and landscape the garden the workshop site. We will find out who can play musical instruments, tell jokes, act and sing, and we will then organises the first concert. We will celebrate our productivity and power and take pride in the way we are providing for each other. We are not just providing vegies and bread but solidarity and the satisfaction that comes from knowing we have started the revolution!

What about food processing, such as buying bulk fruit and bottling or drying, making juices, fruit wines and cider? What then to do with the peelings? Of course, feed them to the newly acquired rabbits and poultry, which we will locate in pens the working bees will build and which will become vegie patches when the animals have cleared them up and fertilized them. The duck ponds will produce large volumes of rich sludge for the gardens. We will plant the communal herb patches, fruit trees, and in time make the fish ponds and the sheds for the beekeeping equipment. Meanwhile sub-groups will research all this and set up committees to look after the fish, rabbits and bees.

We will organise to buy things in bulk, setting up sub-committees to find the best places to get flour, jars, nuts and bolts. We will scrounge the treasure thrown out on council clean up days, to accumulate the wood and iron we can use in the workshop, and the bikes and appliances we can fix to use or sell.

It is difficult to understand why so few charitable agencies, especially churches, have not set up ventures like this. (An inspiring example is The Homeless Garden Project based in California). The standard charitable organization confines itself to merely giving things to 'disadvantaged' people, especially money so they can buy more from supermarkets. Consider the typical old person's 'home' where expensive buildings and staff tend to people who have almost nothing to do all day, when they could have a thriving mixed garden with animals and workers right in their midst. Some could join in and others could just watch and chat... while the institution's food bill was reduced. In Holland such gardens have been found to have beneficial effects on dementia sufferers.

After we get our operations at the garden and workshop site under way and in the backyards of participants, we can explore harnessing other resources in the neighbourhood and taking on other activities there. Are there sheds and trucks, tools, machinery and waste products we can get access to, especially bits of land on which we might plant commons? Can we put in small dams and ponds for water plants and fish, develop pits for clay and earth for building? Can we stack some areas with edible herbs, such as New Zealand spinach that will thrive almost anywhere? Can we arrange with councils how to get access to the vast amount of treasure that goes into waste tips, especially the building and craft materials, the appliances and bikes we can repair. (Eventually we will operate these salvage and recycling depots).

Councils are likely to give us permission to plant and maintain small herb patches, bush tucker, bee hives, bamboos, fruit and nut groves and timber trees on public land. Much can be done without their approval or knowledge though. In some cities 'green guerrillas' just plant on vacant land.

Our working bees and committees will organise and run these activities. These projects out in the community will be very powerful educational devices, enabling us to explain our project to people. We will publicise the up-coming working bees and identify them not as owned by the CDC but as town events in which all are invited to contribute. We will be seen to be working for the good of the town, we will be showing how the town can get together to do important things for itself, and we will be explaining our vision.

We will set up a market day so that people can exchange their garden and craft produce with each other, and sell surpluses to the townspeople. This helps to connect our new economy with the old one, earn us more normal money, and spread awareness of our project to more people. Our market will only sell important items, not trinkets, and only items made locally, not imports. If possible our Saturday morning stalls will be set up in a prominent position. Market day has very important social, political and educational functions. It gives us the opportunity to discuss issues and work towards consensus decisions about what is best for the town.

Remember, the most important work we are doing is not feeding ourselves or providing livelihoods or community. It is educating the town, increasing the numbers who understand our perspective and who will join us, if not now then when the crunches begin. Nothing will be more effective in this campaign than real life visible activities whereby we can be seen to be practising the new ways. Behind one of our stalls will be a big map of the town as we think it could be restructured, with many streets converted to gardens and commons.

Everything will be discussed at the community meetings. The group as a whole will thereby be developing the skills needed to make good decisions about priorities and what's feasible and how best to organise. We will be learning the art of self government.

Leisure, entertainment, celebrations, festivals and culture.

A committee will focus on the possibilities for providing local and free entertainment, eventually including regular concerts, dances, visiting speakers, local artists, craft and produce shows, art galleries, discussion groups, book clubs, picnic days and festivals. Can we form a drama club, a comedy group, a choir, a gym display troupe? After the Saturday morning market we might establish an afternoon working bee followed by a town meeting, games, evening meal, party and performances of some sort? What regular celebrations, rituals and festivals can be organised? Can we get a group to work on the local history, museum, culture and folklore? Eventually we will think about ways in which the town centre could be made into a more convivial space that will facilitate informal meeting, discussion and leisure activities? Of course it is not that these are novel ideas. Many country towns are well aware of the importance of these sorts of activities and projects and most councils engage in some of them But at the neighbourhood and suburban level cars are not necessary for access.

Setting up small family firms and co-ops.

If the CDC's bee keeping operation goes well, and Fred's family really enjoys running it, we might set it up as a fairly independent firm 'leased' to Fred. Thus the CDC is in a position to create firms and livelihoods. It can give people the satisfaction of running their own little enterprise, enjoying making a valued contribution to the community. Our power to do these things derives from the fact that we have working bees, community expertise, our own bank (below) and buying power. Our working bees can quickly build the sheds and we would buy from Fred rather than the supermarket.

But what if Fred tried to become the regional honey tycoon, trying to drive other honey producers out of business and take over their operations? If he tried to do that we would simply refuse to buy from him. But he would not be likely to do it because he would realise that the goal now has to be building town solidarity and security and enjoying a livelihood, a modest but sufficient income, and working for the common good, or we will all go down. The CDC will not be in the business of setting up little entrepreneurs with an opportunity to get rich. It will be in the business of establishing the town's capacity to produce the many basic things it needs and give worthwhile activity to unemployed people, and Fred knows he's there to help fulfil the need for honey, and that if he does this he will get milk and eggs from others making their contributions.

It should be apparent to all involved that the whole approach must be basically collectivist. Although small private firms might make up the biggest sector of the new economy, especially family businesses and farms, it cannot be got going or kept in good shape unless it is guided by concern to work out and set up what is in the best interests of the town. Many crucial functions must be organised, planned, coordinated, monitored, regulated, revised etc. This could not happen in an economy made up of many competing private firms. In conditions of serious scarcity that would quickly lead to a few most 'efficient' winning and driving the rest out of business, and out of town, resulting before long in the collapse of the town.

One problem here is that councils and other agencies have unnecessarily expensive standards, especially regarding house construction. For instance their room sizes, ceiling heights, and materials rules help to make a house cost perhaps ten times as much as it should. Councils also often have silly rules inhibiting the keeping of poultry and animals in suburban areas, food processing and cooperative projects. However, when the time of troubles impacts most of these rules will be quickly swept away as everyone realises that it is essential to facilitate the maximum amount of local productive activity.

The significance of beginning our tiny CDC and the garden and the little productive enterprises and the working bees and commons cannot be exaggerated. To start doing this even in the most humble way is to have begun to develop totally different economic, political, social, geographical and cultural systems. These activities, no matter how small in scale at first, constitute systems that contradict and spurn the acquisitiveness, competition, individualism, power, greed, affluence and growth that drive the normal economy. Just to have got the CDC going is to have put in place astoundingly revolutionary new social forms. All that remains to be done is extend it to include the town, then the region, then...

Go out into the locality and start doing something!

I think it is symbolically important at some early stage for us to find some need in the locality that does not affect the CDC's welfare but which we can take action on. Maybe it's assisting a youth group, or a struggling family, or some homeless people. This is to take our first step towards taking responsibility for and control over our town. We are not going to leave that problem to the officials, who aren't dealing with it anyway. We will go over there and see what we can do about it. This is the stroppy attitude that will drive the new economy – this is our town and its our business what's going on here and we want to know what problems there are around here and we will take action on them.

The suggestion is that it would be good for us to take on a job of this kind, early on, to start getting the hang of such action and building our confidence about it.

Connecting with the normal/old town economy.

So far the discussion has been about starting to create a new economy operating beside the old one, mostly involving people excluded from the old one. Right from the beginning the new economy can achieve miracles but there will be many things we can't produce and which can only be obtained from the old/normal economy. It has many things such as radios and computers that we will want to use. How then can we who have little or no normal money begin to trade with the normal economy?

The core and obvious point here is that we cannot get things from the old economy unless we can sell things to it. The CDC therefore has to begin researching and consulting in order to find items that it can begin selling to firms in the old/normal economy. A likely beginning point might be to trade vegetables, fish, fruit and poultry with the town restaurant in exchange for meals we can buy from it, using our currency.

The restaurant would be very keen to trade with us, because we represent a large amount of potential demand for meals which previously the restaurant was not able to tap (because most of us were unemployed we could not afford to eat there). We open up for him the possibility of selling a lot of dinners, but only if our new currency is used, because we can't pay for meals in the old currency, because we haven't got much/any of it. He can only sell meals to us if he accepts payment in the money we will create for the purpose (see below), and he can't do that unless he can spend that money buying something he needs from us. It is our capacity to produce and sell something that is crucial, not the existence of the currency.

Thus we will begin to trade with the town. The extent of this trade will be limited by how many things it needs that we can produce and the CDC must work hard on this. The problem will be greatly reduced as petroleum becomes scarcer, because that will devastate the capacity of the town's old firms to import goods to sell. They will have to get those things from local suppliers, or do without them, and thus we will have opportunities to take up some of this productive activity.

We will have to make sure everyone understands that our new economic sector with its new firms and money are no threat to the old one. Old firms are not going to see us as taking business from them, because those firms are only going to sell (for our new money) to people who do not have much old money and therefore wouldn't have been buying from old/normal firms anyway. The CDC will not start producing things that are already being produced in the town. For instance if we were to set up a bakery and take sales from the existing bakery that would only be to put it out of business with no net gain in town jobs, bread supply or welfare. However we would not hesitate to compete with and take business from firms that are selling imported goods (and help the locals who worked there to move into our new firms).

Focusing on frugality, sufficiency, what is good-enough.

Right from the start we will make it clear that we reject the affluent consumer way. This will be evident in our attitude to 'standards'. We will insist on providing what is sufficient in the resource, dollar and ecologically cheapest ways. We will in principle reject luxurious and new things and this will be visible in our early projects. We will make do, patch up, be content with what is good enough, and spurn the best, and we will explain why we will assert the moral superiority of out standards, and point to their effect on our footprint and dollar cost of living.

The role of money.

Very important in the development of the new economy is the creation of our own money, which the Community Development Cooperative will use to enable economic activity among those who the conventional economy forces into idleness, unemployment and poverty.

There is much confusion about the nature and function of local currencies and often proposed schemes would not have desirable effects. All money has to be created, somewhere, somehow, and got into circulation. Chapter 4 discussed the absurd and unacceptable way this is done in the normal economy. There is a tendency in alternative circles to proceed as if just creating an alternative or local currency of any old kind would do wonders, without any thinking through of how it is supposed to work. It will not have desirable effects unless it is carefully designed to do so.

What would happen if new money was introduced by giving it to poor people to spend in participating shops? When the poor recipients had spent the money they would still be without a productive role or the capacity to go on earning an income. And on what would the participating shops spend the new money they had accepted? This situation could be avoided only if those low-income people had been able to get into lasting productive roles, so that they could continually produce and sell things to those shops, enabling the shops to use the money they took in.

Similarly, what if the council created new money, spent it into circulation by paying previously unemployed people to build a swimming pool, and accepting part of their rate payments in new money? After the pool had been completed those workers would again be without income and the council would have nothing on which to spend the rate income.

The same general problems arise with LETSystems. These give people the capacity to pay for goods just by writing 'IOUs'.

This can be quite helpful, enabling some people without normal money to trade some things. However the problem is that most people do not have much they can sell, i.e. they do not have many productive skills or the capital to set up a firm. It is therefore not surprising that LETSystems typically do not grow to account for more than a very small proportion of a town's economic activity. (Douthwaite, 1996). What is needed and what LETSystems do not create well is productive capacity, enterprises. A LETSystem will not set up a cooperative bakery in which many people with little or no skill can be organised to produce their own bread.

So the crucial element becomes clear. Nothing significant can be achieved unless people acquire the capacity to produce and sell things that others want. Obviously, unless one produces and sells to others one can't earn the money with which to purchase things one needs from others. So the question we have to focus on is how can the introduction of a new currency facilitate this setting up of 'firms' that will enable those who had no economic role to start producing, selling, earning, buying. The crucial task is to create productive roles, not to create a currency. The new currency should be seen as little more than an accounting device, a necessary but not the most important factor. And the crucial question should be, how can we use a new currency to help get production going by people who are idle.

The way we might best introduce a new currency has been noted above. The CDC has set up the cooperative garden 'firm' and invited people to come along and work in it, recording time contributions, with the intention of sharing produce later in proportion to contributions. The slips of paper issued when one has worked an hour function like an IOU or 'promissory note'. These slips are new money. They can be used to get, buy, garden produce. The key element here is the organising of the productive opportunities, the setting up of the 'firm' which enables people to have 'jobs' and this is not done just by creating a currency.

Note that the bits of paper are not actually promissory notes. We would all understand that all participants share the risk that the crop will fail. (In a satisfactory society all would share the risks associated with major investment decisions, which are made by all of us to achieve goals we all endorse). The slips

312

of paper would be understood as records of what proportion of the product each contributor was entitled to when it became available.

When we then set up the baking venture the time inputs will again be tallied and now those who do the baking can use their time credits to buy vegetables produced by the gardeners, and vici versa. We will have begun to diversify our new economy, and that will function on our new currency.

It would be best to use an hour's work as the unit of currency, regardless of what activity it goes into or what differences the normal economy would put on the various things people produce in their hour. In other words we would be working for 'time dollars.' This is done in a number of communities. Because most or all of us will be using relatively simple skills there is not likely to be a problem of some thinking their hour is more productive or worth more than that someone else puts in. All that matters is that everyone contributes conscientiously, although some will do a bit more in the hour than others.

Consider recessions.

Now let us take a moment to reflect on the appalling fact that recessions, depressions and unemployment are allowed to occur. Hundreds of millions of people are condemned to go without livelihoods, enough money, purpose, or self respect, for years - when all this would be totally and easily prevented, just by doing what the above CDC has done? If the economy begins to slow, causing unemployment, a government could simply set up cooperatives in which unemployed people could - you guessed it - organise themselves to work to produce many of the simple things they need. The start-up and administration expenditure would be far less than the savings in unemployment benefits and social breakdown, let alone in quality of life. These people would be producing, running the organization, largely or wholly off the 'welfare' budget, enjoying life, and paying tax.

So why isn't this done? Why did more than 15% of Australian workers have to endure unemployment and degradation for years after 1929? Why isn't it done now, to eliminate the deprivation and depression of the unemployed millions today? The answer of course is that the kind of solution outlined is totally unacceptable in capitalist society. It would be (gasp) 'socialism', and everyone knows that is stupid, evil and does not work.

So in parts of East Timor and PNG they tolerate unemployment rates of 70%, because everybody accepts that there can be no development unless someone with capital decides to set up an enterprise that will make more money for himself than investing in anything else anywhere else in the world. Then they are surprised and dismayed to find that the bored, hungry and angry young men join rebel gangs and armies, which are of course immediately identified as 'insurgents' (used to be 'communists') and therefore must be crushed to restore (capitalist) order.

Capital; Form a town bank

In general very little capital will be needed to get the new local economy going because the main enterprises are mostly humble and labour-intensive and do not need elaborate premises or expensive machinery or purchased stock. The CDC can organise campaigns to accumulate voluntary donations of capital for particularly important development projects. Some communities have low or zero interest town development accounts into which those who are willing and able deposit some of their savings because they wish to support desirable local development. The CDC can also operate voluntary taxation schemes. (In a sensible world most of the normal tax revenue would be collected locally and spent locally). Note how those developments can proceed even if only a small number of people support them; it is usually not the case that nothing worthwhile can be done unless everyone agrees. On some communes only those who want to see a particular project undertaken contribute capital to it.

The town or region should at some stage establish its own bank or credit union. Normal banks take our savings and lend them to corporations far away. Our town bank should have as one of its rules that the savings of local people will only be lent for projects within the region and that top priority will go to borrowers who intend to develop the town in desirable ways. This means depositors will probably be subsidising town development. The bank which gives low or zero interest loans to worthwhile ventures and does not make the highest returns on all loans will probably not be able to offer to its depositors interest rates as high as they could get from banks that are only concerned with making as much money as possible. Again this is a price we will be willing to pay in order to make sure that (some of) our savings go into developments that will improve our town. (Eventually, in a zero-growth economy, there can be no interest payments). However our bank will not be drained by outrageous executive salaries and bonuses or shareholder dividends, and you will have a say in its lending and investment decisions. All its officers might be voluntary.

Along with the bank we will form a business incubator, to give new little firms assistance with accounting and tax advice, access to computers, perhaps premises, and especially expertise from our panel of the town's most experienced business people. Along with our bank this will put us in a powerful position to take more control over our own economic development. We can set up the firms we want, even if they might not be profitable, create jobs and livelihoods, cut town imports, and reduce dependence on the global economy and on oil.

The remarkable success over many decades of the Spanish Mondragon Cooperative movement testifies to the power of these institutions and this approach. Largely because the town formed its own cooperative bank and advisory institutions it has been able to build many modern and powerful businesses capable of succeeding in international trade (not that we will want to do that). Similarly the achievements of the Spanish Anarchist collectives of the 1930s showed how socially beneficial development can take place rapidly when people have control over factories land banks.

Another important task right from the earliest days is to make links with groups that can be enlisted and assisted — and helped to see what we are on about... the charities, churches, welfare agencies, aged people's homes, Lions and Rotary service clubs, farmers markets, youth-off-the-street initiatives, indigenous, drug and alcohol rehabilitation, parole support, slow food, Men's Shed movement...

Building a new local economy which we run.

Now look what we have done. We have built a radically new economy, one which all of us participate in making rational decisions about what we need and therefore are going to produce cooperatively. Even though it might be tiny for a long time, it is an economy which we run to do what we want done. We can therefore begin to eliminate unemployment and poverty and homelessness in our town and provide livelihoods and security to all. We have not waited for government or the economy to provide for us, we got out there and did it for ourselves. Do we have lonely old people or bored youth around here – well let's just see what we can organise to get rid of these problems.

The significance of this attitude could not be exaggerated. Although for a long time we might not have the capacity to exercise much control over anything important, that's where we must be clearly determined to go from the start. So our orientation will not be centred on encouraging little entrepreneurs to set up, or households to take up gardening, or the town to plant an orchard... within the old framework of individuals and groups functioning in a town that's part of consumer capitalist society and whose fate is mostly left to global market forces and officials from the council and the state. What we are about is gradually taking cooperative responsibility and control over our town and talking it out of consumer-capitalist society and running it to meet our needs.

The two level economy.

We should be keenly aware that what we are doing can be put in terms of building and running Economy B, the one which ensures that all our basic needs are provided for. Many will live well almost entirely within Economy B because they opt to live very simply, produce much in their home gardens, contribute to community working bees and networks, and meet many needs via commons and the giving/gift sectors. However for a long time most of us will probably also be involved in Economy A which will be the (possibly large) remnant of the present economy. In this economy mostly non-essential but desirable goods and services will be produced for sale, we will work for money, and we will be able to purchase imports to the town. However economy A could collapse without harming us because Economy B is the one that will provide and guarantee our quality of life. No matter what happens to the global economy we know we can always produce all the carrots, repairs, jobs and concerts we need, totally secure because we are in complete control of these processes.

The transition will be a gradual stepping from Economy A to Economy B. At first we will not be able to provide much for ourselves but as we get more activities going our dependence on the normal economy will decline. In the very long term it will probably make sense to completely shift Economy A's remaining components into Economy B, so that everything is rationally planned and cooperatively organised.

Learning to govern ourselves.

As our scope increases we will be making more and bigger decisions and this will involve us in working out by trial and error and a lot of careful thinking what are the best ways for us to do this. The first tiny CDC discussions around the pot belly stove in the workshop will grow towards eventually becoming town meetings and along the way we will be focussed by our circumstances on what is best for the collective, what are the best ways to find agreement, how best to handle disagreements, to make sure all feelings have been expressed, how to monitor, review and revise our decisions. We will be learning a very different political process, one that cannot be about engineering 51% majorities that force the rest to comply. We will be in situations where it is glaringly obvious that we must find ways that all can see are the best, and therefore ways all will willingly support.

Reducing town importing and exporting; making the town more self-sufficient

In time we must work on enabling the town and its nearby region to produce as many of the things it needs as possible from local resources. At present most people live in suburbs which must depend almost entirely on imported goods and services. This means huge costs in terms of energy, resources, footprints, and dollars, and it means dependence on the fickle, treacherous and predatory global economy. People must export a lot to earn the money with which to import a lot via the supermarkets. So when a poor country has sold off all its forests it will have to find something else to sell. It must worry that at any moment the global economy could trash it. The main export from Rich World suburbs is labour and this cannot be sold without travelling a long way to work. The coming petroleum crunch will wreak havoc on that arrangement. You and your neighbours will wish desperately that you could provide for yourself without this dependence on exporting and importing.

There are five areas in which the CDS must work in order to help increase local economic self-sufficiency.

a) Setting up import-replacing firms.

The CDC must look for items which can be imported into the town but might be produced locally. Can we encourage and assist existing firms to take on such ventures. What firms do we need? Do we need and can we organise a bike repairer, shoe repairer, bee keeper, butcher, jam maker, fish farm, poultry farm, baker, house insulator, mini-dairy? Can we develop some local energy sources, windmills, water wheels, woodlots, ethanol plants? What firms are producing non-necessities and might be persuaded that their fate is precarious and that they should try to deal in local wares. How can we help them to do this? How can we make sure no one crashes into bankruptcy and has to leave town? We are in a powerful position to lever the transition of firms, because we can bring into play our working bees, town banks and business incubators, new money and our power to purchase or boycott. We can for instance build the dirt-cheap mud brick premises for the baker or bee keeper.

As petroleum becomes scarce the town will be rapidly increasing its understanding that we must assist these developments by at times subsidising, paying more and helping, or the town will not have affordable honey or bread.

b) Set up co-operatives.

Given that at first the town or suburb will be highly dependent on imports when these begin to become problematic many people will be threatened with unemployment. Many who were travelling long distances to work will also run into serious difficulties. For the CDC these firms and people represent abundant resources to be redeployed into local co-ops. We must be thinking ahead, preparing to help threatened firms and people to foresee the

318

restructuring they will have to deal with and how they could start producing some of the things the town needs. Does the town need a poultry farm, or acquaculture – then just form a co-op and set these ventures up.

c) Increase household production.

Of course town self-sufficiency also depends greatly on increasing household self-sufficiency. The more goods that are produced in home kitchens and workshops, craft rooms and gardens the less that will have to come through supermarkets. The CDC can greatly assist here, for example by developing recipe books for great dinners from the abundant plants that thrive locally, including the garden and roadside 'weeds'. It will develop formulae for cleaners, solvents, oils, dyes, glues, paint, etc. that can be made from local ingredients, within households or small firms. It will put out designs and recipes for soap making, tanning leather, bread baking, weaving, leatherwork, pottery, blacksmithing, preserving, and making sandals, hats, baskets and basic clothing.

The CDC will develop craft groups to increase home production of many items for use within the home. It will organise classes, skill sharing, display days (no prizes!), local sources of materials and the listing of skilled people willing to give advice or run classes. The CDC will develop and make available information on gardening, repairing, and how to cut household costs.

Many highly enjoyable leisure activities can be central in our skill development, such as field days, craft demonstrations and displays, talks by experienced practitioners from other towns, visits to gardens and systems.

d) Building up the commons.

Commons are very important in increasing local self-sufficiency because they provide lots of 'free food', materials and services for all. The CDC's early experience with this powerful device at the garden site will put it in a position to lead the town in thinking out what to locate where, and how best to organise the working bees that will do the building and maintenance.

319

e) Living simply!

The literature on local economic development usually fails to recognise that its prospects depend greatly on the readiness to reduce consumption in the first place. Our chances of providing most or all we need locally will be much better if we can cut back on the demand for stuff, especially high tech items that have to be imported via transnational corporations. We must keep in mind that the planet would not benefit much even if we produced all we use locally but went on consuming as much as before. Localisation gets rid of the transport and packaging costs but much more important is all the unnecessary consuming presently going on.

The supremely important 'educational' function of the CDC.

As I have said a number of times, by far the most important task is to do with developing the ideas and values that will lead people to work for the transition. At the start few if any people in the town or suburb will have thought from the perspective argued in this book.

There are two goals here. One is increasing the realisation that the alternative ways are enjoyable and effective means for achieving extremely important economic and social goals firstly in the era of increasing scarcity, such as providing good food and building community solidarity, escaping oil depletion, and raising the quality of life. The second element is increasing the realisation that consumer-capitalist society is unacceptable, that it is the cause of serious global problems – and that it can't be fixed and can never solve our problems let alone those of the poor majority in the world, that it is likely to plunge us all into chaos soon, that it is not compatible with ecological sustainability or justice and therefore that we must move on from it soon. There is no better base from which to develop these critical global understandings than through the activities under discussion.

Ask yourself how else could we go about trying to develop general public understanding that this social system is deeply flawed and has to be replaced? We can't force people to attend lectures or read books. We can't walk into people's homes and start telling them about the global situation. We can't explain these things via the media, because we have almost no influence on what they present. But we can make these connections clear throughout all the CDC's activities. When we are glaringly visible doing things in the neighbourhood we will explain that the ultimate point of what we are doing is to eliminate the global problems consumer society is causing and to illustrate and pioneer much better ways, and persuade more people to join us.

This public education function can also be carried out via the CDC's many research activities. Various surveys and audits will need to be made, such as into what goods are being imported and might be replaced by local products, what items existing firms would be willing to buy locally if they were available, what problems and needs people are experiencing, and what attitudes people have towards our project. While door knocking to collect this evidence we can explain the global significance of what we are doing and invite people to meetings and events.

Among the devices a small group can use are, organising public meetings to discuss the town's situation in view of the coming oil problem, drawing up a possible new town geography showing what roads could be dug up for commons, surveying what people think are the most neglected needs in the area, listing the most urgently needed new co-operative businesses the town might consider setting up, listing possible working bee projects, and reporting the results of door knock surveys of town opinion on these kinds of issues. We could put our findings into reports and newsletters. These activities will always involve reference to succinct analyses of the global situation, so people can see the rationale for our projects and proposals.

The community garden site can be crammed with information boards, displays, dioramas and examples. Wonders can be done with a few bits and pieces. For instance earth building can be illustrated by a mould, a heap of mud, a few mud bricks, and lots of stunning pictures. A waist-high sand tray can enable people to move model houses to design an ideal settlement, and redesign the suburb they are living in. A few such items enables a very-informative school visit. A similar venture involves examples located in various households in the neighbourhood, a chicken pen here, a mud brick dog kennel there, a mini orchard, a park we have plans to cram with useful plants, the place where a mud brick quarry and pond might go. We then take people on explanatory tours.

One of the many concerns of the CDC will be to develop (or find) good indices of per capita ecological footprint, and of the quality of life. It will also develop measures of cohesion and social wealth; e.g. how well the working bees and town meetings are attended, how many feel excluded or stressed, how the old and the young are faring. The CDC will liase closely with other localities on these issues, refining measures and sharing information and ideas. Right from the earliest days some of these measures will be valuable educational devices, for example having a town footprint figure prominently displayed on the big noticeboard outside the garden.

The CDC will make sure people realise from the start that the overall goal is not 'prosperity' as is conventionally understood. It is not raising the town's 'living standards' defined in terms of GNP per capita. It is not bringing more income into the region. The immediate goal is to enable the town, suburb or region to provide itself with many of the basic goods and services needed for well-being and security, and to enable all those excluded by the old economy to have access to productive activity and incomes. The ultimate goal is to develop the consciousness that will lead people to eagerly work hard to build settlements, economies and lifestyles that make a sustainable and just world possible.

Conclusion.

My argument has been that there is a powerful logic leading to the strategy outlined in this Chapter. After hundreds of years in which progress was indubitably identified with getting richer we have suddenly run into an era of scarcity that will oblige us to scrap many of the ideas and values that have driven Western culture. An examination of this situation gives us no choice but to accept that a sane, sustainable and just, and satisfying society now has to be defined in terms such as frugality, self-sufficiency, stability, participation, localism and cooperation.

The implications for the transition process are just as coercive, inescapable and radical, contradicting many classic theories and strategies. The new society cannot be imposed or even given. Unless it is willingly developed it will not work, and it must be learned. Communities must bumble their way to the geographies and practices that suit them in their conditions. This then means there is little choice about how to proceed. The only way to get there from here is to start now, where we live, building the new ways.

If we ever do make it to a sustainable and just world order then we could not have got there unless tiny groups of people had begun to take on this task of working out how they can start the transition in their town or suburb. The Eco-village and Transition Towns movements have got us started on this path. Before long we want to be able to derive from their accumulating experience the recipe book that will enable many more groups to quickly and easily apply the strategies the pioneers have found to be most effective.

But what matters most is not that we start building new ways but that we use these activities as the educational devices that will enable us to increase the understanding that huge and radical restructuring is needed. If we can succeed at that task then the remaking of our settlements will romp along.

None of this will happen anywhere unless people just like you and me take up the challenge. No one is an expert on how to do it and governments aren't going to do it for us. Don't think there are lots of people out there much better qualified than you are. It can only be done in your locality by the ordinary people who live there. Even if we had experts in the process they could not come in and start telling your neighbours what to do; that would not work. The people who live there are the only ones who know that scene, and they are the only ones who can work out how best to go about achieving the goal within their conditions.

You could not be offered a nicer revolution! No need for sacrifices or suffering, or to contend with secret police or tanks. Many good people feel very disturbed at their Rich World comfort and security and worry about what they should do. This book derives a clear and emphatic answer. If you are concerned about the fate of the planet and want to know what is by far the most important thing you can do about, then form a CDC!

BIBLIOGRAPHY

Appfel-Marglin, P., (1998), *The Spirit of Regeneration; Andean Culture Confronting Western Notions of Development*, London, Blackwell.

Baran, P. and P. Sweezy, (1996), *Monopoly Capital*, Harmondsworth, Penguin.

Barker, P., (2006), *The Cognitive Structure of Scientific Revolutions*, New York, Cambridge Univerisity Press.

Beder, S., (1997), *Global Spin, The Corporate Assault on Environmentalism*, Melbourne, Scribe.

Benholdt-Thomsen, V. and M. Mies, (1999), *The Subsistence Perspective*, London, Zed.

Berg, I. E., (1970), *Education and Jobs; The Great Training Robbery*, New York, Praeger.

Bernard, T. and J. Young, (1997), *The Ecology of Hope*, Babriola Island, New Society.

Birol, F., (2003), 'World energy investment outlook to 2030', IEA, *Exploration and Production, The Oil & Gas Review*, Volume 2. Paris.

Bidelux, R, (1985), *Communism and Development*, New York, Methuen.

Blazey, C., (1999), *The Australian Vegetable Garden, Diggers Seeds*, Dromana, Victoria.

Bookchin, M., (1987), *The Rise of Urbanism and the Decline of Citizenship*, San Francisco, Sierra Club.

——, (1990), Introductory Essay, in Dolgoff, S., Ed., *The Anarchist Collectives : Workers' Self-Management in the Spanish Revolution, 1936-1939*, Montréal, Black Rose Books.

——, (1991), *The Ecology of Freedom*, Montreal, Black Rose.

——, (1994), *To Remember Spain*, The Anarchist Library.

Bossel, U., (2004), 'The hydrogen illusion; why electrons are a better energy carrier', *Cogeneration and On-Site Power Production*, March – April, pp. 55 – 59.

Brecher, J., (2000), *Globalisation From Below; The Power of Solidarity*, London, South End.

Brown, L., (2006), *Plan B 2.0*, New York, Norton.

Brundtland, G. H., (1987), *Our Common Future*, London, Oxford University Press.

Carey, A., (1995), *Taking the Risk Out of Democracy*, Sydney, University of NSW Press.

Chomsky, N., (1986-92), *The Prosperous Few and the Restless Many*, New York Odonian Press.

Chossudovsky, M., (1997), *The Globalisation of Poverty*, London, Zed Books.

Climate Safety, (2009). http://74.125.153/search?q=cache;17nCMUmiDl1s J;climatesafety.org/download/climatesafety.pdf

Coppin, P., (2008), 'Wind energy', in Newman, P., (Ed)., *Transitions*. CSIRO Publishing, Canberra.

Dalton, G., (Ed)., (1968), *Ancient, Primitive and Modern Economies; Essays of Karl Polanyi*, Boston, Beacon Press.

de Hart, R., (1984), *Ecosociety*, Dehra Dun, India, Natras Publishing.

Dolgoff, S., Ed., (1990), *The Anarchist collectives : Workers' Self-management in the Spanish Revolution, 1936-1939*, Montréal, Black Rose Books.

Douthwaite, R., (1992), *The Growth Illusion*, London, Greenprint.

———, (1996), *Short Circuit*, Dublin, Lilliput.

Easterlin, R. A., (1972), 'Does economic growth improve the human lot? Some empirical evidence.', in D. A. David and M. W. Reder, (Eds)., *Nations and Households in Economic Growth*, Stanford, Stanford University Press.

Eckersley, R., (2004), *Well and Good; How We Feel and Why It Matters*, Text Publishing, Melbourne.

Ehrlich, P., (1972), *Population, Resources and Environment; Issues in Human Ecology*, San Francisco, Freeman.

Eisler, M., (1990), *The Chalice and the Blade*, San Francisco, Pandora.

Flannery, T., (2006), *The Weather Makers: The History & Future Impact of Climate Change*, Melbourne, Text Publishing.

Foote, D., (2009), Review of R. Solnit, *A Paradise Built in Hell; The Extraordinary Communities That Arise in Disaster*, Viking Press, in *The Guardian Weekly*, 18th Sept, p.41.

Foster, J. B. and F. Magdoff, (2008), 'Financial implosion and stagnation', *Monthly Review*, December, 1 – 29.

Fotopolous, T., (1997), *Towards an Inclusive Democracy*, London, Cassell.

———, (2001), 'The end of traditional anti-systemic movements', *Democracy and Nature*, 7, 32, Nov., 415 – 446.

Freudenberg, G., (2008), *Churchill and Australia*, London, Macmillan.

Fulton, L., (2005), *Biofuels For Transport; An International Perspective*, Paris, International Energy Agency.

Garnaut, R., (2008), *The Garnaut Climate Change Review; Final Report*. http://www.garnautreview.org.au/index.html

Global Eco-Village Network, (GEN), http://gen.ecovillage.org/about/index.html

Goldsmith, E., (1993), *The Way*, Boston, Shambala Press.

Grayling, A., (2007), *Towards The Light*, London, Bloomsbury.

Hamilton, C., (2000), *Is Life Getting Better? The Genuine Progress Indicator*. Canberra, Australia Institute.

Hamilton, C. and R. Deniss, (2005), *Affluenza; When Too Much is Never Enough*, St. Leonards, Allen and Unwin.

Hansen, J., et al., 2008. 'Target atmospheric CO_2; Where Should humanity aim? Climate Progress'. http://climateprogress. org/2008/03/17/hansen-et-al-must-read-back-to-350-ppm-or-risk-an-ice-free-planet/

Hazledine, S., (2009), Professor of Sedimentary Geology, Edinburgh University, interviewed on ABC Science Show, 19th Sept.

Heinberg, R., (2003), *The Party's Over*, Gabriola Island, New Society.

——, (2007), *Peak Everything; Waking Up to the Century of Declines*, Gabriola Island, New Society.

Henderson, H., (2006), *Ethical Markets; Growing the Green Economy*, London, Chelsea Green.

Herman, E. S., and N. Chomsky, (1988), *The Manufacture of Consent*, New York, Pantheon.

Hodge, G. A., (2000), *Privatization: An international review of performance*, Boulder, Colorado, Westview Press.

Hopkins, R., (2009), *The Transition Handbook*, London, Chelsea Green.

Hyde, L. (1983), *The Gift : Imagination and the Erotic Life of Property*, New York, Vintage Books.

Illich, I,. (1973), *Celebration of Awareness; Tools for Conviviality*, Harmondsworth, Penguin.

Institute for Self Reliance, (1982), *The New City State*, Washington,

Inter-governmental Panel on Climate Change, (IPCC), (2007), *Climate Change 2007, Fourth Assessment*, Geneva, Switzerland.

Jackson, R., (2000), *And We are Doing It!*, R. Reed Publishers, San Francisco.

Khor, L., (1957), *The Breakdown of Nations*, London, Routledge and Kegan Paul.

Kitching, G. N. (1989), *Development and Underdevelopment in Historical Perspective: Populism, Nationalism, and Industrialization*, New York, Routledge.

Klein, N., (2007), *The Shock Doctrine; The Rise of Disaster Capitalism*, New York, Metropolitan Books/Henry Holt.

Kohn, A, (1993), *Punished by Rewards*, New York, Houghton Mifflin.

Koont, S., (2009), 'The urban agriculture of Havana,' *Monthly Review*, January, 44 - 63.

Korten, D., (1999), *The Post Corporate World*, West Hanford, Connecticut, Kumarian.

Kunstler, J., (2005), *The Long Emergency; Surviving the Converging Catastrophes of the Twenty-First Century*, New York, Grove/Atlantic.

Lach-Newinsky, P., (2009), *The many deaths of socialism*, (Duplicated MS).

Leahy, T., (2009), *Permaculture Strategy for the South African Villages*, Palmwoods, Qld., PI Productions Photography.

Lenzen, M., (2009), *Current state of development of electricity-generating technologies – a literature review. Integrated Life Cycle Analysis*, Dept. of Physics, University of Sydney.

Lovelock, J., (2007), *The Revenge of Gaia: Why the Earth Is Fighting Back — and How We Can Still Save Humanity*, London, Allen Lane.

Luzzi, A. C., (2000), 'Showcase project; 2 MWe solar thermal demonstration power plant', *Proceedings of the 10TH Solar PACES Int. Symposium on Solar Thermal Concentrating Technologies*, Sydney.

Magdoff, F., and M. Yates, (2009), *The ABCs of the Financial Crisis*, New York, Monthly Review Press.

Marshal, P., (1992), *Demanding the Impossible: The History of Anarchism*, London Harper Collins.

Mason, C., (2003), *The 2030 Spike: Countdown to Catastrophe*, Earthscan.

Maybury-Lewis, D., (1992), *Millenium: Tribal Wisdom and the Modern World*, New York, Viking.

Meadows, D. H., D. Meadows and J. Randers, (1972), *The Limits to Growth*, New York, Universe.

Mies, M. and V. Shiva, (1993), *Ecofeminism*, Melbourne, Spinifex.

Monbiot, G., (2006), *Heat : How to Stop the Planet Burning*, London, Allen Lane.

Monkerod, D., (2009), 'US inequality continues to grow', *The Capital Times*, (Wisconsin), 17th July.

Morris, D., (1987), 'Healthy cities: Self Reliant Cities, *Health Promotion International*, Vol. 2, No. 2, 169-176. http://heapro.oxfordjournals.org/cgi/content/abstract/2/2/169

Murphy, P., (2008), *Plan C: Community Survival Strategies for Peak Oil and Climate Change*, Gabriola Island, Earthscan.

Newman, P., and I. Jennings, (2008), *Cities as Sustainable Ecosystems*, Island Press.

Newman, P., T. Beatley, and H. Boyer, (2009), *Resilient Cities: Responding to Peak Oil and Climate Change*, Washington, DC, Island Press.

Norberg-Hodge, H., (1991), *Ancient Futures; Learning From Ladakh*, San Francisco, Sierra.

Odum, H. T., (2000), *A Prosperous Way Down*, Colorado, Univ of Colorado Press.

Papworth, J., (1995), *Small is Powerful*, London, Adamantine.

——, (2006), *Village Democracy*, Exeter, UK, Imprint Academic.

Pepper, (1996), *Modern Environmentalism*, London, Routledge and Kegan

Quinn, D., (1999), *Beyond Civilization*, Three Rivers Press, New York.

Rai, M., (1995), *Chomsky's Politics*, London, Verso.

Relocalise, (2009), http://www.relocalize.net/how_do_we_relocalise

Rosling, H, (2009) 'The best statistics you have ever seen', http://www.ted.com/talks/hans_rosling_shows_the_best_stats_you_ve_ever_seen.html

Rude, C., (1998), 'Postmodern Marxism; A critique', *Monthly Review*, November., 52-57.

Sahlins, M., (1974), *Stone Age Economics*, London, Aldine.

Samana, U., (1988), *Papua New Guinea; Which Way? Essays on Identity and Development*, North Carlton, Vic., Arena.

Schumacher, F., (1999), *Small is Beautiful; A Study of Economics as if People Mattered*, Washington, Hartley and Marks Publishers.

Shannin, T., (1995), *Late Marx and the Russian Road*, New York, Monthly Review Press.

Shiva, V., (2005), *Earth Democracy; Justice, sustainability and Peace*, Cambridge, Mass, South End Press.

Smith, J., (2010), *The Coming Collapse of Civilisation*, Mellen.

Speth, G., (2001), *A Bridge At The End Of The World*, New Haven, Connecticut, Yale University Press.

Stephan, W., (2009), (www.worldchanigng.org).

Stern, N., (2006), *Review on the Economics of Climate Change*, H.M.Treasury, UK, Oct. http://www.sternreview.org.uk

Tainter, J. A., (1988), *The Collapse of Complex Societies*, Cambridge, Cambridge University Press.

The Simpler Way Website, (2006), http://ssis.arts.unsw.edu.au/tsw/

Trainer, T., (2005), "Social responsibility; the most important, and neglected, problem of all?", *International Journal of Social Economics*, 682-704.

——, (2007), *Renewable Energy Cannot Sustain a Consumer Society*, Springer, Dodrect.

——, (2008a), *Renewable energy – Cannot sustain an energy-intensive society.* http://ssis.arts.unsw.edu.au/tsw/REcant.html

——, (2008b). *Estimating the limits of solar thermal power.* http://ssis.arts. unsw.edu.au/tsw/

——, (2008c), *The Garnaut Report: A critical comment.* http://ssis.arts. unsw.edu.au/tsw/Garnaut.crit.html

——, 2010. "Can renewables etc. solve the greenhouse problem; The negative case", *Energy Policy*, 38, 8, August, 4107-4114

——, (in press), 'A critical discussion of the stern and IPCC analyses of carbon emission mitigation possibilities and costs', *Energy and Environment*.

Trieb, F., (undated), *Trans-Mediterranean Interconnection for Concentrating Solar Power; Final Report.* German Aerospace Center (DLR). Institute of Technical Thermodynamics, Section Systems Analysis and Technology Assessment.

Walker, Liz, (2005), *Eco-Village at Ithaca: Pioneering a Sustainable Culture*, Gabriola Island, BC, Canada, New Society Publishers.

Ward, C., (1973), *Anarchy in Action*, London, Allen and Unwin.

Waren, B., (1980), *Imperialism; Pioneer of Capitalism*, New York, New Left Books.

Wilkinson, R., and K. Pickett, (2009), *The Spirit Level; Why Equal Societies Almost Always Do Better*, London, Penguin.

Wood, E. M., (1998), 'The Communist Manifesto after 150 years', *Monthly Review*, May, 14-36.

Wright, J., (2009) *Sustainable Agriculture and Food Security in an Era of Oil Scarcity; Lessons From Cuba*, London, Earthscan.

THE SIMPLER WAY WEBSITE:

Materials on the themes dealt with in this book.

http://ssis.arts.unsw.edu.au/tsw/

Issue Summaries:

❑ Summary of the simpler way – our unsustainably affluent society.

❑ The limits to growth predicament – the environment problem.

❑ Third world development – the economy – our empire – peace and conflict.

❑ Social breakdown – the alternative society; The Simpler Way (Thoughts on the transition to The Simpler Way).

Collected documents

The limits to growth. Globalisation. The economy. The Empire.

Pigface Point

Pigface Point is a site introducing visiting groups to simpler way themes. A slide show tour of the site.

Alphabetical list of topics

This is a list of topics on which accounts are offered from The Simpler Way perspective.

The way it could be

A fictional account of a town that has adopted the simpler way.

Contact: Ted Trainer, c/- Social Science and International Studies, University of New South Wales, Kensington, Australia, 2050.